FIGHTING FOR A LAUGH

FIGHTING FOR A LAUGH

ENTERTAINING THE BRITISH AND AMERICAN ARMED FORCES 1939–1946

RICHARD FAWKES

MACDONALD AND JANE'S LONDON

First published in Great Britain in 1978 by
Macdonald and Jane's Publishers Limited
8 Shepherdess Walk, London N1 7LW

© Richard Fawkes

Designed by David Fordham
ISBN 0 354 04201 7
Filmset and printed in Great Britain by
BAS Printers Limited, Over Wallop, Hampshire

CONTENTS

FOR
CHERRY

INTRODUCTION

Someone once said that war is five per cent fun, five per cent fear and ninety per cent boredom. It's during that long time of boredom that the need is greatest for some sort of diversion. This book is about the entertainers who helped fill those spare hours for British, American and Allied troops during the Second World War. It traces the development of ENSA and USO Camp Shows Inc., the two largest civilian entertainment agencies ever, and the rise of service entertainment: GI shows, Stars in Battledress, the RAF Gang Shows, Unit and Divisional Concert Parties.

For the first time the place of entertainment in service life was accepted by the military authorities and the colonel who thought the only relief his men needed was a game of football and a cold shower, while not becoming quite obsolete, was certainly in the minority. As an army doctor said to Joe E Brown, 'The only thing that can relax a body as taut as these bodies is a tub of hot water, or a good belly laugh. And we can't get the hot water.' The sheer volume of entertainment required throughout the world gave countless opportunities for untried artists, in and out of uniform, to learn their craft in front of a captive audience. Many of today's top stars found their performing feet while entertaining troops, in particular those with a talent to make their fellow-sufferers laugh, like Harry Secombe, Norman Wisdom, Dick Emery, Peter Sellers and Harry Worth.

The Second World War brought many changes to everyday life at home. People travelled half way round the globe, tasted foreign food and gazed on some of the wonders of the world. Class barriers, while not quite tumbling down, had their foundations undermined. Men who were bored and prepared to watch anything went to see plays, ballet, opera and concerts, perhaps for the first time, and discovered they enjoyed what they were seeing. As a result audiences were built up which enabled the post-war arts in Britain to reach their present position of eminence. This book is a tribute to the many men and women who helped creat those audiences while making such a valuable contribution to the war effort.

Because there was so much more happening in entertainment than could possibly be covered in a book of this size, I have deliberately omitted films, radio and what was happening in POW camps, and with more than 10,000 artists working for ENSA and USO alone, it has obviously not been possible to mention more than a few by name. To those who have been omitted and to those who find an artist they remember with particular affection is not named, I can only apologize.

RICHARD FAWKES

ACKNOWLEDGE-MENTS

For a book of this kind I have harassed and badgered many very busy people, all of whom have given freely of their time, memories and souvenirs. I would like to thank them and the many people who sent me photographs, cuttings and reminiscences. In particular, I would like to mention the following: Larry Adler, Chesney Allen, Avril Angers, Irene Ansell, John Arnatt, Marjorie Baldwin, Felix Barker, Bruno Barnabe, Peggy Thorpe Bates, David Benson, Bridget Boland, Christopher Bond, Sir Adrian Boult, Faith Brook, Basil Brown, Patricia Burke, Barbara Burton, Douglas Byng, John Carlsen, Ian Carmichael, Charlie Chester, George Chisholm, Alan Clare, Kenneth Connor, Roland Coombs, George Cooper, Sam Costa, Margaret Courtney, Fred and Frank Cox, Charles Craig, Colin Cunningham, Basil Dean, Norman del Mar, Michael Denison, Florence Desmond, Winifred Doran, Deanna Durbin, Victor Fawkes, John Foskett, Geraldo, Sir John Gielgud, Tommy Godfrey, John Gostelow, Joyce Grenfell, Norman Hackforth, Stanley Hall, Dorothy and Robert Harbin, Doris Hare, Vera Harley, Jack Healy, Richard Hearne, Ronnie Hill, Michael Hordern, Frankie Howerd, Noel Howlett, Cyril Hunt, Michael Jackson, Dudley Jones, Geoffrey Keen, Reginald Kilbey, Muriel and Waldo Lanchester, Arthur Lane, Michael Langdon, Evelyn Laye, Eddie le Roy, Reg Lever, Jack Lindsay, Richard Llewellyn, Hugh Lloyd, Arthur Lowe, Murray Macdonald, Michael MacOwan, Gordon Marsh, Queenie Masters, Diana Menuhin, Walter Midgley, Michael Mills, Billy Milton, George Mitchell, Stephen Murray, Dame Anna Neagle, Laurence Neal, Greatorex Newman, Cyril Ornadel, Brian Oulton, Ivor Owen, Hugh Paddick, Nigel Patrick, Jon Pertwee, William Pleeth, Sandy Powell, Sam Rabin, Ralph Reader, Hugo Rignold, Cardew Robinson, Edmund Rubbra, Charles Sadler, Jeffrey Segal, David Shipman, Eddie Shrimpton, Donald Sinden, Bill Stevenson, Richard Stone, Bill Sutton, Frances Tanner, Terry-Thomas, Dame Sybil Thorndike, Eric Tissington, Stan Tracey, Tommy Trinder, Dame Eva Turner, Gordon Turner, Andre van Gyseghem, Reg Varney, Sidney Vauncez, Bill Walsh, Jack Warner, Peter Warren, Stanley Watson, Peter Watts, Elisabeth Welch, Leslie Welch, Eric Weston, Audrey White, Emlyn Williams, Lord Willis, Norman Wisdom, Harry Worth and Chris Wortman.

I would also like to thank Terry Charman, the staff of the Imperial War Museum and Alan W Kravath of the United Service Organizations Inc., for their help with my research; Felix Barker and Reg Lever, for allowing me to read their, as yet, unpublished accounts of their war years – *Sand In My Shoes* by Reg Lever and *Soldier in Greasepaint*, a history of *The Balmorals* concert party, by Felix Barker; and acknowledge the following books from which I have quoted extracts: *A Proper Job* by Brian Aherne (Houghton Mifflin), *The Theatre At War* by Basil Dean (Harrap), *Pillars of Drury Lane* by W MacQueen Pope (Hutchinson), *The Man who was Bilko* by Phil Silvers (W H Allen) and *Bing* by Charles Thompson (W H Allen). I am indebted to the estate of the late Sir Noël Coward for permission to reproduce 'Lines To A Remote Unit' and an extract from *Middle East Diary* (Heinemann).

Also I should like to thank the following publishers for permission to quote:

W H Allen & Co. Ltd (London) Hawthorn Books, Inc. (New York) for *All My Yesterdays* by Edward G Robinson and Leonard Spigelgass

A S Barnes (New York) *Laughter is a Wonderful Thing* by Joe E Brown

Elm Tree Books (London) for *Anything for a Quiet Life* by Jack Hawkins, copyright © 1973 by Mrs Doreen Hawkins and the Estate of the late Jack Hawkins.

For permission to reproduce illustrations I would like to thank the following copyright holders or owners:

The Imperial War Museum, Radio Times Hulton Picture Library, the Mander and Mitchenson Collection, RAF Gang Show Association, USO, *Illustrated London News*, *Punch*, BBC, Popperfoto, *Stars and Stripes*, The National Film Archive, Larry Adler, Chesney Allen, Marjorie Baldwin, Felix Barker, Bruno Barnabe, Faith Brook, Basil Brown, Harry Brydges, Patricia Burke, John Carlsen, Ian Carmichael, George Chisholm, the estate of the late Sir Noël Coward, Deanna Durbin David, Manja Geraldo, John Gostelow, Robert Harbin, Vera Harley, Jack Healy, Ronnie Hill, Michael Hordern, Michael Jackson and Harvard Theater Collection, Dudley Jones, Waldo Lanchester, Eddie le Roy, Hugh Lloyd, Gordon Marsh, Queenie Masters, Diana Menuhin, Michael Mills, Dame Anna Neagle, Cyril Ornadel, Brian Oulton and Peggy Thorpe Bates, Ivor Owen, Nigel Patrick, William Pleeth, Hugo Rignold, Jeffrey Segal, Donald Sinden, Bill Sutton, Gordon Turner, John Vickers, Elisabeth Welch, Norman Wisdom.

Every attempt has been made to find the copyright owners. The author and publishers regret any omission that may have occurred and will willingly correct any in all future editions.

CHAPTER ONE

1939-EVERY NIGHT SOMETHING AWFUL

Everyone knew that the war would open with a blitz. The Luftwaffe would strike massively, decisively and immediately. Millions would be gassed, burnt or blown to pieces. Seven hundred tons of bombs would rain on London during the first week and the city would be reduced to rubble.

When Hitler walked into Poland on 1 September people knew that the time had come; there could be no more compromises, no more flights to Germany and waving umbrellas. The fear and apprehension were mixed with relief that at last something positive was about to happen. Forty-three per cent of those interviewed on 1 September by Mass Observation said better to have done with it; let's get it over. For the second time in twelve months (it had happened previously at the time of Munich) London's children were evacuated. Schools were closed and roads out of the city made one-way to speed them on their journey. The rich slipped quietly away to the country to what those left behind called their 'funk holes'. Under Plan Yellow, 25,000 file-clutching civil servants joined the exodus and plans were rushed ahead to remove Eros from his perch in Piccadilly Circus to the safety of Egham in Surrey. At Alexandra Palace the infant television service closed down 'for the duration' without announcement, leaving the 20,000 set owners vainly twiddling the knobs for the advertised programmes. The official explanation was that transmissions would help guide enemy bombers to their targets. In reality, television cost twenty times as much to produce as radio and the BBC wanted to marshal all its resources for the more popular service. Those who had just paid between thirty and sixty guineas for a set they could no longer use or get rid of were understandably peeved. Radio broadcasting shrank to a single Home service, consisting of non-stop news, patriotic speeches and endless recitals at the theatre organ by Sandy McPherson. The BBC was attacked for the utter boredom of its output, particularly by Hannen Swaffer who suggested that the entire operation should be handed over to C B Cochran. Most listeners felt they had heard enough organ music to last them the duration, however long that might be.

The war was finally announced at 11.15 am on Sunday, 3 September. Tommy Trinder had been booked to give a concert that day in Bridlington, Yorkshire. 'I left London in my car and, on the way, stopped for a cup of tea. A bus came along carrying about forty expectant mothers. As they climbed off the bus I looked at the conductor and said "Blimey! You've had a nice time!" Continuing my journey I was listening to the car radio when I heard that war had been declared. I decided to turn back. I reversed the car and had started on my way when an air raid warning went. I saw a shelter and everybody running to it and I thought: oh yes, one has to go to a shelter. We'd been brainwashed

From the beginning, ENSA and its units were favourite reading in the newspapers and magazines. Every wartime effort was subject to security restrictions which not infrequently let something slip by; viz the pith helmets the girls are sporting would not imply that they were about to entertain the troops in Scotland.

what to do. I stopped the car and left the engine running in my haste. A warden was ushering everyone down and they were taking off their shoes and socks because there was about six inches of water on the floor of the shelter. I said "If I'm going to be killed, at least I'll die with dry feet." So I stood up top. Nothing happened. I got in the car and went home.'

The sirens had sounded within minutes of the declaration and people ran to the shelters convinced the Germans must have had their planes in the air early. It was a false alarm. 'An aircraft was observed approaching the South Coast of England at 11.30 am,' an Air Ministry bulletin announced later. 'As its identity could not be readily determined, an air raid warning was given. It was shortly afterwards identified as a friendly aircraft and the All Clear signal was given.'

The Government wasn't prepared to take chances. Blackout restrictions were imposed immediately and all places in which crowds might gather and where casualties would be high were ordered to close, with the exception of churches. That meant no football (and even more upsetting no pools), no dogs, no race meetings, no speedway, no dances, no films and no theatres.

Overnight the entire entertainment profession found itself out of work. Many in it decided not to wait for their call-up and went directly to the recruiting offices. Others volunteered to drive ambulances, become ARP (Air Raid Precautions) Wardens or joined the Civil Defence. Most simply went home and waited.

The clamp-down on all forms of entertainment provoked a howl of protest. George Bernard Shaw fired off a letter to *The Times*:

'May I be allowed to protest vehemently against the order to close all theatres and picture-houses during the war? It seems to me to be a masterstroke of unimaginative stupidity. During the last war we had 80,000 soldiers on leave to amuse every night. There were not enough theatres for them and theatre rents rose to fabulous figures. Are there to be no theatres for them this time? We have hundreds of thousands of evacuated children to be kept out of mischief and traffic dangers. Are there to be no pictures for them? The authorities, now all-powerful, should at once set to work to provide new theatres and picture-houses where they are lacking. All actors, variety artists, musicians and entertainers of all sorts should be exempted from every form of service except their own all-important professional one. What agent of Chan-

Basil Dean wearing the army-style uniform ('Basil dress') which became compulsory for all artists entertaining overseas after 1942.

cellor Hitler is it who suggested that we should all cower in darkness and terror for the duration?'

If few would have agreed with Shaw that artists should be exempt from military service, one man with whom the sentiment struck a sympathetic chord was Basil Dean, newly-created Director of Entertainments for the Naafi (the Navy, Army and Air Force Institutes).

Fifty-one year old Dean, a theatrical producer, director and film magnate, had been a pioneer of troop entertainment during the 1914–18 war and had been responsible for building the first Garrison Theatre. He had seen how disorganized and wasted most efforts had been and remembered with horror the endless rounds of children from dancing academies and troupes of talentless amateurs who had tried to cheer up the unfortunate soldiers, most of them in hospital beds from which there was no escape. He knew from his own experience that if ever the need for troop entertainment arose again something much more professional would be required. Against considerable indifference and opposition he had pushed ahead with plans to organize an army of entertainers, embracing all branches of the profession, ready to go anywhere troops were stationed, whenever wanted.

The name of his embryonic organization was the Entertainments National Service Association, known universally as ENSA. Few of the men to whom ENSA played knew what the initials stood for. Most tended to believe Tommy Trinder's definition – Every Night Something Awful – or thought it was Every Night Same Act.

ENSA became the voluntary mobilization of the entertainment industry, employing by the end of 1944 nearly 4,000 artists, a figure exceeded only by the American equivalent USO (United Services Organization) which used 5,424 salaried performers. ENSA cost £14 million to run, played to more than 500 million people and four out of five members of the profession appeared under its banner at some time during the war. Its artists, from unknown comedians to great stars, played in every theatre of war under conditions that were always difficult and sometimes dangerous. For six-and-a-half years, ENSA made a valuable contribution to the nation's morale. Yet this brilliant, imaginative idea ended in a sordid and sour manner. There was no place for ENSA artists in The Victory Parade through London; Basil Dean, for all his hard work, received only the CBE; questions were asked in Parliament and Dean himself was embroiled in a mesh of innuendo and accusation of mismanagement and dishonesty, none of which was true.

The reasons are not hard to find. 'I don't suppose that even the world's most unsuccessful agent has ever had to handle quite so many deadbeat acts as were sent to me,' wrote Jack Hawkins, ENSA's organizer in India, in his autobiography, *Anything For A Quiet Life*. In fairness to Dean, it simply was not possible to put on 500 first-class shows a week around the world with a war on. Another reason was Dean's personality: he was not an easy man to get on with and few of the artists who worked for ENSA would have chosen him to run it. He was arrogant and autocratic, with a strong dislike of the freewheeling variety performer. In order to pilot his scheme through he stamped on a great many toes whose owners were unforgiving and had long memories. Every opportunity to do down Dean was seized. There can be no doubting Dean's sincerity nor that he achieved results where less resilient men would have failed. It is one of the tragedies of the war that the man who conceived, guided and inspired ENSA should ultimately, if unwittingly, have been the cause of its demise.

ENSA had started to take shape in the summer of

1938 when Dean outlined his plans to three other veterans of the first war, Leslie Henson, Owen Nares and Godfrey Tearle. Although they thought him slightly mad, they agreed with his premise that if another war came a central body would be needed to co-ordinate the theatre's contribution and agreed to help. Dean set about enlisting further support but in the aftermath of Munich and 'Peace for our time', few were prepared even to listen. George Black Snr, the great Palladium producer, laughed in Dean's face and Gracie Fields' agent told him that she would be making her own arrangements but they would be unnecessary since 'there won't be a war.'

Stubbornly, Dean pushed ahead. Early in 1939 he revitalized his small committee (of Henson, Nares and Tearle) and brought in the widely respected Sir Seymour Hicks as Controller and figure-head. Dean wrote a pamphlet setting down his ideas, unsuccessfully lobbied MP's and, together with Hicks, pounded the corridors of the War Office trying to obtain official approval. What the War Office thought was summed up by an officer who told them that if actors wanted to do their bit they should join the Army and fight.

Getting nowhere with the Army and becoming increasingly desperate, Dean turned next to the Naafi, successors to the Navy and Army Canteen Board with which he had worked in the First World War. The Naafi was already running entertainments in a small way as a corollary to its work providing food and drink for the forces and readily agreed to use Dean as a link between itself and the theatrical profession. What is more, it agreed to finance the new organization.

On Leslie Henson's suggestion the name of the organization became the Entertainments National Service Association. Committees and sub-committees were set up at the beginning of August to work out how the association should function. Their early meetings were bitchy in true theatrical tradition. No one agreed with anyone else, agents were unhappy that their clients should receive the paltry wage offered (with a much-reduced ten per cent for them), the Incorporated Society of Musicians claimed to represent a higher class of performer than the Amalgamated Musicians' Union, and everyone was suspicious of Dean and his motives. He was suspected of making a bid to take over the entire entertainment profession.

Frustrated by the lack of progress Dean made a scathing attack on the agents, accusing them of wrecking ENSA before it had started. He was

The Theatre Royal Drury Lane, the home of ENSA throughout the war, was handed over to that organization when the enforced closures of all theatres brought Ivor Novello's The Dancing Years *to a halt.*

forced to write an open letter of apology (his first draft had to be rewritten in a more conciliatory tone) before they would attend any more meetings.

3 September arrived and although the daily meetings took on a more urgent air, nothing was resolved. The committees had been so busy deciding who should do what that they had overlooked one detail – there were no artists to organize. Within hours of the declaration artists and managements were announcing their own plans to entertain troops. Dame Marie Tempest, at seventy-five, said she would tour in *Dear Octopus*; Harold Holt, the music impressario, detailed plans for his artists to give a series of concerts; theatre managers and repertory companies offered their services to local garrisons and camps. Dean knew that he had to act fast and with both the Naafi and the War Office keen to see if he could provide the goods he had so extravagantly

promised earlier in the year, he decided to by-pass his committees and sought the help of Thorpe Bates, Chairman of the Concert Artists' Association and ENSA's own concert section. Bates assembled a star studded party and the very first ENSA concert was given to Scots Guards waiting to be sent to France at Pirbright Camp on Saturday, 9 September. The show was repeated the next day at Old Dene Camp. A week later another celebrity concert took place for the RASC starring Jack Warner, Beatrice Lillie and Annette Mills.

Meanwhile the committees continued to wrangle. A particularly vitriolic meeting between agents, theatrical managers and ENSA officials took place on 8 September. It was described by W MacQueen Pope, ENSA's publicity officer, in his Book, *Pillars of Drury Lane*:

'There were scenes of strife and dispute from the very opening and Sir Seymour Hicks, in the chair, had a terrible job on his hands. Nobody agreed

14

with anything or anybody – many distinguished Theatre people walked out, shaking the dust of ENSA free from their shoes. Outside, the press was waiting, licking its lips for a good scandal story. Inside, a riot raged and at times it looked like personal violence. Something had to be done and done quickly.'

It was. Earlier that week Dean had been offered the use of the closed Theatre Royal, Drury Lane as a temporary headquarters. News that permission had been granted for the move came while the meeting was still in progress. MacQueen Pope made the announcement. 'By a miracle the storm died down. The Lane as headquarters! – this was something important – this mattered. The immense prestige of that building had its effect. A new feeling came over the scene and more friendly discussions ensued. Drury Lane had won the first battle for ENSA.'

The next Monday, 11 September, ENSA's small staff moved into the theatre, the dressing-rooms becoming offices and the Board Room, in which Sheridan wrote *The School For Scandal*, becoming the ENSA Conference Room. Dean decided the time had come to stop talking and start work. He announced to the press that the organization had

been set up and that a regular service of entertainment for troops would begin in two weeks time, on 25 September. Twelve concert parties – ten from England, two from Scotland – would open simultaneously throughout the country and play two or three shows a day for a month. Since Dean knew nothing about concert parties he relied on Rex Newman, producer of the famous *Fol-de-Rols*, to find them for him. On Friday, 22 September, the ten English parties made their way to Drury Lane for a press conference and the official send-off.

'We all supplied our own costumes and props,' says Reg Lever who led the *Bouquets* company. 'Since we had been playing at various seaside places we had everything ready, which was the whole point of choosing us. We had been at Southend, Cecil Johnson had been at Margate, Murray Ashford had been at Scarborough, Wilby Lunn had been at Folkestone.

'All the press were at Drury Lane. Sir Seymour Hicks climbed on a basket and made the big speech: we were artists going to do national work, as essential to the soldiers as food and rest. "As members of a great profession," he said, "you are going to help Great Britain win the war. But you'll

Drury Lane boardroom. Left to right. Greatorex Newman, Thorpe Bates, R. Layton, B. Lecardo, J. Waller (representing Geraldo), Henry Oscar, C. Morris, Alec Rea, Gracie Fields, Basil Dean, Lancelot Royle, Sir Kenneth Barnes, E. P. Clift, Stanley Bell, Walter Legge, Virginia Vernon, Lilian Braithwaite, William Armstrong, W. Macqueen Pope, W. Abingdon and E. Everett.

find you will have to rough it when you get out there."

'We managers then went to the front of the house and were given sealed orders which we were told not to open until we were on the train. A coach took us from Drury Lane. We were carted all round the outskirts of London and dumped at King's Cross. We hadn't been given movement orders or anything like that so I had to open my sealed orders to find out where we were going so I could buy the tickets! We were going to Catterick, a peacetime camp, just like Aldershot. Everybody knew about Catterick so what all the secrecy was about, I don't know.

'When we got there we had to go to the Hooge Lines, to a proper Naafi with a proper stage. There hadn't been a show on there for months and it was filthy, but we had been told about roughing it and assumed this was it. The girl in charge knew nothing about us but she found some pails and scrubbing brushes and scrubbed the stage, while we climbed up to the rafters and fixed our curtains. Two sergeants then said they would rustle up some lads. They arrived looking forward to seeing Jack Buchanan and Phyllis Robins; since we hadn't either, that was it as far as they were concerned. We ended up with about 150 men, started the show and were doing very nicely indeed when, halfway through, there was a banging on the door. A brigadier came in playing bloody hell about everything. I was on stage. "Bloody well get him off!" he shouted. It turned out that we were in the wrong place – we should have been in the Aisne Lines where there had been 2,000 men waiting for us for an hour and a half! We stopped our show and went over. When we got there, they had been running an impromptu entertainment – chaps getting up, singing and so on – and an escapologist was on, tied up, trying to get loose. We bundled him off, still tied up, into the wings and got on with our show. I never knew what happened to him!'

A week later some troops stationed in the Home Counties were lucky enough to see Jack Buchanan when a second, smaller, but more glamorous wave left Drury Lane. With Buchanan, in his own coach, his name emblazoned on the side, went Elsie Randolph, Fred Emney and Sid Millward's band, to give sixteen special concerts. Harold Holt, who had joined forces with ENSA, organized twenty-four musical concerts and Jack Hylton, head of the Light Music section, and Geraldo, his deputy, took their bands out. Film shows started

and a section to tour hospitals was set up under Dames Sybil Thorndike and Lilian Braithwaite. The daily papers were full of pictures of stars 'somewhere in England' meeting their audiences.

In spite of the early difficulties ENSA had become a reality. Offers of help poured in to Drury Lane from every branch of show business. One old lady, who wanted to do her bit, arrived with programmes of her last performances, forty years earlier. ENSA's staff was unable to cope and some embarrassing mistakes were made. Sidney Bernstein (subsequently Lord Bernstein, head of Granada TV, then a noted cinema impresario) offered his services to the film section and received a postcard advising him he would be called upon to entertain His Majesty's Forces at the earliest possible moment.

ENSA, however, faced a much more serious problem than the confusion caused by a raw and inexperienced administration. With a few exceptions ENSA was unable to obtain the services of those stars and good competent professionals who would have set the standard for the years to follow. Two weeks after the war had started they became unavailable.

On 5 September, Aberystwyth claimed a niche in history by being the only place in Britain to have a cinema open in defiance of the Government ban. The magistrates closed it the following day but the first shot had been fired in the campaign to have places of entertainment reopened. Since no bombers had been seen over Britain the Government found it hard to resist the growing clamour. On 15 September cinemas and theatres in rural areas were given permission to open until 10 pm, provided a member of staff was posted where he or she could hear an air-raid warning. The following week those in cities, including London, were also allowed to reopen. The BBC, stung by criticism that its non-stop news and organ music had actually lowered the nation's morale, slipped drama, music and variety (in the shape of *It's That Man Again*) back into the schedules.

Managers and theatre owners, anxious to recoup some of their losses, assembled their companies as fast as possible. Because of a 6 pm curfew in the West End which lasted until the beginning of December, London productions were sent to the regions. The Crazy Gang headed north for five weeks, Sandy Powell opened in Oxford, the Old Vic Company set up at the Victoria Theatre, Burnley. Suddenly performers were in demand again. By Christmas there were more shows in the

West End than there had been the year before with audiences swollen by troops on leave. Why should an artist play for ENSA's peanuts (top rate £10 a week irrespective of billing; £4 a week for the chorus) when £50 a week or more could be picked up in the commercial theatre? Many artists on the first ENSA tours left as soon as their contracts expired.

Most applications to reach Drury Lane were from those branches of the profession hardest hit by the war – the concert party performers who had not been allowed back to the seaside resorts, the pub comics, the Masonic and cabaret entertainers. ENSA saved many of them from almost certain starvation. Then there were the 'has-beens' (the old timers who saw in ENSA a chance to recapture some of their former glory), people who sang in church choirs, who had appeared in amateur dramatics or been told they ought to be on the stage by a doting aunt. After the war Dean calculated that ENSA received 50,000 applications, mostly from amateurs, had auditioned some 14,000 and offered employment to 800. Of the women engaged only fifty stayed on in show business afterwards.

The early auditions were held on stage at Drury Lane, the only chance most applicants would ever have of appearing in a real theatre.

Chris Wortman, star and manager of an ENSA show produced by Archie de Bear, attended one. 'One morning during rehearsals Archie said to me "We've got an audition going on. Come down. It might be fun." I sat between him and Lilian Braithwaite with Basil Dean on the other side. This poor soul, who was well over fifty, came out wearing a blue dress, her hair heavily tramlined, iron-waved, especially for the occasion. She only had one leg and a crutch which she put down in the wings. She then hopped to the centre of the stage and started to sing, very off-key, 'Abide With Me.' Archie turned to me and said, "God, I should hate to!" The auditions went on and on. They were pathetic. He told me that for every two or three hundred they saw, they might find two or three they could use.'

Even that ratio was too high. Much of the criticism of ENSA stemmed from the fact that it became too big. But Dean was faced with a difficult decision: either keep ENSA select, with high standards (which would have been to his and

'Look, dear, a contract from ENSA!'

ENSA's glory) or try to meet every demand made on him. He chose the latter. That, for him, was the purpose of ENSA. It was his duty to supply as much entertainment as requested and since there were more than a million-and-a-half bored men under arms, there were many requests which had to be granted.

By the end of its first month ENSA had put on 500 shows. After two months the figure had climbed to 1492 and audiences totalled 600,000. At any one time 700 artists were employed. Programmes covered plays, variety, concert parties, classical music, dance bands, one- or two-handed shows that needed no theatre, lectures (Will Hay spoke on his hobby, astronomy), wrestling and film shows. There simply were not enough Jack Buchanans to go round even if Dean had been able to get them. He was forced to rely on the unproven and ultimately second-rate artists who attracted scorn. As a soldier wrote to *The Performer* after watching an awful show and reading the impressive list of well-known names connected with ENSA, 'The lads prefer the goods to the Invoice.'

Stan Tracey, now one of Britain's leading jazz musicians, was one of the very few talented amateurs to audition for ENSA. On leaving school he answered an advertisement for musicians to join an accordion band. 'Criticism of ENSA never upset me because it was true and you can't knock the truth. We used to get cat-calls in the band because they insisted we wear this bloody make-up. We used to put on the minimum and the band-leader would say, "Oh, come on, lads!" We would end up looking as if we'd been in California for four years lying in the sun, with a terrible white line round the neck. We had no idea and nobody showed us. We would have great black eyebrows, red lips and this terrible tan, and we had to wear highly-coloured gipsy costumes. We must have looked like a band of ravers.

'Obviously there were some artists in that mass who were worth watching but I never came across them. The people I worked with were not much as performers, nobody of any quality. We had two old birds, Nina and Norah; my God, they must have been sixty! They did a juggling act which was pathetic. Then there were a couple of soubrettes, one of whom was a big, jolly, plump-buttocked girl who fell on her arse nearly every night; she was terrible; a blind siffleuse, an impressionist and conjurors who had the most ghastly magic tricks, one in front of the magic set you buy for your kids.

They were all old and they always had their old lady with them as assistant. We also had a couple who were supposed to be Apache dancers. They were old, too. He had a gut that had to be seen to be believed and the act was terrible. When you're on a stage no more than twelve feet wide it was ridiculous. It always used to end up with him whirling her around his head like a lunatic and, regular as clockwork, he would come off the stage and throw up.'

In spite of attempts by producers at Drury Lane to keep standards high too many shows were thrown on and despatched without proper rehearsal and with inadequate performers. To the growing number of complaints that units were being neglected or did not receive enough shows were added those about the quality of the ones that did arrive. Often the complaints were only too real.

'I was sent to join a variety company in Taunton,' remembers Winifred Doran, 'about which there had been complaints, particularly that some of the material was blue. It was one of those companies where they had really been scraping the barrel. We were all called to rehearsal by this fat man whom I shouldn't think had ever had anything to do with the business. He wanted to see our acts. He stopped a double-act of two men and said he didn't like them at all. He then pulled out a load of postcards on which jokes had been written, spread them out and told them to pick the ones they wanted. When my turn came he didn't like the number with which I finished although I'd been using it for years. He said it was no good and told me to go to the shop round the corner and buy myself a comic song.

'When we were sent to France they picked things for us to do from old concert party albums they got cheap from the publishers. It was really dreadful material and, of course, a lot of people, not being professionals, would stick to what they were given. As soon as we got away from Drury Lane those of us who were professionals would drop everything we had been given and put back our own acts.'

The reluctance of many top performers to join the early ENSA was not just a question of money, important though that was, but was because they had made their own arrangements to entertain troops. Before the war show business and top society mixed happily. Nearly everyone had a brother or relative who had joined up, knew an admiral, a general or an air vice marshal.

(Below) *Soon after war was declared Elisabeth Welch and several other performers were amongst the first to entertain the troops independently of any organization.* (Above) *ENSA troupes had to prepare for any eventuality for wherever they were to play.*

'A lot of artists would call up friends and get parties together, sometimes with War Office permission,' says Elisabeth Welch. 'If we went out of London, transport was laid on for us. I went to Salisbury a lot. Wherever we went the boys were very pleased to see us. Sometimes they were a bit stunned, agog at who was up there on the stage in front of them – people like Vivien Leigh, Kay Hammond and Michael Wilding. Often we had no stage. I've been on a truck, with a terrible broken-down piano, to sing to about six men on an Ack-Ack site in the middle of nowhere. I don't think they really wanted me to sing – though, as the piano was there, I did – they just wanted somebody to talk to. They were bored, lonely and tense, waiting for enemy planes to come over. A good shoot-up, they told me, was a relief.'

Actor Richard Hearne, better known to millions after the war as Mr Pastry, also organized his own concerts. He persuaded friends like Leslie

Henson, Fred Emney and Douglas Byng to join him in shows for troops stationed near his home in Kent. Since most big names were appearing in the theatre during the week such concerts had to take place on Sunday. They were a great success until the Lord's Day Observance Society complained and had them stopped.

From the outset there was controversy about the type of entertainment ENSA ought to be sending to the troops. Being a drama director and producer Basil Dean was keen to include plays. There was, however, a strong feeling amongst members of the various committees that troops would not want anything that smacked of highbrow. It was agreed that until a full survey of facilities available around the country had been carried out only variety, concert parties and light music should be offered.

A start was made with drama at the beginning of October when two repertory productions were borrowed to open the refurbished Garrison Theatre at Woolwich for a two week season that was reasonably successful. The first play produced solely by ENSA was not so fortunate. *Eight Bells*, starring James Mason, gave its first five performances to average houses of ten. When the curtain rose on the sixth and there was only one soldier in the audience, the play was withdrawn. John Gielgud, Ivy St Helier and Beatrice Lillie, a company West End audiences would have paid over the odds to see, fared little better when they took excerpts of Wilde and Coward to RAF Honnington. Although the hangar was packed they had to struggle to make themselves heard. When Gielgud asked the stage manager how long to make the interval he was advised not to have one if he wanted to get back on. The men were only waiting for them to finish so that they could listen to the Station dance band and its new crooner, Sam Costa. Emlyn Williams, touring his own play *Night Must Fall*, was horrified to see soldiers being marched into the theatre. 'We thought: Oh, dear, is this what ENSA is going to be like? We were very put off the whole idea. In fact, the only times we ever had trouble were when the audience had been marched in. We found them very naive. They just were not used to theatre. They talked, they read papers, they were not interested in the play. What they really wanted was girls.'

In the early days this was true. The majority did want only variety, comics and dancing girls – 'Tits and tinsel' as Charlie Chester put it. Few regular soldiers had been to a theatre to watch a play or

even wanted to. What drama they had seen was in the cinema where it didn't matter to the actors on screen if they talked or made comments. And in variety they were expected to join in. The habit was hard to break. It took great perseverance on the part of the actors to get themselves and their plays across. Gielgud found that, without a tradition of play-going, even if an audience did try to listen, it quickly lost the sense and became bored. His solution was to write an introduction to each act outlining the plot, delivered by one of the characters. It was a ploy adopted by many ENSA play productions.

The reception a show received, not just a play, depended almost as much on the local commander's attitude as on the ability of the performers. Some officers were grateful for any entertainment and nothing was too much trouble to ensure a performance ran smoothly. Others suffered entertainers and did nothing to encourage or help them. One crusty relic from the First World War refused to allow girls near his men – far better for them to have a run and cold shower – so only the male artists could appear. Some units, determined to have a good turn-out, made ENSA

'We're booked for some ENSA visits – see what you can do about entertaining the troupes.'

ENSA provided the artistes, but the troops provided the concert hall – and very cheerfully, too. Frances Day, wearing surely the longest pair of slacks ever, encourages the workers.

concerts parades. An alternative to jankers was being made to sit in the front row. Other units reserved the first few rows for officers and wives who failed to turn up leaving a gaping hole between stage and audience.

Invariably shows went down best in places which were cut off from theatres, cinemas and dance-halls, and without their own proper facilities for a full-scale production. It was out with the remote units, on balloon sites and in Ack-Ack batteries, off the beaten track and difficult to reach, that ENSA's most valuable contribution was made, reminding men that they were not forgotten but played an important part in the war. Heavy equipment had to be dragged across fields ankle-deep in mud. Pianos refused to go through hut doors. Stages were no more than trestle tables or planks on ammunition boxes. There was nowhere to change and no mirror for make-up. The only shows to get through were the small ones.

'I went with the Gerry Allen Trio to a searchlight battery in the wilds where they'd had nothing,' recalls Tommy Trinder. 'We couldn't get the organ into the hut so that meant we couldn't have any accompaniment. Along came the man in charge. "You, you and you!" he said. "Get this off!" They took down the side of the hut, put in the organ, then put back the side.

'At that time there were no models as we know them today – all top models were showgirls. If you opened *Harper's Bazaar* you could pick out the girls who used to model during the day and appear in the theatre at night. I took some of them with me to one camp. The sergeant came out in his shirtsleeves and said, "The dressing-room's in here." I said, "Thanks, but where do the men dress?" "In here." "Where do the ladies dress?" "In here." "We can't dress in the same room," I said. "Why not?" he asked. "Had a bleeding row?" And he walked away!'

In December ENSA introduced admission charges, an imposition which did nothing to improve feelings towards the organization. Until then all shows, even the most star-studded, had been free but there were grumbles that men who had no wish to be entertained were subsidising those that did through Naafi profits which belonged to everyone. Dean had other reasons for welcoming the decision: the money was required to expand the service and he was convinced that audiences would appreciate a show more if they had paid for it. He worked out a scale of charges which, after the customary bickering, was accepted. Its adoption aroused as much anger as the free concerts had. Soldiers wrote to their MP's accusing the Naafi of profiteering; Naafi managers complained they were losing bar sales while shows were on in their institutes; several companies were refused permission to appear and were returned to Drury Lane in protest.

There was one further difficulty with which ENSA had to cope. Its artists were civilians and, as such, were considered a security risk. (It was not until much later an officer-style uniform was issued to performers going overseas. Known popularly as Basil Dress, it brought another attack on Dean for trying to run a private army.) Particularly during 1939 and 1940 when a German invasion was feared imminent, the War Office refused to reveal troop locations in case the information fell into wrong hands. Very often all an ENSA driver had to find a unit was an incorrect map reference or name of a village, and all signposts were taken down to confuse German paratroops. Many units received an unscheduled concert from a party tired of scouring deepest Hampshire for the right location. The Lanchester Marionettes became the first ENSA show to play one remote unit. They were not the first to be routed there, just the first to arrive, two years after the war began. John Gielgud was astonished to be presented with a bill for excess petrol after a tour spent mostly looking for audiences. A Drury Lane official had worked out the route on a map and assumed the extra miles came from joy-riding.

Nor were some Entertainments Officers as helpful as they might have been. Jumping at the chance of visiting Drury Lane to arrange concerts and availing themselves of the West End night-life, they would creep back to their units the following morning unable to remember what had been booked. By the time a concert party arrived two weeks later the men would be out on exercise or had actually moved camp. A company manager who took his troupe to the pub when he found his venue occupied by local amateurs was promptly, if unfairly, sacked.

Scale of ENSA admission charges introduced on 4 December, 1939:

CATEGORY A *For permanent Garrison Theatres and Cinemas.*

Plays, musical and dramatic, Concert Parties and other full-scale entertainments, including standard-size film programmes (35-mm) 1/– (1/6d reserved), 6d and 3d (5p or 7½p, 2½p or 1.25p).

CATEGORY B *For institutes, converted gymnasia and other buildings used temporarily for entertainments.*
Programmes similar to those in Category A but given by smaller mobile companies carrying their own portable stages: 1/–, 6d and 3d.

CATEGORY C *Mobile cinemas (16-mm, substandard): Free.*

CATEGORY D *Sing-songs: Free.*

In spite of War Office precautions security at the camps themselves was never as tight as it might have been. Brian Oulton was touring in a play by Val Gielgud in which he and Desmond Jeans played German officers. 'Desmond wanted to buy some cigarettes and we had to go out of the camp to get them. As we passed the sentry he saluted us. On our way back he saluted us again. The absurd thing was that, although not a word passed between us, we were wearing German uniforms!'

Tommy Trinder drove in convoy with the Crazy Gang to give a show at an RAF station in Essex. 'We drove up to the gates and the sentry shouted halt. We told him who we were and that we were coming to do a show but he told us to wait outside. So we lined our cars up and waited while he went off to check we were who we said we were. Then Eddie Gray, who drove much slower than the rest of us and was way behind, arrived, sailed straight past us, parked his car by the sentry and got out. He clicked his heels, raised his hand in a Nazi salute and said, "Heil Hitler! I haf come for zee plans of zee Blenheim bombers!" The sentry roared with laughter and let him in. "Why him and not us?" we asked. "He's one of the Crazy Gang," he said. "I'm not sure about you lot."

To try and sort out some of these teething troubles a network of area officials and Entertainments Officers was established in every Command. Their basic task was to collate requests, route the shows that were sent to them, arrange hostels and food for the artists and monitor complaints.

Against her doctor's orders, Gracie Fields went to the French front to sing to an audience that literally overflowed the auditorium in the local cinema.

While ENSA struggled to find its feet in Britain, the British Expeditionary Force sat in France, waiting for action. Dean was eager to send them entertainment both because it was urgently needed and also because sending companies overseas would help confirm ENSA's role in the war. In October he succeeded in obtaining permission to visit the Adjutant General, Lieutenant General Brownrigg, at his headquarters in Northern France. Brownrigg readily agreed to the provision of mobile film units for forward areas (the first two were on their way five days later) but was reluctant to commit himself to live entertainment. Dean persisted and finally was given consent provided no women were included in the parties. Dean returned home triumphantly and announced that six star parties, already rehearsing at Drury Lane, would open the French service at the end of November.

The first ENSA show on French soil immediately broke the Adjutant General's 'No women' provision. Gracie Fields, who had just undergone a major operation which threatened her career, contacted Dean. She planned to return to her home on Capri to convalesce and would be driving through France; could she sing for the troops? It was too good an opportunity to miss. Dean phoned GHQ in Arras and sought permission for a concert. To his surprise it was granted.

Gracie Fields was too weak to undertake a complete programme on her own so, at twenty-four hours' notice, a company was assembled at Drury Lane. Sir Seymour Hicks (who was to have led the first official party) acted as compere with Dennis Noble, Claire Luce, Tom Webster and the Three Exquisite Ascots. When news got out the demand for tickets was so great that Gracie had to agree to give a second concert the same day. On the way to the first, in Douai, her car became entangled with a convoy. Some soldiers recognized her and demanded a song. One became two and what looked like becoming a full impromptu concert for 200 men and a handful of astonished French villagers only ended when the air raid sirens went. In the theatre foyer at Douai a large banner proclaimed 'To Gracie from the boys.' Inside it was crowded, two people to a seat. She made her entrance in the second half, unannounced, and walked slowly to the centre of the stage. 'What an odd moment of silence it was,' wrote the *Daily Express* reporter. 'Then, uproar. The floor shook to 2,500 pairs of stamping feet, the men whistled and cheered.'

'For three months I had rarely sat even on a chair with a wooden back,' John Gostelow recalls of that afternoon. 'Then I was one of a small number of men from my AA battery selected to attend the concert. I sat in the stalls and relaxed in the supreme luxury of a plush theatre seat and enjoyed the wonderful artistry of Miss Fields. I can remember the warmth and luxurious feeling to this day. It was the cold start of a bitterly cold winter of which I'm reminded by every winter's day that is frosty and foggy at the same time.'

Fields was given just as rapturous a welcome for the evening show at Arras. The theatre was again bursting and the guest of honour, the local mayor, couldn't get into his reserved box which was occupied by several Scots Guards. He retreated to the only available place, behind the stage, and watched the show through a hole in the backcloth.

ENSA's efforts overseas were off to a rousing start. While Gracie Fields continued her journey south, Hicks and company returned to London. Ten days later he was in France again leading the first show of the regular service. On the same train out of Victoria Station were two other companies – Leslie Henson's Gaieties and Ralph Reader's all-male Gang Show, designed to tour the forward areas.

'There were about thirty people seeing off Leslie Henson and his party, and about the same number for Sir Seymour,' says Reader. 'When we got to the station there must have been two- or three-hundred to see us off – all Scouts and their families, some with kids in their arms. It was like a scene from *Cavalcade*. As the train steamed out into the dark, blacked-out night they started to sing 'Crest of a Wave.' It was the most emotional experience. Leslie Henson was standing next to me and when I looked at him he was crying.'

'We were,' remembers Bill Sutton, a member of that Gang Show, 'very, very choked. We felt that was it – that we would never see England again.' In fact, they spent that night at a hotel in Folkestone. The sea was rough and with a danger of mines in the Channel the ship's captain refused to sail.

'We were supposed to have given a show that night at Seclin, near the Belgian frontier,' continues Bill Sutton. 'They had assembled the troops, mostly Guardsmen, and they waited and waited until a call went through explaining that we were still in Folkestone. They called them all back the next night to the local town hall in the hope that there would be a show then and it was packed. When we landed at Calais there was a coach waiting to rush us across France. The audience had been assembled as we were landing and they gave a town-by-town commentary on our progress. I don't think there was ever a bigger build-up to a show than that one. When we finally got there, a mistake had been made with the posters outside – instead of *Ralph Reader and the Ten Blokes* they read *Ralph Reader and the Ten Blondes*. Well, we got on stage and they let it go for a while, then they started to shout, "Where are the women?" When they discovered there weren't any, that did it. There was uproar. They'd been given free beer while they'd been waiting, to keep them quiet, and they were riotous to say the least. We decided not to stop and just carried on. For the first three-quarters-of-an-hour it was impossible to make ourselves heard but gradually they settled down and started to laugh and we finished up having a terrific show.'

Other companies soon made the Channel crossing. Jack Buchanan took Elsie Randolph, Fred Emney and Sid Millward with him; Will Hay led the first *ENSA Music Hall*; Joe Loss, Billy Cotton and other bandleaders took their bands for a minimum four week tour at the standard rate of £10 a week. Before the end of the year thirty companies, of all sizes, were on the French circuit.

Once overseas ENSA units were at the disposal of local military commanders and subject to Army regulations. If troops moved suddenly it could mean getting up early to give a show before they departed or rearranging the performance many inconvenient miles away. Having to change and make-up in a lavatory before climbing on to a draughty, improvised stage did not equate with the star status some girls assumed. The work also interrupted the round of cocktail parties in the Mess. Despatches flew back to London that ENSA abroad was every bit as bad as ENSA at home. Receiving more publicity from knocking ENSA than ever their talent had brought them, the detractors told bigger and better stories. A Sheffield paper ran a piece on three girls who objected to signing the official secrets act: 'As if we would tell people where we have been!' they whined, before recounting a town-by-town itinerary of their travels.

That winter was the worst within living memory. Arriving anywhere or getting back to a hotel became a major triumph. Icy roads, swollen rivers and endless delays while passes were inspected, or the chorus girls, wandering round in civilian clothes, were rescued from suspicious Military Police, were everyday hazards for which ENSA took the blame. When Billy Cotton's Band failed to complete a sixty mile drive to a concert because a temporary pontoon bridge collapsed with the band on one side of the river and their instruments on the other it was headlined as a typical example of ENSA's waste and muddle.

Thoroughly alarmed by the activities of its foster-child, the Naafi ordered a complete investigation into ENSA's affairs. The majority of charges were proved to be groundless but too late to stop ENSA-baiting becoming a public sport. Throughout the war, whenever news from the front was dull, reporters knew they could rely on attacking ENSA for a few popular, controversial paragraphs. In an organization employing thousands and giving thousands of shows a week around the world, ammunition was never hard to find.

CHAPTER TWO

MESA AND THE ARMY CONCERT PARTIES

The demands for entertainment were always greater than ENSA could meet, but ENSA, much to Dean's annoyance, was not the only source available. Up and down the country there were hundreds of worthy citizens determined the troops should not be forgotten. Within weeks of the declaration church choirs, amateur dramatic societies, operatic groups, Women's Institute revues, YWCA concert parties and troupes of performing children were queuing outside the barracks to give a show. Urgent appeals for amateur entertainers to make themselves known appeared in the press alongside requests for knitted comforts for the troops. Organizations were formed to co-ordinate their efforts, the one in Northern Command involving more than fifty amateur operatic societies and concert parties. Half the nation seemed to harbour a secret desire to climb on a stage and entertain.

Ronnie Hill, revue artist, writer and composer, had joined the Royal Navy and become Entertainments Officer at Portsmouth. 'There were many pretty dreadful amateur companies around Portsmouth consisting very largely of children – five or six year olds – doing little tap dances and so on. Every time they came I would go into the theatre with my heart in my mouth because I thought they would produce the biggest mickey-take of all time. The incredible thing was, it never happened. The sailors became very sentimental about children and would sit there crying their eyes out. It didn't matter how bad they were.'

A camp in the West Midlands was paid a visit by a concert party formed by a group of housewives.

The group's stage manager was Eddie Shrimpton. 'Before the show began the local padre held a short service which finished with him calling for a few moments silent prayer, "that we may all be granted what we desire." The show opened with half-a-dozen girls doing a can-can. It was not very well done and had never gone down particularly well – until this night. The reception was marvellous. The men cheered and cheered and wouldn't let the girls off stage. We found out why, afterwards. One of them had forgotten to put on her knickers. My job then, for the rest of the war, was to check it never happened again. It said a lot for the power of prayer.'

Popular though some amateur shows undoubtedly were, there were few that would have been welcomed back quickly. Enthusiasm could not make up for lack of talent and most were pretty poor.

Another drawback to amateur groups was that their members had full-time jobs or family commitments and if a key member couldn't find a baby-sitter, that was it, no show. They were unable to commit themselves to a regular programme of concerts and were never able to travel far from home. Most Entertainments Officers found it easier to omit them from their plans.

That didn't mean the field was left open for ENSA. In every Command there were alternatives. In some of the more neglected and remote areas concert parties which started as amateur, occasional groups were adopted by the troops and became semi-professional, playing regular engagements for which they were paid expenses. Manaagers of Repertory and Variety theatres were prepared to arrange performances and some even set up companies just to play to the forces. One such manager was Charles F Smith, philanthropist director of the Theatre Royal, Brighton. He disapproved strongly of ENSA's policy of categorizing shows so that only troops stationed in large garrisons or towns (which had a lot of entertainment anyway) saw star productions while men with remote units received sing-songs. He decided to produce his own units which would play to men in Southern Command no matter where they were stationed or the size of audience. He called his venture Mobile Entertainments for the Southern Area, which, like everything in service life, became known by its initials as MESA. Every night except Sunday, Smith sent out two plays, two concert parties and a film show.

This MESA production was one of the most popular enterprises and it was played to the forces throughout the war before finally going to SEAC sponsored by ENSA.

Donald Sinden, fresh from school and planning a career as an architect like his grandfather, failed his army medical and spent his war years in one of the MESA play units. 'My cousin was a very keen amateur actor in Brighton and when the RAF called him up in the middle of rehearsals he phoned me and asked if I would take over. I had never wanted to be an actor or even go on the stage so I said, "What do I have to do?" "It's easy," he said. "All you have to do is learn the lines and go on; no problem at all." I did just that and played for four performances one of which was seen by Charles F Smith. He asked me to join his company and I thought it must be because I was the world's greatest. I discovered later he couldn't get anybody else – they were all being called up!'

Sinden made his professional début in *George and Margaret* on 26 January, 1941. 'We played six nights a week, with variations: we might be booked to appear at some camp one night and they had moved, or suddenly they didn't want us. We were paid 7s. 6d. (37½p) a performance and, as always, no play, no pay. It should have averaged out at just over £2 a week but it never did.

'We went out in a single-decker bus from which half the seats had been removed to hold the scenery, such as it was. Because the size and shape of the stages varied so enormously we had to be very adaptable; we used the minimum and filled in with black curtains. At Aldershot or Southampton we had a full-size theatre but most often we played in a hut, a room or a village hall near the barracks. We also played a lot of country houses which the army had taken over, including Goodwood where we were in the ballroom. It had semi-circular ends and when they built the stage from mess tables, since oblong shapes don't fit into a semi-circle, there were quadrant-shaped holes dotted around the edge of the stage. Most of them were all right except for one right outside one of the doors of the set. When we entered we all had to open the door over the hole and take a large step on to the stage; the same going out. Now a juvenile in the company, younger than myself, was so nervous that when he went to open the door and make his exit, he just turned and went straight down the hole. There he was up to his waist. Instead of climbing out and starting again he tried to close the door over his head, in full view of the audience which roared with laughter and held the play up for a good ten minutes.

'On another occasion we played *George and Margaret* in a room where the stage was minute. In

French Leave *was typical of the many plays produced to entertain the forces, in that it travelled with the barest essentials, and despite the village hall amateur appearance, was enthusiastically received by its audiences. Donald Sinden (standing at the back) had made his debut before the troops in* George and Margaret.

the first scene the family came down to breakfast, just like any family, at different times and as each person came on he or she had to take his breakfast from the sideboard, cross to the table and sit down. On this particular stage there wasn't room for anything but a dining table, a sideboard and a couple of chairs. Once the actors were on, the stage was full. The dining table was a folding card-table, about two feet square, and, as each actor came on, he had to bring his own chair then, when he'd had breakfast, take it off. There was a marvellous moment when, through stepping up on to the stage all the time, we loosened the boards and gaps appeared. The sideboard, another small table with a telephone, the breakfast and a bowl of fruit made up with a wax banana (being war we couldn't get real ones) and tennis balls painted to look like apples and oranges, suddenly went down one of these gaps. I was in the middle of a love scene, with the girl in my arms, when apples and oranges went bouncing past us and out into the audience.'

These sort of conditions awaited any company playing to troops. One night they would appear in a real theatre, the next in a Nissen hut on an improvised stage with a handful watching and rain on the tin roof drowning the lines. The following night would be spent in a cavernous hangar in front of two-thousand men, and heaven help the actor who could not adjust his performance to be heard at the back.

And still the work of amateurs, professional companies, individuals and ENSA could not satisfy demand. There was, however, a further source to which the Services could turn, the hundreds of professional performers, some of them household names, who were in their own ranks. Most of them had joined up reluctantly when their call-up papers came through and were only too pleased to put in as much time as they were allowed entertaining. Should someone refuse to put on a show or appear he could always be ordered. But few needed a second invitation.

'The day I joined up,' remembers Charlie Chester, 'I had my photograph in the paper: "Cheerful Charlie joins an Irish Regiment." Well, my regiment was newly formed so it had no money, no equipment, no gym shorts even, just a few old First World War rifles. When we arrived at Newtown we were marched from the train to a great big hangar just outside the town, in our civvies. We were told to take off our clothes, take off our trousers, take off our pants and put them on back-to-front, with the fly-hole at the rear. We then had to run all the way through the town to the other side for a medical!

'There was one little cinema in Newtown called the Regent. I formed a concert party called The Craziliers and we did a show there every Sunday. We made so much money that we were able to buy pipes, drums, Irish kilts, football gear, sports equipment and start a PRI (President of the Regiment's Institute) fund. We made the regiment fairly wealthy.'

A sensible commander like Chester's would be quick to utilize talent in his ranks. Happy men are efficient men and entertainment helped keep the men happy. It was an equation older, more conservative officers had difficulty making. To them an actor or performer was an embarrassment. A butcher could be sent to the cookhouse, a doctor to the Medics, a mechanic to the workshops, but what could be done with an actor? He hadn't a trade and unless he showed officer potential was fit only for general duties. Cellist Reginald Kilbey was sent to the Royal Engineers because he was considered to be good with his hands.

'The tragedy was,' says Peter Warren, former stage manager who joined the Royal Artillery, 'to see violinists, whose hands were their living, peeling potatoes or scrubbing floors. The thing was most of us were never any good as soldiers. I was the most god-awful soldier you ever saw. I had minocular vision and when I was on the rifle range I committed the unforgivable sin – I hit the next man's target. They thought I was taking the mickey and sent me to the toughest hospital, where they sent all the bad boys, at Hatfield. The occulist took one look at my eyes and said, "What do you expect me to do?" "Please tell them!" I said. When I got back the first thing they asked me was where was my rifle? "Here," I said. "Give it to us," they screamed. I never saw that rifle again. I tried, God knows, I tried.'

Not even officers were immune from sarcasm and misunderstanding if they had been entertainers in civilian life. 'Certainly at the beginning of the war entertainers were regarded as pariahs,' says Nigel Patrick. 'I was stationed in Yorkshire when a very distinguished general came to inspect us. All the officers were waiting in a room on the first floor, chatting away, when the colonel saw the car with the red flag fluttering away and rushed down to receive him. This old boy staggered out, looking as though he had commanded something at Waterloo, staggered up the stairs, came in and said, "At ease, gentlemen, at ease." He was then solemnly introduced to everyone by the colonel. "How do you do?" he said. And then, because it was a Territorial battalion, "What do you do in peacetime?" "I have an antique business," replied the first man. "Really? That must be most interesting buying all those lovely things. I don't suppose you like selling them, what?" "Not much, sir, but I like the money." "Jolly good, jolly good." And so on, down the line, talking to everyone, until he came to me. The colonel made the introduction: "This is Patrick, sir, one of the subalterns in 'A' Company." "And what do you do?" "I'm an actor, sir." He looked at me, grunted and turned straight to the next man.'

Ian Carmichael had just finished his training at the Royal Academy of Dramatic Art and landed his first job in a Farjeon revue when his call-up papers arrived. After ten weeks square-bashing at Catterick and a course at Sandhurst he was commissioned into the 22nd Dragoons.

'My colonel was a regular cavalry man, a pukka-pukka Indian Army-type, who looked down on entertainment. I always got on with him strangely enough, even after he discovered I had been an actor, although he always thought I had been in the back row of the chorus at the Windmill. Once he found out he treated me like a court jester. I was *commanded* to entertain in the Mess, which irritated me enormously. If there was a visiting general, when we were in the ante-room having

Ian Carmichael, seen here with Nigel Patrick in Spring Time for Henry, *August 1940, appeared in this same vehicle in Oxford some 35 years later.*

coffee after dinner, I would be summoned: "Come and amuse us, Carmichael." I did recitations and various impersonations of personalities within the brigade and I must have been successful because I was continually being called upon: "Come and sit by me. Entertain me." If I hadn't been I would have been banished to the other end of the table.

'A decree came from headquarters that the four regiments in the brigade should each put on a show in the camp theatre. That was an official decree from the brigadier so suddenly my colonel pricked up his ears. When ordered to do something by the brigadier he bloody-well did it. Any pleas of mine to put on entertainment had fallen on very stony ground but this was an order. He sent for me. "You will put on a show, Carmichael, and it will be the best in the brigade." So, fools rush in; with the impetuosity of youth I went back to him after twenty-four hours and said, "I've thought about this and I'll do it." (I'd do as I was told!) "But," I went on grandly, "I want to be able to take anybody I need from the regiment and I want them off all duties for a fortnight. We've got to be able to rehearse this properly and I can't do it in the evening." I laid down a number of impossible requests such as two grand pianos – one for the stage and one for the pit – an impossible amount of money so that I could costume everything from London and I insisted on having the regimental signwriter and carpenter to do the scenery. Everything was agreed. Eventually we put on this show called *Acting Unpaid*, all with regimental talent and it was quite a success.'

The prize catch for any unit wanting to form a concert party was the professional who could lick a few keen amateurs into shape.

'I was in the first batch of militia,' recalls Kenneth Connor. 'Hore-Belisha's Gentlemen they called us – and a finer load of rough you've never come across. I had to report to Mill Hill barracks and was immediately stopped at the gates by the orderly officer. "Have you just come from the Open Air Theatre in Regent's Park?" he asked. I said I had. I was the only actor in an intake of a thousand men. "I want you to start a concert party and get a show on for tonight," he said. He gave me 10/– (50p) to pay for any props I might need. This was in the afternoon. I didn't know anybody and there was nothing I could do except post notices asking who wanted to join. One or two did and I got the show on. The hit of the evening was a little Jewish tailor who just read an imaginary letter he'd written to his Mum about Mill Hill depot. He was a born raconteur and brought the house down. I tried to get some things going on the Minstrel line. We'd all been issued with mugs, knives, forks and spoons, and they were hidden beneath our chairs. We sang a verse of 'Jingle Bells' then, in a military movement, dived under our chairs and came out rattling the eating irons in the mugs for the bells. Since most of the audience had their mugs with them, they joined in and it worked very well. Afterwards we had a night out in the Sergeants' Mess, for two hours.

'At six o'clock the next morning, I was shaving when the orderly corporal bashed me on the shoulder and said the major wanted to see me. I went, braces dangling and covered in soap. He said, "Would you give me the, um, the er, change out of the 10/– to help defray the cost of the, er, drinks in the Sergeants' Mess?" This was the morning after the concert! I had bought three pairs of black stockings, large, which could go over the head and have eyes cut in them to make Minstrel masks, a few pins and some elastic. I owed him 3/4½d. I dived my grubby paw into my rotten, stinking uniform trousers and said, "Take your bloody money! I can't get away from this place with a guard on the gate and you come round asking for change out of ten bob! From an impresario!" It didn't go down too well I'm afraid.'

Ian Grant, lyric writer of the popular *Let There Be Love*, also came up against the mean military mind when he arranged for revue star Douglas Byng to top the bill of a show he was putting on at Winchester barracks. For the show he had managed to scrounge £4,000-worth of lighting equipment and drapes from the Dorchester Hotel where he had been working before the war. Arriving back at the barracks in a taxi crammed with booty he was refused the 4/2d. fare (21p) and told he should have gone by bus.

Actor John Arnatt, a chorus boy for C B Cochran before his call-up, was sent to the BEF in France with a detachment of Royal Engineers.

'At the end of parade they used to fall out the various trade categories. Then they would finish with me – 'Fall out, Sapper Arnatt' – and that was the end of my day. I became a staff car driver until the car packed up and I had no job again. One day the sergeant-major came to me and said, "There's a concert on tonight and you're in it." I tried to explain that I was either a chorus boy, in which case I had a routine worked out for me, or an actor, in which case I had a script to work from,

but this didn't go down at all well. "You are an actor and you are going to appear." So I went to this concert and discovered it was a talent contest which I won with a Marriott Edgar monologue, 'The Battle of Trafalgar.' After this success the sergeant-major said there was to be a broadcast from France of service entertainment and I would be in it. Again I tried to explain that although I might get away with pinching somebody else's material in a camp concert there was such a thing as copyright for a broadcast. I also thought, though I didn't say so, that Stanley Holloway was doing monologues rather better than I was. However, my objections were waved aside with "There will be a concert and you will appear." So I wrote an act for myself based on a lecture about the rifle given by this same sergeant-major. I tried it out and it went down very well, lasting me, on and off, for the rest of the war.'

The broadcast from France never took place. The Germans finally made their push in the Sedan and Arnatt, along with thousands of others, joined the dash for the beaches of Dunkirk. Back in England his unit was sent to Bury St Edmunds to clear a site for a new camp.

'Anyone in 'ere got any talent?'

The March 1941 Spotlights and Sweet Music production of the RAPCATS concert party was typical of the many such performances throughout the land. The balding, bemedalled gentleman in the centre was the producer Clifton James who later gained fame as Montys 'double'.

'The CO sent for me one day and said, "I want a concert party." Again I pointed out that we were under canvas, in the middle of a wood, we had no piano, no musical instruments of any kind and no talent. This was waved aside in typical Army fashion: "You've got no other work to do" – which I hadn't – and, "You will perform in a concert party." "We have one Nissen hut," I replied. "If you let me have that I can keep all the props in there and build a stage on to the side. And there is a man here who tells me he can play the accordion. If you give him forty-eight hours leave he could go and fetch it." Eventually, after a great deal of arguing, all this happened and I went round the unit (it was a company so there were about 200 men to choose from) and held auditions in the woods. We got some packing cases, some ammunition boxes and bits of wood, and built a stage. We still had no songs or material. The accordionist had brought back one or two numbers but they were a bit dated. I couldn't write music and neither could he but he could play by ear so I made up some words and he picked out a tune. Eventually we formed a show with about eight or nine men in.'

Arnatt's woodland party flourished for a few performances only to wither when he was transferred to an OCTU (Officer Cadet Training Unit.) But the sort of entertaining he had been doing was happening everywhere. People got together, either because they wanted to or because they had been ordered, put on a show and then went their separate ways.

It would be wrong to imagine that the Services were full of professional actors busy acting or that every performer in uniform appeared on the stage. Those who had been commissioned were invariably not allowed to tread the boards – military duties came first – and those in special or skilled units such as the Parachute Brigade didn't have time. Even a regular unit concert party would not give a show more than one night a month at most.

For those who were involved, concerts made great demands, particularly when the producer, scriptwriter and star were one and the same, as often happened with a professional. During the day they had to be soldiers. Writing, auditioning, rehearsing, painting scenery, had to take place in the evening, in off-duty hours, most of the time without much sympathy or help from fellow

The Salvation Army organized Carol Concerts such as this in a gymnasium near Dover which could just as likely be repeated in a small village hall, Nissen hut or tent anywhere in Britain.

Servicemen. Not even the Mess provided a refuge where a comedian or musician could relax. He was expected to be at everyone's beck and call, ready to entertain the moment he was asked. It didn't matter that he had just sat down for the first time in twelve hours or was involved in conversation; if someone wanted him to, he had to get up and do his party piece. It was forgotten that he, too, had to be on parade at seven the next morning.

'I used to find it very difficult ever to refuse to play in the Mess,' says Reg Varney, who had been playing the piano at the Windmill before his call-up in 1941. 'If I didn't go to the piano willingly all sorts of dire penalties would be muttered. And in the Army, if you were at the bottom, you could take a hint.'

As well as having to play into the small hours, night after night, Varney was spending every evening with *The REME Revels*, the concert party he had started. 'During the day I was metal-bashing on Churchill tanks. In the evening there were auditions, rehearsals, preparing material

(most of which I wrote), organizing the others and performing. After that I had to go into the Mess and play the piano. It was too much for one person. After six months I collapsed from exhaustion. Fortunately we had a very good show which the padre liked and he managed to get us relieved of some of our duties. He also took it upon himself to become our agent, arranging performances in other camps. But I still had to pay people to do my guard and picket duty while I went to rehearsals.'

Men of God exercised considerable influence over troop shows. With half the male population in their temporary care they saw themselves as Guardians of the Nation's Morals, the last bastion between the wholesome world of the civilian and the depravity of the Forces. And depravity, for them, meant entertainment. Every performance came under the closest scrutiny to ensure it was free from taint. Visiting shows were especially suspect and came in for much criticism. ENSA, of course, bore the brunt of the attacks. A sermon on the theme that ENSA catered for 'all that is lowest, disgusting and immoral' received banner headlines and when the *Daily Sketch* entered the lists with an article entitled 'Cleanse the ENSA stables' it was able to print three-and-a-half columns of supporting letters.

Naturally the case was overstated but there was some substance to the accusations as Basil Dean was well aware. He insisted on a clause being inserted into the standard ENSA contract directing artists 'not to give expression to any vulgarity, words having a double meaning, nor to use any objectionable gesture.' Nor should they 'make personal reference to officers or others while on the stage' nor 'invite the participation of any officer, warrant officer or non-commissioned officer on the stage or in the audience to take part in the performance.'

The sort of performer Dean was trying to guard against is described in his book *The Theatre At War*:

'There is a type of bludgeoning performer who wears a proboscis of another hue, best described as "blue nose", whose reliance upon lavatory jokes and indecent gesture is sickening when it is not frankly boring. The thirst for entertainment was so great that indifferent performers of this type got more applause than they deserved, and this encouraged an inordinate belief in their abilities . . . The pest arose, too, when little parties designed to give entertainment lasting an hour or so were called upon to expand their programmes to last two hours. The artistes ran out of material and began to pad out their turns with tap-room gags, often of the most abysmal vulgarity. (The majority of variety artists work with a limited repertoire; their fund of invention seems limited.)'

A further safeguard against the 'blue nose' performer was the vetting of all scripts at Drury Lane. A signed copy, approved by headquarters, had to be carried by an artist at all times. Failure to do so or repeated complaints meant suspension and ultimately expulsion from ENSA. When there was so little work around for the artist most likely to offend this was a very real threat. Typical complaints are to be found in this official letter sent to an ENSA company manager:

'The following stories were noted at a performance of your show:–

1. In the number "The Colonel and the Girls", the "Colonel" is asking questions and one of the girls replies: "I always go to bed between six and seven," to which the "Colonel" replies "Far too many in a bed."

2. The Comedian also gives the old rhyme which has been cut out of several ENSA shows of the land girl who "to milk a cow was unable" but "practised at night with sausages under a table."

3. Another old gag used when some member of the audience leaves the hall also appeared, ie 'Is your journey really necessary?" Not very objectionable, but to it was added "I expect it's the cold weather," leaving no doubt as to its application.

4. Another story of the girl who went on a cruise and later having had a baby was asked: "Was it the cruise?" and replied: "No, the Captain's."

5. In a sketch of a domestic scene between husband and wife the latter refers to a neighbour who hasn't left his wife for two years and remarks that that was love. The husband retorts: "That's not love, It's paralysis."

Three at least of these stories have been ordered to be cut out when told previously in shows, and it is not credited that they can be in the script passed by Drury Lane. Will you please see that they are deleted at future performances.'

Hardly the most *risqué* of jokes any of them but what would pass unnoticed on television today was, in 1940, considered very blue. Even the most innocuous remark could be misinterpreted. And it wasn't just unknown ENSA comedians who were criticized. Tommy Trinder was frequently reported for vulgarity (though his material was never offensive and the troops never complained); Beatrice Lillie created a furore with an act she had played in the West End and in New York; and Freddie Frinton, telling a joke that comics had used for years, fell foul of a padre as Kenneth Connor recalls:

'I saw Freddie in a show at divisional headquarters in Northumberland when he did the old gag about a vicar losing his umbrella and only remembering where he'd left it when he reached the seventh Commandment, Thou shalt not commit adultery. Of course everyone laughed but the senior chaplain got up and went out, closely followed by his number two.

'The following morning I saw Private Frinton standing by the kerb and told him how much I'd enjoyed his act. "Well, there's somebody who didn't," he said, "Holy Joe. He's sent for me. He's took offence at last night." On my way back I passed the same spot and there was Freddie, leaning up against the wall, crying. I thought he'd been threatened with being shot at least. He was actually laughing! "It were terrible," he said. "He

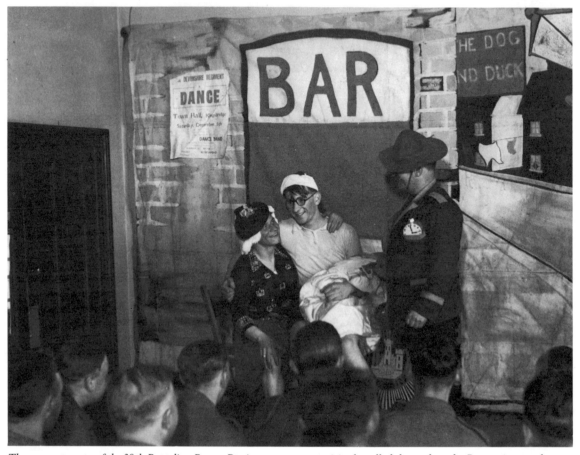

The concert party of the 30th Battalion Devon Regiment not unsurprisingly called themselves the Devonaires to play to their fellow soldiers as here in Falmouth. Also, not unsurprisingly, they appeared with the minimum scenery, costumes and props.

told me off for filth and all that and being disrespectful to Holy Orders with a Chaplain of the Forces sitting in the front row by telling that joke. I told him the vicar might have remembered he'd left it on a bus – it's people's minds. 'Stand to attention!' he said. I told him I couldn't discuss the matter unless we could talk man to man. 'Right,' he said, 'you can stand at ease.' Then I told him I go all over the country entertaining, making the lads laff. I go to make people laff, not to offend. He destroyed the fun last night by getting up and going out. If he didn't like the show he could have waited until the interval and not come back. Everyone looked. They knew something was wrong. He told me I must be more careful in future and asked me to have a cup of coffee with him at the Queen's Head. When we got to the door he said, 'Hello, Frinton, it's raining. Just wait here.' I were waiting for a long time.

When he came back his bloody face, it were redder than ever. You should have seen it! He looked me straight in the eye and said, with a twinkle, 'Frinton, I can't find my umbrella.'"

Tommy Trinder was one of the first civilian entertainers to visit the Home Fleet in the Orkney Islands. He too suffered the vagaries of the uniformed cleric.

'The very first show we did the padre came with us. He put down a chair in front of the stage and sat facing the audience. He didn't watch the show at all. He was looking to see how the men reacted. Well, he was so off-putting that we used to try and lose him. We would tell him that we were going to one place and then go to another. We would say we were going to Flota, then go off to Hoy in the hope that he would end up at Flota.'

As well as looking for blue material padres and other self-appointed censors were on guard against any references to marital infidelity or girls becoming pregnant. Such ideas were bad for the morale of men away from their homes. In fact the majority of comedy routines revolved around service life. Old gags were redressed into uniform: the doctor became the medical officer, the park attendant or authority became the NCO. Trinder now admits that much of the material he used was not very funny but it worked at the time. The men themselves didn't want to hear crude jokes. When they went to a show they wanted to be entertained and there was nothing that could be said on stage which they hadn't heard already in the barracks. Women might be in the audience, too, or in the chorus on stage and crudity then was only an embarrassment.

When it came to concerts put on by troops the content depended entirely on the talent and professionalism of the artists available. Anyone who could sing, dance, tell jokes, recite, conjure, give bird impressions or play an instrument would be pulled in to help. Sketches were usually written by the performers about local personalities and life

'*Apart from the fact that the first two rows are reserved for officers, AND that you're sitting in the Air Commodore's seat, I personally can't see any objection to your remaining here.*'

in uniform and rarely rose above the level of school-boy humour. Sometimes there might be a variation on a half-remembered West End revue number or a complete Crazy Gang routine would be used. Nigel Patrick explains what went into a concert party he organized:

'Early in 1940 I was posted to South Wales. It was the time of 'Cromwell', which was the codeword for the expected invasion of this country by the Germans, and nobody was allowed out of the camp. Our commander said to Frank Lawton (Evelyn Laye's husband) and myself, "You're the experts; arrange something." So we arranged a concert which was, I suppose, typical of the sort of thing people were putting on. We found out who could play the piano or mouth-organ, recite or do something, had a parade and weeded them out. The performance was held in a huge tent. The duty officer came on stage and said, "We're going to have an entertainment and first on the bill is Rifleman Snooks from 'B' Company. Right, come on." And this chap was yanked up to play the piano for three minutes, then sat down. Then Corporal Jones from 'C' Company juggled, and so on.

'Frank and I thought we ought to do something so when the duty officer said, "Now here's someone who ought to be able to do something for us," Frank climbed on stage and started to recite the poem "The Green Eye of the Little Yellow God" by Milton Hayes. There was a very famous parody of this by Reginald Purdell which involved someone shouting from the audience. So Frank started: "There's a one-eyed yellow idol, to the North of Katmandu, there's a little marble cross below the town. . ." At that moment sitting in the third row, I called out, "Have you been there recently?" "What?" "Have you been there recently?" That's how the sketch progressed – or was supposed to. I got as far as the second "Have you been there recently?" when the second-in-command, who was sitting in front of me, turned round and said, very fiercely, "Shut up!" He ruined the sketch.'

Many of the regiments and divisions that had fought in the First World War had a tradition of concert parties and were quick to revive them. Other units followed suit once they discovered the value of on-camp entertainment. The importance of the uniformed entertainer increased dramatically, creating a problem for those CO's sympathetic to the idea of home-grown productions. If the men involved were craftsmen their work

'Right-o, I'll tell you what I'll do : I'll swap our second piano-tuner for one of your six comedians if you'll give me a written guarantee that he isn't a female impersonator.

suffered as a result of the long hours spent rehearsing and performing. If, on the other hand, they were appalling soldiers was there any point in trying to teach them to dismantle radios or solder wires? The solution was to utilize their talents in keeping up morale. Wherever practicable men were released from all but token duties to concentrate on entertaining with the proviso that if need be they would revert to fighting soldiers.

One of the best of these more-or-less permanent companies was *The Balmorals*, the concert party of the 51st Highland division. *The Balmorals* had been a famous name during The First World War when the divisional concert party had been the mainstay of entertainment for men in France. When the Highland Division returned to France in 1939, with the BEF, *The Balmorals* was revived only to be taken prisoner along with most of the division at St Valery-en-Caux in June, 1940. The division was reformed in Scotland the same year and with it another *Balmorals* concert party. Fleet Street journalist Felix Barker had been conscripted into the Gordon Highlanders and found himself posted to a remote corner of the Shetlands where he was asked if he would like to submit a sketch for the opening production.

'In the bottom of my kitbag I had a typewriter. It was rather a strange thing to take on active service but one clung to the vestiges of one's civilian life. I sat down on the three wooden planks that were my bed and tried to write sketches suitable for the concert party. As soon as I started to type a sort of reverential hush came over the hut and everyone turned to me as though I was playing with a time-bomb. Eventually someone asked, "What's that thing?" "A typewriter," I replied. That seemed to satisfy everyone except the corporal in charge because when the platoon commander came round to switch off the lights, as he did every night, he said, "Please, sir, Private Barker's got a typewriter," as if I was concealing a wild animal. The officer came to the end of my bed and asked severely if this was true. I said it was but that it was only a very small typewriter. "In that case, jolly good show," he said. And such was the way of the Army that the following day I was transferred to brigade headquarters as a typist.

'It was while I was there that I conceived the first of the sketches I wrote for *The Balmorals*. It showed an outpost very much like the Shetlands in which all the staff had gone to pot. No one bothered to change out of his pyjamas and, indeed, a major had his crown on his pyjama shoulders as though it were an epaulette. All this was completely revolutionized when it was announced that three ATS girls were about to arrive on the island.'

The sketch appealed to Stephen Mitchell in charge of *The Balmorals*. Producer of the West End production of *The Corn Is Green* and other plays by Emlyn Williams, Mitchell was a major himself. Within forty-eight hours of submitting his manuscript Barker was on his way to join the concert party at its temporary base in a requisitioned distillery. After endless auditions at which, Barker recalled, every cook-sergeant seemed to specialize in bird imitations, the company reached its final strength of thirty. Twelve became performers, ten formed a band and eight worked on production. Only half-a-dozen had had any sort of previous theatrical experience.

The standard at which Stephen Mitchell aimed was a mixture of popular concert party and Farjeon, the emphasis being on Farjeon (Herbert Farjeon had been running small, intimate, highly sophisticated and successful revues during the Thirties.) As far as possible he wanted to use original material and approached such distinguished Scottish writers as James Bridie, Eric Linklater, A G MacDonald and Alan Melville to provide it. The company also contributed ideas, especially Felix Barker.

'Stephen told me the sort of sketches he wanted and gave me various ideas. "Above all," he said, "I want you to try to write something which will suggest that we are going to win the war." Well, in September, 1940 it was extremely difficult to think of anything one *could* write that would suggest Britain was in any way likely to win. However, I went away, found myself a little corner in the distillery where I could set up my typewriter and got to work. By one of those flukes of imagination I hit on the idea of Hitler and Macbeth being one person, with the Highland Division eventually attacking Berchtesgaden and killing Hitler in exactly the same way Macduff kills Macbeth, with the three witches as commentators. This made what proved a most unusual sketch and one which had rather considerable success.'

Barker now thinks that many of his initial ideas for sketches were too rarified for the world they had to inhabit. A piece about an *avant-garde* art gallery might have worked well in a West End revue but it didn't go down at all in a Garrison theatre. By trial and error in front of an audience

Felix Barker as the Führer in the sketch he wrote himself called 'The Tragedy of Hitler' which was based on Macbeth and meant for production by The Balmorals.

The Balmorals discovered what would work and what wouldn't, and the show settled down to its right level.

A permanent concert party was the sensible way of utilizing talent and providing a commodity that was in short supply. Actors and variety artists who previously were very aware of their shortcomings as soldiers suddenly found themselves playing an important role, even if, in many cases, they had to work harder than if they had stayed put with their units. A concert party had to be self-contained. Scenery, props and equipment had to be loaded on to a lorry, off-loaded at the venue and put up before a performance could take place. When the curtain fell on a show everything had to go back on the lorry before the company could return to barracks and bed.

Removed from regular duties *The Balmorals* toured throughout Scotland playing to every division in Scottish Command. From the first performance in Aberdeen until the Division left for the Western Desert in 1942 they worked non-stop in a series of one-day fit-ups and one-night stands in marquees, converted garages, requisitioned castles, huts and the occasional theatre. They had become, in effect, a professional revue company which happened to be in uniform and happened to be receiving Army pay.

Until the idea of the Army concert party had become established and an accepted part of the war effort great care had to be taken never to incur a charge of skiving which could have brought about the disbanding of a unit. Too many people were convinced an entertainer worked only for the time he was seen on stage and it was essential that soldier artists should be seen to be working. Those who ran the units were very wary of antagonizing the military hierarchy and did their best to ensure some kind of standard was attained.

Conscious of his responsibility when he was promoted sergeant and took over running *The Balmorals* from Stephen Mitchell, Felix Barker decided to issue separate Daily Orders for the company. Those for 11 May, 1942, just before the Division left Aldershot for North Africa, read:

DETAILS FOR THE BALMORALS CONCERT PARTY

1. The entire company will parade in best battledress, shoes and walking out hats at Corunna Barracks at 1000hrs. Haversack rations will be drawn.
2. At 1015 hrs they will embus on own transport and proceed to London. Those who find this too uncomfortable and are prepared to pay their own fares may be dropped at Aldershot Station.
3. The company will rendezvous at Drury Lane Theatre at 1200 hrs for briefing and issuing of detailed orders. A party consisting of the band under L/Cpl McLellan will proceed with the upright piano to Bond Street and will sell it to Messrs Chappell for the best possible price. The cast under L/Cpl Playfair will proceed to Fox's for return of costume and purchase of travelling wardrobe, make-up, etc. Pte Millar and Pte Ward will proceed to the ENSA workshops in Drury Lane to contact Mr Henry about all electrical and stage manager's equipment to be taken overseas.
4. Lunch will be eaten at convenient public houses under party arrangements. The NCO i/c each party will be responsible for the first round.
5. L/Cpl Clarkson will be responsible for the contacting of the Services' Entertainment Bureau and obtaining tickets for theatres that evening. A return of names and theatres for which tickets are required will be made to him by tea-time tonight. Recommended theatres see Appendix A.
6. On the completion of duties the truck will be parked by Dvr Wilson in an authorized WD Car Park or private garage which ever is the more suitable. In the event of a garage the cost will be defrayed by voluntary contributions which will be made by every member of the company.
7. The company (less rail party) will embus at 2230 hrs in Piccadilly Circus, map ref. unnecessary. The truck will proceed by the most amusing route back to Aldershot.
8. Lights out, if possible, at 2359 hrs.

signed: Felix Barker (Sgt) NCO i/c *Balmorals*

Appendix A: The following theatres are recommended as being particularly valuable to *The Balmorals* training programme:

His Majesty's:	Big Top
Vaudeville:	Scoop
Saville:	Fine and Dandy
Hippodrome:	Get A Load Of This

The commanding officer happened to notice these orders pinned up while he was inspecting the barracks and was absolutely delighted. Turning to the CSM who accompanied him he said, 'I'm glad to see *The Balmorals* are starting to soldier up a bit, Sergeant Major.'

CHAPTER THREE

STARS IN BATTLEDRESS

O n Friday, 10 May, 1940, the Phoney War came to an end when the Germans marched round the northern end of the impregnable Maginot Line into Holland and Belgium. Two days later Basil Dean, who with customary foresight had already planned for the evacuation of the 207 ENSA artists playing to the BEF in the event of such an emergency, arrived in France to supervise the operation. Twelve companies playing in the front lines near the Belgian border were immediately withdrawn and sent back down the line to await a passage to England. The only problem came in locating Will Hay who was rushing up and down in the street screaming abuse at the Germans for interrupting his performance. The Vic-Wells Ballet, with Margot Fonteyn, Frederick Ashton and conductor Constant Lambert, which was on a goodwill tour of Holland for the British Council before going on to the BEF for ENSA, just made it to the Hague in front of the advancing Germans and caught the last boat out.

On 25 May it was officially announced that all entertainment services to the BEF had been suspended. On 27 May the evacuation of the British Army from the beaches of Dunkirk began and side-by-side in the boats with troops they had gone to entertain were many ENSA performers. Other artists and personnel headed for ports further along the French coast and by mid-June everyone was safely back in London. The only casualties were several baskets of props and costumes abandoned in the rush. The German soldiers who found them must have wondered quite what sort of army they were up against.

Among the thousands of soldiers who escaped from Dunkirk was Lieutenant Basil Brown of the West Yorkshire Regiment. Brown, a businessman in his native York who had been involved with the York Repertory Theatre, had been posted to the 46th Division in France where he had sought permission to form a Divisional concert party. His basic concept differed from that of *The Balmorals*

Stars in Battledress was finally established by Basil Brown in October, 1941.

and other conventional concert parties in one important aspect: instead of a single company he wanted to divide his performers into groups of three or four men and send them to the least accessible spots so that the shows went out to the men rather than the men having to come to the shows.

Wounded during the evacuation Brown spent several months in hospital where he worked on an idea of a central pool of entertainers, to be drawn from the entire Army, whose prime function would be to perform in the more remote areas. The idea was not original. At the same time Eric Maschwitz, a former Head of Variety at the BBC seconded to the War Office, was trying unsuccessfully to interest his chiefs in a similar plan. Maschwitz got to hear of Brown and the two men met to discuss how such a scheme might be made to work. The War Office finally decided there might be something in it. Worried by the effect on morale that the humiliation of Dunkirk was having, Army Welfare was directed to set up an entertainment branch which would include radio broadcasts, films and live shows. Basil Brown was chosen to head the live entertainments section.

'The mantle fell on me,' says Brown, 'because, by then, Eric Maschwitz had been posted away from the War Office. I went to work writing a series of papers for my superiors about the advantages of a central pool of men who, after their basic training (which was very important), could be used as entertainers but were available to go back to regimental duties if there was trouble. All sorts of people expressed interest but it was turned down again and again until finally the Adjutant General at the time, Sir Ronald Forbes Adam, gave authority for a limited number of men. "Let him have fifty men," he said, "and in six months we'll see what he's done with them."'

The promulgation was made in October, 1941. It had taken Brown more than a year to overcome the opposition of those superiors who couldn't be bothered with him or his idea because, as they never failed to remind him, 'There is a war on.' It was an important round to have won, for nothing could function in the Army without an Establishment. There was no way of clothing, feeding, bedding or, more importantly, paying a man who was not part of an established unit.

The main drawback to the regimental or divisional concert party which Brown wanted to overcome, was that it relied too much on the goodwill and the whims of senior officers. Because performers were putting on a show in place of peeling potatoes or doing guard duty, an officer could cancel the performance at a moment's notice if he took a dislike to an artist or a production; and there was nothing a producer could do about it. A brigadier in the Western Desert made sure that Clifford Odets's play *Waiting For Lefty*, which he considered subversive, never went on by posting key members of the cast each time it was about to open. Although Brown's men would be soldiers they would not be subject to such vagaries since their prime military duty would be to entertain. 'Every artist a soldier, every soldier an artist,' was how broadcaster Gale Pedrick summed them up.

By persuading the War Office to sanction an establishment, even on a trial period, Brown made sure that a Corps of Entertainers became as much part of the Army structure as the Signals or the Medical Corps.

One other factor helped influence the War Office's decision. This was the deepening enmity between Army Welfare and ENSA. Senior officers, in particular Major-General Willans, the new Director of Army Welfare, did not like to see such an important area of welfare being run and masterminded by a civilian, especially one as forthright as Basil Dean. They felt that anything Dean could do they could, and would, do better. While admitting that ENSA did valuable work, Willans declared that Army shows must provide the backbone of troop entertainment.

The hub of Brown's new empire, for its six month's trial, was Nissen Hut 13 at the Royal Ordnance Depot, Greenford. At the end of October, 1941 the adminstration arrived: Michael Carr, composer of 'South of the Border' and 'We're Gonna Hang Out The Washing On The Seigfried Line', to be the unit scriptwriter; George Black Jnr, son of the Palladium producer, to become the unit's first commissioned officer and producer; Sydney Grace, an agent's booker, and Stanley Hall, a make-up supervisor from Denham Studios, to become the unit's Quartermaster.

Sydney Grace persuaded *The Stage* to run a paragraph on the new unit and shoals of letters arrived from frustrated artists in units up and down the country asking to join. George Black and Basil Brown set out on a tour of every Command looking at divisional and unit concert parties and holding auditions. It was then left to Brown to obtain the artists they wanted. He wrote a polite request, on War Office notepaper, asking for a man to be transferred. Although it was only a request some COs took it as Holy Writ and complied immediately. Others had already discovered the usefulness of having an entertainer in the ranks or were alerted to the talent under their noses and refused. Sometimes the artist himself, having found a comfortable niche, declined to be moved. 'I should think,' says Brown, 'we probably got three-quarters of the people we asked for.'

'The unit came in for a lot of criticism at first,' remembers Stanley Hall, 'mostly from the cheaper Sunday papers because people said "Look at them doing their own job when they ought to be fighting for their country." In fact, we did a very tough job, working very long hours, under great difficulties. But we had to be very careful not to withdraw someone from the Parachute Regiment, somebody from something important or someone with a trade. Then the War Office would have stepped in and said no. We were only allowed to have the ordinary soldier.'

Forty-two artists reported to Greenford, all of them professional entertainers before their call-up, many of them well-known, like Charlie Chester, Harold Childs, Terry Huson, Nat Go-

Boy Foy, already well known, was among the first stars of . the 50 men called up to form Stars in Battledress.

nella, Boy Foy (a juggling uni-cyclist who had peddled round the top of the RKO building in New York), Eddie le Roy (brother of 'Monsewer' Eddie Gray), George Melachrino and Alec Pleon, the comedian who had been fined £20 the previous year for telling a joke about Hitler which hadn't been passed by the Lord Chamberlain. Greeting them on the wall of Hut 13 was a notice which read: *Temperament will not be allowed.*

The official title of Brown's new unit was the Central Pool of Artists, to become much better known by its soubriquet, 'Stars in Battledress'. The nickname was a chance inspiration, as Basil Brown recalls:

'In 1941 Norman Marshall was producing a big charity show at the Coliseum in aid of one of the Army charities. He was looking for talent in the Army and somebody sent him to me at the War Office because I knew where so many people were and, because Army Welfare was sponsoring it, it was a simple matter for me to authorize a man to make an appearance. Walking across Trafalgar Square one day Norman said to me, "I'm so glad I came to see you because, after all, today all the stars are in uniform." It was just one of those things. It clicked: stars in uniform, stars in battledress. They were known as Stars in Battledress from that moment on.'

Stars they may have been but their daily routine was decidedly terrestrial. The day at Greenford began with 7 am breakfast parade and roll call. Since the nearest billets were a mile away that meant an early start. At 8.30 there was a full Depot parade.

'The Pool, as we were called,' recalls Peter Warren, 'fell in at the end of the line, bringing with us a strange assortment of props, musical instruments and things ready for the day's rehearsals. These were left in a pile on the path behind us while we stood freezing for a quarter-of-an-hour waiting for the officer-of-the-day to come and inspect us. Nat Gonella would usually arrive with a couple of minutes to spare, flashing by in his car, smoking a cigar. It was generally considered that he had given the officer a lift because the inspection would always commence after Nat's arrival. When this was over the parade was marched off in sections to make tanks, machine guns or whatever it was they did make (nobody seemed to know) and Stars in Battledress picked up their props and instruments and marched away to their hut to rehearse.'

The Central Pool of Artists on parade was a disheartening sight for the militarist. Men wore coloured socks, Nat Gonella insisted on wearing brown suede shoes, a performer appeared with diamante ear-rings on and a musician always paraded with a furled umbrella. In spite of the efforts of those performers who came from a disciplined background (Charlie Chester had been a sergeant in the Irish Fusiliers and continued to blanco his stripes throughout the war) there was never a real possibility of turning the majority of the Central Pool into smart soldiers. They came from various units with differing drill and routines and temperament would not allow many of them to take soldiering seriously. When one of their number fainted during an important inspection, his platoon immediately crowded round to offer assistance.

'To say Hut 13 was cold in winter would be an understatement,' remembers Peter Warren. 'In any weather it was always warmer outside. There was one old stove in the middle of the hut but never any materials to light it and it was the hardest job in the world to coax any out of a neighbouring hut. Looking back I can see us all now, at nine o'clock in the morning, teeth chattering, fingers blue with cold, trying to work out comical sketches. Only at half-past ten, when the canteen opened and we were able to get a really hot cup of coffee, were we able to settle down to work and rehearsing the new show.

'How the administration ever worked in those days was also a mystery. They didn't even have a telephone and every time they wanted to make a call they had to go from the hut to the main depot. To do this it was necessary to have a pass signed by the local CO, which took at least a quarter-of-an-hour to obtain and was needed four or five times a day. As Stanley Hall and Sydney Grace spent their entire time dashing between the two and queuing up at a call-box to phone Basil Brown at the War Office, it was a miracle the shows were ever produced.'

But produced they were. In December the first-ever performance by a Stars in Battledress company was given in the Greenford Depot theatre before a packed house curious to discover exactly what had been going on in Hut 13. Leading the company was Yorkshire comedian Tom Kendall and with him were ventriloquist Peter Brough, Slick Snelling, Denis de Marney, George Clark and Ken Morris. Immediately after the try-out Kendall took his unit out on the road to gun and balloon sites in London and the Home Counties. Peter Warren went with them as a performer even

though his entire professional life had been spent backstage. For his début he sang a comic song. It was not very funny and when he forgot the words half-way through his career on stage came to an end. He returned to Greenford to become the Pool's Production Manager, responsible for dressing the shows and acquiring props and equipment.

A week later the second unit, under Charlie Chester, played a week in Croydon raising funds for Army charities and before long six parties, each of seven men, were in action.

The winter of 1941–42 was bitterly cold and disturbing reports reached Greenford of the appalling conditions the artists were having to suffer. As pioneers in many areas they were discovering, as ENSA had before, that no one knew about them and they were never anybody's responsibility. Unlike ENSA, which had hostels to put its performers in, Stars in Battledress were billeted on camps for their stay in an area. They were given disused sheds or lorries in which to sleep or put in with local soldiers who naturally resented being awakened at two or three in the morning when the unit arrived back from a distant engagement. No matter how late they were, it was up at 6.30 am for breakfast – or go without. In the evenings they missed the meal again because they were setting up the show and it was too much trouble for anybody to feed them separately. Basil Brown let it be known that unless his artists were treated better the units would be withdrawn. The hint was taken; for the early performances had gone down so well that any suggestion they might be cancelled in the future would not have pleased the troops. Their success is not hard to understand. The productions were professional and slick and up on stage were household names the audiences would have paid good money to watch in Civvy Street. More than that, the stars were soldiers; they belonged to the same Army as the audience. There was a rapport between them that few civilian shows could hope to match.

The six months' trial period came to an end. The decision on whether or not the Central Pool of Artists should continue was taken after a command performance given to Sir James Grigg, Secretary of State for War, and numerous Whitehall top brass. Charlie Chester's unit was chosen to appear.

'The man who nearly wrecked it was Charlie himself,' recalls Basil Brown. 'In those days, believe it or not, although there was a war on and the permissive society, permissive anything,

GRAND CONCERT IN AID OF DEVON COUNTY ARMY WELFARE

CIVIC HALL

FRIDAY, APRIL 17th, at 7 p.m.

THE CENTRAL POOL OF ENTERTAINERS PRESENTS A BRILLIANT COMPANY OF

STARS IN
A NONSENSICAL HIGH-SPEED
ALL-LAUGHTER EXTRAVAGANZA

BATTLE DRESS
with

THE B.B.C.'s POPULAR NON-STOP COMEDIAN
SERGEANT "CHEERFUL"

CHARLIE CHESTER

EDDIE LE ROY
(L.-CPL. CHARLES GRAY)
LAUGHTER LET LOOSE

4 BOW BELLES
THEY WERE AS PURE AS SNOW—BUT THEY DRIFTED

CORPORAL KEN FRANKS
THE LAD FRA ILKLA MOOR

RIFLEMAN ARNOLD ENGLISH
A GOOD BOY IN BAD COMPANY

GUNNER LOUIS ALMAER
THE BRITISH ARMY'S LARRY ADLER

PRODUCTION BY
2nd-Lt.
GEORGE BLACK

PRIVATE FRANK BEHRON
THE BRILLIANT BROADCASTING PIANIST OF HATCHETTES SWINGTETTE FAME

MORE LAUGHS THAN THE CRAZY SHOW!
EVERYTHING YOU WANT! SKETCHES! SONGS! DANCING! MUSIC!

TICKETS, 2/-, 1/6 & 1/-, obtainable from Messrs. MOONS, Messrs. WHEATON & Co. and ARMY WELFARE OFFICE, 9, Dix's Field; and at the Door

This billing was the second unit to go on the road and was the one that gained the approval of the authorities and gave Stars in Battledress its lease on life.

hadn't been thought of, there was a terrific blitz going on about dirty material. It was the biggest headache I had at the War Office: letters from padres and people like that about my men going out and cracking blue gags. Anyway, in front of the Secretary of State and a lot of very senior officers, Charlie cracked a doubtful gag. I got the wind-up very badly. I was terrified that someone would turn round and say "This is going too far." That performance was like being on trial. I knew that if it registered in a big way authority would come through to make it a really big unit.'

'I did a gag,' says Charlie Chester, 'about Hitler at the end of the war when the Russians got hold of him: he was going to be dragged through the streets of Moscow by the Bolsheviks. When I was told that my unit had been chosen to give the trial show for Sir James Grigg I was told to keep it nice and tidy. I knew what they meant but I thought it's

no good kidding this man; he knows what sort we are and the shows we've been giving to the troops. So I told the gag just as I would normally and that meant with a gesture. I got into trouble not because of the gag but because of the actions.'

Grigg loved the show and permission was given to a relieved Basil Brown to expand the Pool. In May, 1942 the headquarters were moved to the Duke of York's Barracks, Chelsea, and George Black set about finding more artists. Among those he chose were Terry-Thomas, Peter Cavanagh ('The Voice of Them All'), Ted Gatty, Walter Midgley, Freddie Frinton, Bruce Trent and Sid Millward. By 1944 Stars in Battledress was 200 strong.

Sid Millward, who was to become internationally known with his band The Nitwits, heard about the Pool only forty-eight hours before his commissioning parade was due to take place at Barmouth. He knew that once he became an officer his chance of entertaining would vanish. As officer-of-the-day Millward lined up his company on the seafront, marched them across the promenade, down the beach and into the sea. He was put on a charge but instead of finding himself on the first train out of Barmouth, as he had planned, he was told that so much money had been spent on him already he must start his course again. His CO was spared further humiliation when a request arrived for his transfer to Stars in Battledress.

Not all the second wave of performers were professionals. Many amateurs auditioned for George Black, among them Arthur Haynes who was desperate to become a comedian.

'If you haven't got an act there isn't much point in doing an audition,' says Charlie Chester. 'Arthur Haynes didn't have an act – he was just a keen amateur. He didn't pass his audition. George Black, who hated sending people back to their units, offered him a lift to the station in his taxi and with George was his little boy. Arthur loved kids and he was trying to make the boy laugh. But the kid had a face as long as a kite. In the finish Arthur said, "You're as hard to make laugh as your old man." George felt so sorry for him he told him to come back and join us.'

The success of Stars in Battledress was not only due to the fact that they could call upon 'names' the audiences wanted to see, but above all to the dedication and professionalism that went into every production. The professionals already had their established acts; George Black had access to the Palladium library, which included all the Crazy Gang routines; top stars such as Arthur Askey, Max Miller and Tommy Trinder gave the Pool permission to use their sketches. The additional material written by Michael Carr and his fellow performers was of an equal standard. No show was allowed on the road until George Black was thoroughly satisfied it was ready.

'We used to produce the shows at either Olympia, in the café which had been turned into a theatre, or in an office over the Brompton Road tube station,' says Peter Warren. 'I remember one night at Brompton. There were Stanley Hall, Syd Grace, George Black and myself, and we had just been watching a first night. We were talking about it and we went on and on. Suddenly Syd Grace said, "By golly, we're talking about a five-handed concert party as though it's a £25,000 West End show." "Yes," I said, "and that's where the success is." '

Like all shows that went to troops, Stars in Battledress played their quota of Nissen huts, fields and woods, and performances had to be adapted to meet local conditions. If bombs fell during the show or guns outside started firing, jokes had to be told to coincide with the lulls. When Freddie Frinton's party arrived at a searchlight battery, seven of the nine men there were manning the searchlights. The group told a few jokes, sang a few songs and then settled down to play poker for the rest of the evening. Charlie Chester remembers a concert at a large ammunition dump:

'There was a miniature railway there that was used for hauling ammo. and bombs. We gave our show on one platform while the audience sat on the other. There's nothing more disconcerting than trying to crack a few gags when all you can see of the audience is a glimpse between trucks every few seconds. Every time I got to the punch line another truck would come past and drown it. I don't think I finished a single joke. The thing about troop shows, though, was that if you went down well, you went down really well; if you died, you died. I died on my feet in Cornwall. The audience enjoyed the songs and everybody got big laughs until it came to me, the star of the show. After it was over I said to the sergeant-major, "What's the bloody matter with that audience? They didn't laugh at a single joke?" "I'm not surprised," he said, "This is the Polish Brigade and none of them speaks English." '

Variety was the most popular form of live

'I want the back few rows to sing Rachmaninoff's Prelude and Fugue in G flat minor, the centre rows to sing Shostakovich's Scherzo, opus 2, and those here in front to sing 'Daisy, Daisy' – right; everyone ready?'

entertainment throughout the war but with so many people from every walk of life being drafted into uniform demands began to be made for entertainment that catered to minority tastes especially in music. There were hundreds of people in the Services who didn't want non-stop dance bands and crooners, but preferred more middle-of-the-road music. Stars in Battledress responded by sending out a sextet led by violinist Eugene Pini. Reginald Kilbey played the cello:

'We played Strauss waltzes and some marvellous arrangements for string quartet and clarinet of the tunes of the day, the ones that are still played today, like 'Dinah' and 'Beautiful Dreamer'. John Duncan sang ballads and songs from *Merrie England* and *Faust*, and I used to play some serious cello solos – Chopin's *Nocturne in E*, Schumann and the repertoire of cello composer David Popper. In fact, we played anything. On one occasion we played the last movement of Dvorak's *American Quartet*. The chaps went mad about it. They thought it was a jazz tune and a lot of them who hadn't heard it before used to say what a wonderful piece of music, what is it? When we told them it was chamber music they wouldn't believe us: that rubbish was for the long-haired chaps, as they called them.'

The concerts were an outstanding success. Men who went to them only because there was nothing else to do were surprised to discover no hushed concert hall atmosphere and that the show contained a lot of comedy. This was provided by the sophisticated compere, Terry-Thomas.

Terry-Thomas had drifted into show business via film work as an extra and a job compering a second-rate cabaret. He had spent some months touring *Cabaret Parade*, his own show, for ENSA before his call-up in 1941. He was seen appearing in a Sunday show in York by George Black and was soon posted to Stars in Battledress. His time in the Army allowed him to develop his public *persona* as an upper-class twit. The expensively tailored man who introduced 'Tales From The Vienna Woods' was very similar to the Terry-Thomas of countless post-war films. The cigarette holder, the toothy grin, were part of a carefully cultivated image which was allowed to spill over into everyday life.

'Terry managed to get hold of one of those leather jackets issued to drivers,' remembers Basil Brown. 'He also got a great big fur collar which he had put on it and a service cap which he succeeded in pulling back so that it looked like an officer's in peacetime. He looked very smooth and wherever he went he was saluted by the troops, left, right and centre. And Terry, who never rose any higher than sergeant, acting unpaid, took in everyone, as only Terry-Thomas could, even up to the brigadier.'

As well as introducing the musical items, Terry-Thomas had a solo spot in which he performed monologues with sound effects (a creaking door from the cello) and 'Technical Hitch'. Terry-Thomas was a brilliant impersonator and this sketch, which he wrote himself, gave him full rein to display his talents. Inspiration for the piece was BBC announcer Bruce Belfrage whose only fluff while reading the news when a bomb fell on Broadcasting House was to repeat one line. In the sketch a BBC announcer arrives to present a record programme only to find he hasn't any records. Such is his devotion to duty that rather than cancel the programme he impersonates every one of the singers, from Richard Tauber to Leslie 'Hutch' Hutchinson.

'The idea came to me,' says Terry-Thomas, 'when I was sitting in a Norwich pub, on an ENSA tour, drinking the worst beer I had ever tasted in my life. It was a ghastly, dreadful day, snowing and sleeting and I was waiting to go and see Richard Tauber a friend of mine who was in *Old Chelsea* at the local theatre. Sub-consciously I think I must have been looking for a vehicle to do a Tauber impersonation. That coupled with the Bruce Belfrage incident sparked off the idea. It took me a long time to work up and I didn't actually do it until I was in Stars in Battledress.'

The sketch made Terry-Thomas's name when he performed it in *Piccadilly Hayride* after the war.

'I've never had so many laughs as I had in the Army,' says Reginald Kilbey. 'Terry-Thomas was so funny and both he and Gene Pini had a keen sense of humour. We were strolling players really, moving around on a lorry driven by a poor ATS girl who had a terrible time because we travelled everywhere via the pubs.

'We got to Mill Hill barracks one night when an air raid was on. Since it was an artillery barracks everyone was on duty so we adjourned to the pub and got terribly sloshed. Then we got back on the lorry, with our piano, to return to the Duke of York's because there obviously wasn't going to be a concert that night. The raid was at its height. Flares were coming down, bombs were falling and guns were going off right next to the lorry. It was absolutely devastating. Terry was hanging on the crossbar, where the canvas goes, giving a marvellous impersonation of a German, with a lovely German accent, when his hat blew off. "Stop the lorry!" he screamed. We stopped the lorry and there we were, shrapnel all over the place, walking around looking for his hat. The whole party was an absolute shambles. This went on day after day, although we always gave our concert first, if we could find the place, and saved our drinking for afterwards.'

Stars in Battledress parties were conceived as all-male, go anywhere units 'As a last resort, only soldiers can live as soldiers,' says Basil Brown. The finest dresses and costumes Peter Warren could exchange his handful of clothing coupons for ended up on the backs of hairy soldiers. Many female impersonators felt an audience's resentment when 'The Belles of the Ballet', for whom chocolates and flowers had been bought, or even 'The Antiseptic Sisters', were discovered to be men in drag. Some of the disappointment vanished when a young ATS girl arrived at the Pool for a three week trial. Janet

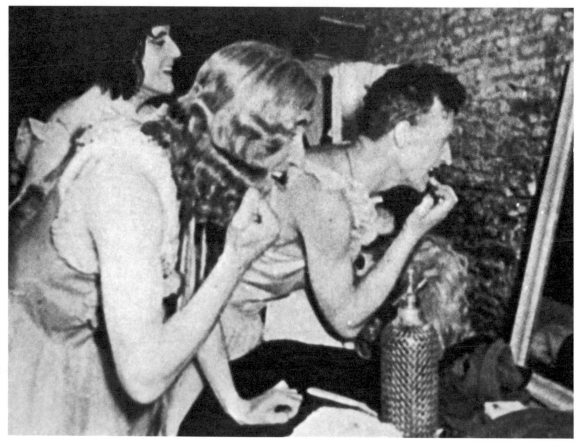

Make-do facilities were the order of the day wherever Stars in Battledress performed. The only amenity in the dressing room afforded to Bert Scrase, Harold Childs and Jack Browning was the soda syphon (whisky not in evidence).

Brown, the singer and impressionist, had been recommended to George Black by Henry Hall, conductor of the BBC Dance Orchestra, after he had heard her singing in Glasgow prior to her call-up. Audiences were astonished and delighted to see a 'Janet' who really was a Janet, without size twelve boots beneath the dress. She made her début on two table tops in a field and was an instant success even though she had fallen into a cesspit while crossing the field in the dark. Being the only girl in the show and coming in for special attention wherever the unit played, Janet Brown's frequent encores began to irritate her fellow artists. When they appeared in a village hall which still had up the set of the last dramatic society production, they decided to take their revenge. Alan Clare was the unit's pianist.

'This set took up the entire stage and there was no way off except through the doors of the set. I had to play the piano in front of the stage because there was no room to put it anywhere else. After one encore Janet came down to me and whispered, "What shall we do next?" "I don't know," I said. "You think of something." She sang another number then went to leave, only the other guys had put a chair under the door handle and she couldn't open it. She ran across the stage to the other door – and the same thing. The audience began to giggle and Janet was saying, in a loud stage whisper, "Let me off! Let me off!" She started to throw herself against the door and all I could hear were the boys behind saying, "Give them another song, Janet!"'

It may seem obvious that soldiers would enjoy seeing and hearing pretty girls – chorus lines were always top of their list of priorities – but Army Welfare was cautious of allowing females to join entertainment units. Girls would be touring with men, living in poor conditions and one breath of scandal could have sounded a death knell for the

46

entire Stars in Battledress. The success of Janet Brown's three week trial proved that there were no problems in a girl touring with men that couldn't be overcome and that a lone girl appearing in an all-male camp was not a signal for riot and rape. The way was open for women to become a permanent part of the Central Pool of Artists. This, in turn, meant a wider variety of entertainment could be put on, in particular, plays. Audiences would accept men dressed up as women for sketches in a variety show – it often added to the fun and some boys were prettier than women – but in a play, with conventions an audience was not used to, it could be ludicrous.

First moves to set up a specific play unit within the Army occurred at the time the Central Pool was struggling to establish itself. Towards the end of 1941 actor Charles Cameron formed the London District Theatre Unit to tour productions around the area where ENSA didn't go. He obtained the release of twenty people including Stephen Murray, a drill instructor in the Royal Army Service Corps, who became sergeant in charge. Although the unit received official blessing it was never an established company.

'We had an extraordinary collection of people,' recalls Stephen Murray, 'some professional actors, some completely non-actors, one or two people who were ostensibly electricians, a carpenter who had once worked in a film studio and two or three ATS girls who were not actresses at all. We had an equally scratch collection of timber, canvas, old lights and things like that, mostly scrounged. There was no set-designing to begin with; we just had to rig up curtains. We began with a comedy by Philip King called *Without The Prince*. We had to ring up units and ask if they would like a show. "What is it?" they would say and when we said a play they would reply, "Oh! Well, we could try it, I suppose." Our area went as far as Woolwich, Eltham and Windsor and we had quite a rough time in the beginning. We found that, in the average unit, seventy-five per cent had never been inside a theatre and weren't going to. To begin with they were marched in and they rolled their beer bottles down the aisles and so on. We had to fight them. They were very tough indeed. But once we'd got them, they were marvellous. At first we had to force ourselves on units but within two or three months we had eighty or ninety units around London ringing up and clamouring for us, wanting more plays.'

The enthusiasm which greeted the production

of *Without The Prince* encouraged Cameron to obtain the transfer of more professional, uniformed actors. Among them was Brian Oulton, rescued from the depths of Salisbury Plain where he had been helping defeat Hitler by sweeping up leaves. Oulton's wife, Peggy Thorpe Bates, although a civilian, was brought in to play female roles.

Transport for the unit was either by lorry or train and arrangements did not always proceed with military precision.

'There was always great secrecy about our destination,' says Peggy Thorpe Bates. 'Stephen Murray, who was the only one who knew where we were going, would meet us at the station and shepherd us all on to the train. One time, Brian, Terence Morgan and I got into a carriage and although we didn't know where we were going the others were next door so that was all right. We were talking away like mad when I suddenly thought we seemed to have been travelling a long time. I looked out of the window and there was nothing! The rest of the train had vanished! From having lots of carriages joined to us, there was just our little carriage and something propelling us. Eventually we arrived at a station called Tattenham Corner, which was only ever used during Derby week, got out and found a ticket collector who said we shouldn't have been there. We had no tickets and didn't know where we should have been. Fortunately Stephen realized what had happened, found out where we were and sent a lorry to collect us.'

Three new productions were added to the repertoire: *Arms and The Man, French Leave* and the ever-popular *Journey's End*. For Christmas 1942 the unit decided to put on a farce. Reports filtered back that much as the men had enjoyed the performances they had come to expect something rather better from the unit.

From touring London District, the unit was sent on a tour of all Home Commands including Northern Ireland where it played to an audience of two (its smallest ever) and a leading lady went missing.

'In *Without The Prince*,' explains Stephen Murray, 'we had a hen which was an integral part of the show. We travelled her round with us all over London District, all over England, Scotland and Northern Ireland. She was called Hetty and from time-to-time she laid eggs. In Ulster we played at an American camp and Hetty was stolen. We made a formal complaint to the American

Characters in Order of their Appearance —

Dr. Haggett	.. ..	CLIVE MORTON
Susan Haggett	..	BEATRICE RADLEY
Gwenny	.. .. ..	EDITH EVANS
Mrs. Haggett	..	PHYLLIS MORRIS
Ada Haggett	..	RONDA KEANE
Bruce McRae	.. ..	TOM COLMER
Tallant	.. ..	BRUNO BARNABE
Rosen	.. .. ..	LIONEL HARRIS
Davenport ..	..	CLIFFORD EVANS

THE PLAY PRODUCED BY EDITH EVANS

Stage Director	..	EVELYN BRIERLEY
Decor by	..	HUBERT GURSCHNER

Emlyn Williams adapted Réné Fauchois's play Prenez Garde à la Peinture *as* The Late Christopher Bean *which was presented by Southern Command Entertainments Branch at the Garrison Theatre in Salisbury. After the war this theatre became the home of the Salisbury Repertory Company.*

colonel and had to find an understudy. That night we were given Chicken Maryland for dinner and none of us could touch it! We moved to our next date, about sixty miles away, with the understudy which was not at all good, when suddenly a jeep arrived with Hetty intact; tied up but safe and sound. She had been found in the cook's locker.'

By 1943 the work of the London District Theatre Unit, ENSA play companies, repertory theatres, independent managements and occasional one-off Army productions had convinced Army Welfare that there was a demand for plays. The success of Janet Brown in the concert party and repeated requests arriving at the Duke of York's barracks to locate actors and actresses in uniform for local productions, persuaded Stars in Battledress that the time was ripe to set up its own play section. Murray Macdonald (who, as Captain Honeyman, had been running a highly successful season of plays in the Garrison Theatre, Salisbury, using such Army talent as Peter Ustinov and Bruno Barnabe and civilian guests like Dame Edith Evans who directed and starred in *The Late Christopher Bean*) was invited to direct the inaugural production, Terence Rattigan's West End success, *Flare Path*. In the cast were John Longden, Wilfrid Hyde White, Kenneth Connor and Faith Brook. Simultaneously another West End play, *Men In Shadow*, by Mary Hayley Bell, began rehearsals with Geoffrey Keen (a corporal in the medical corps and the first straight actor to join the Pool), William Kendall and George Cooper. This production was chosen for a performance in front of Queen Mary at her war-time retreat, Badminton.

'We were in Oxford when we were told we hadn't been booked for the following day because we had a special assignment,' recalls George Cooper. 'The next day we were picked up by our lorry and taken to the village hall in Badminton. A lot of villagers were there, Princess Margaret and the Duke of Gloucester. And in the middle, on a very high-backed, upright chair, all red and gold like a throne, sat Queen Mary. The play opened with the French resistance looking after some RAF men in a barn which had just been searched by the Germans. The opening line was, someone coming out of the loft and saying, "I'm glad those bastards have gone." In those days that was out of the question in front of Royalty, of course, but Queen Mary had said she wanted to see the play without alteration.'

The stage in the village hall was so tiny that when the set was up there was no room for anyone to walk behind it. An actor exiting on one side of the stage and required to enter from the other had to sprint out of the building, round the back and in through another door.

'All of us not in that opening scene were crowded in the wings picking holes in the scenery to watch the Queen's face,' Cooper remembers. 'When the opening line came she just smiled. We left about one in the morning to return to the YMCA in Oxford where we were staying. It was pouring with rain. After this glorious day we had a miserable ride back in an old canvas-covered lorry which was leaking. When we got to the YMCA it was locked. We banged on the door and the superintendent came and asked what we wanted. We told him we were staying there and he said, "Oh, no, you're not! I'm not having drunken soldiers in here." And he locked the door again. We had to call the police to explain that we had been entertaining Queen Mary, otherwise we would have been left out in the rain all night.'

Queen Mary also saw some unrehearsed business during another Stars in Battledress command performance, given by Harold Childs's variety unit. In one of the sketches Jack Browning pulled off Bert Scrase's trousers, a part of the routine it

April, 1942, somewhere on the Salisbury Plain – as the current jargon went. Today we can safely identify Sergeant 'Cheerful' Charlie Chester standing to the right and his unit: Lance Corporal Eddie Le Roy, Rifleman Arnold English, Corporal Ken Franks, Private Frank Behron, Gunner Louis Almaer and unnamed driver.

was decided to drop for Badminton. In the heat of the moment Browning forgot the decision and whipped off not only the unsuspecting Scrase's trousers but his underpants as well. Queen Mary, it was reported, laughed as loudly as anyone.

Plays like *Men In Shadow* and *Flare Path* made no attempt to escape the war. Set during the war they utilized the contemporary experience and helped strengthen the resolve of the audience. The process of involvement occasionally worked in reverse as Kenneth Connor remembers:

'*Flare Path* went down particularly well with RAF boys. They liked the writing, which was full of RAF slang of the time, they liked the story and the love triangle, and they liked the cocky little gunner I played, always coming in at the wrong moment. It often got very emotional. I got very stewed in a Mess one night and got talking to a real air gunner, somebody who had just come back from hell in time to see the show. When he told me

he thought I was the best air gunner he'd ever come across I couldn't stand it. I went to the air commodore, who was there, and demanded an immediate transfer from the Army to go off on a flight with these lads. Directly five of them took me into the cloakroom and hung me up behind the door to stop me making a bloody fool of myself. I was quite prepared to go off; in my condition it seemed the logical thing to do. I damned near strangled on that door. It was only by kicking my heels against it, at the risk of my neck, that I attracted the attention of our lorry driver before the unit all drove off.'

Although Stars in Battledress play productions had casts and directors who could have commanded large fees in the West End, they, like their variety cousins, went where they were needed and that meant rarely playing in a theatre. The cause of much of the resentment building up between Stars in Battledress artists and ENSA artists came from the fact that ENSA productions always played better locations and the performers were paid while Army units received only Army pay. But unlike variety artists, who could stand on a table to sing or tell jokes, plays required a set which had to be taken everywhere. Astonished gasps were heard when audiences realized that doors in a flat actually opened. Geoffrey Keen was asked by a general if he was always lucky enough to find a mill-wheel (part of the *Men In Shadow* set) in the right position wherever they played. The cast came to expect such comments. A favourite was, 'I would like to see this done by real actors.'

Wilfrid Hyde White was another actor, like Terry-Thomas, who used his immense charm to avoid being suffocated by military regulations. His constant complaint was that he suffered from the cold and on top of his Army greatcoat, which he refused to take off even on stage, he wore a three-quarter length coat made from a blanket and, if it really was cold, a moth-eaten fur coat. His appearance startled both soldiers and Military Policemen, and his condescending mode of address convinced them he was an eccentric officer. Not for one moment did they guess he was a driver from the Ordnance Corps. On stage, if there was a single footlight which might provide some warmth, he would huddle over it and refuse to move. The other actors were expected to adjust their performances around him.

In the same production with Wilfrid Hyde White was Faith Brook, actress daughter of film star Clive Brook, one of the first ATS girls to join a Stars in Battledress Play Unit.

'There hadn't been many women in Army entertainment before me and that proved very difficult at first. Even though we didn't get back until three in the morning the girls in the company had to report to the local ATS barracks at 8.30 am. When we arrived with traces of make-up, the hair perhaps not quite two inches above the collar and possibly nail polish left on, we were very severely wrapped over the knuckles. It was a very schizoid existence behaving like a soldier during the day and becoming an actress at night. Some ATS ladies did their best to make life unpleasant. Either they were half-male already or as soon as they put on uniform their butch side appeared. They didn't like what they considered the glamorous theatre. It became a great strain but fortunately everything was changed. We were billeted out and only had to report once a month.

'Being female, the boys wouldn't let me carry anything but in return I had to darn their socks and look after the costumes. When we arrived at a site I would get out the wardrobe and perhaps iron things while they were putting up the set. Afterwards I would put the wardrobe away in a big basket while they struck the set so that we could get away quickly. This applied particularly to *Flare Path* because if we didn't hurry after the show we very often wouldn't even get a drink before we had to be back on the truck. Whatever could be taken off stage during the third act was put in the appropriate basket. Things like cigarette boxes that weren't going to be used any more. Cushions would be kicked off and candlesticks whipped away. We would end with practically nothing on stage except the furniture we sat on.'

Plays which most people had once agreed would never go down well in front of a troop audience had become a definite cog in the entertainment wheel. The principle that it didn't really matter what type of show was on stage as long as the presentation was good, applied to a play as much as to variety or music. If troops saw quality they would accept it, and the Stars in Battledress Play Unit provided quality.

'We took *Men In Shadow* to Arborfield,' remembers Peter Warren, 'and we were rehearsing the opening, in which a wounded airman with a broken arm is dragged through a trap door – a very tough scene – during the afternoon. George Black was in charge and he was checking the lighting and so on. He asked me to go to the back of the hall to set up something. Standing at the back, watching the rehearsal, was a very pukka sergeant. As I passed him he said, "You know, there's more to this acting lark than you think, isn't there?"'

CHAPTER FOUR

THE RAF GANG SHOWS

The Second World War – the war of Pearl Harbour, Taranto, the Blitz, Dresden and the Battle of Britain – was the first in the long history of human conflict to utilize fully the potential of the skies. Less than forty years after the Wright brothers made their historic flight in a heavier-than-air machine, aircraft had become an important fighting weapon. Success on land and often at sea depended on supremacy in the air in what was a new and, at times, exciting form of warfare.

The men who joined the RAF felt themselves to be special as did the public who admired them. During the Battle of Britain young fighter pilots, alone and brave, became a symbol of Britain herself. They were the 'Few' to whom so many owed so much. To wear the light blue uniform had a glamour that neither the Army nor the Navy could match, and yet it was a glamour dearly bought. Billy Milton remembers taking his ENSA company to play at an RAF station near Dover.

'It was idyllic. The sun was shining and there were a lot of young men in the bar looking very handsome in their uniforms, enjoying themselves. We gave our show and immediately after it the padre came into my dressing-room and asked me to hurry over to the Sergeants' Mess as soon as possible to play the piano. I asked him what the rush was since I needed a moment to cool off. He said, "We've lost at least three-quarters of those men who were in the bar. The Germans were up there waiting for them." And it dawned on me that all those people I'd had the pleasure of talking to and entertaining were never coming back.'

'The saddest places of all to play,' agrees Kenneth Connor, 'were the RAF stations. In the Messes where we had a meal before the show or a drink afterwards one end would always be banked high with the most expensive wreaths and gorgeous floral tributes for the mass burials they were carrying out. Throughout a performance we would hear the Tannoy going: "Crash crew, stand by." Planes would come limping in from raids and people would come limping in to the end of the play.'

In 1939 the Royal Air Force was just twenty years old. Being the youngest service by several hundred years it took wilful pleasure in being different and discovering its own traditions and values. Life in the RAF wasn't all heroics. It was tough and dangerous but at times of inactivity it could be boring and from the start the Air Ministry recognized the role of entertainment. Stations were encouraged to form bands and concert parties and the RAF was keen to recruit professional entertainers, especially musicians. Provided a musician volunteered and hadn't waited to be conscripted he would be assigned to general duties and allowed to keep playing. When conjuror Stanley Watson arrived at Henlow the sergeant in charge of his intake was so pleased to find an entertainer amongst the recruits that he insisted on carrying Watson's suitcase and gave him a weekend pass to return home and collect his props.

Fred and Frank Cox, professionally known as the Tornado Twins, were identical twins whose careers had started as child entertainers. When they decided to volunteer for military service they went to their local recruiting office. 'After our medical, at which all the doctors were fascinated by our identical body structure and ignored everyone else to examine us, we were sent upstairs to see an Army colonel. "What can you do? Can you drive?" he asked. We told him we were acrobats, we could dance, play several instruments and entertain. "That's not a trade, that's light-headed," he said. "You're no use to us. Pioneer Corps." And that's what we were down for until a friend advised us to try the RAF. We went to see this man at the RAF recruiting office who said, "We'd love to have you; we can use your talents. What do you know about planes?" We looked at one another and both said, "Well, we've got a Meccano." "Right," he said, "you're in."'

The Twins were posted to Blackpool, at the time a major centre for RAF training with several thousand airmen stationed in and around the town. As in peacetime, the town brimmed with entertainment. The commercial theatres were all doing good business and local amateurs, professionals and RAF performers gave frequent shows to raise funds and entertain Servicemen. Every Sunday RAF Welfare mounted a concert in the Opera House in which RAF personnel appeared in the first half and guest artists such as Max Wall and the Crazy Gang in the second. The orchestra, made up of RAF musicians, was conducted by Sydney Torch. Outlying stations also had their own concert parties, one of which the Cox Twins joined.

Impressed by their guitar playing, a sergeant

Fred and Frank Cox, the Tornado Twins, had been appearing on stage since childhood, and continued to perform in the Gang Shows during their military careers. After the war they married the Miles sisters who are also identical twins, and all four still appear on the stage together.

suggested that they should join Alfredo's Band Show in London. Since neither of them had ever heard of Alfredo nor his Band Show, they asked the sergeant to dictate a letter of application for them. Alfredo turned out not to be the leader of a refugee gipsy orchestra but the muddled sergeant's rendering of Ralph Reader, and his Band Show, the RAF Gang Show.

'Eventually we heard that we had been accepted. We went down to London and were immediately sent out to Debden to meet Ralph Reader for the first time. We were due to meet him at eleven o'clock outside our billet and we were there a good half-an-hour early. Then we saw this man in the distance looking like an American – belt tied round his middle, forage cap on one side – with this incredible walk. He had an air of energy and we could tell he was a special man, an individual. We decided to give him a tremendous simultaneous salute and when he reached us we gave him the best ever: all stiff arms, tingling nerves and so on. There was silence as he looked at us in astonishment. "Forget it, kids." he said. "Let's go and have a drink."'

Ralph Reader's name is now synonymous with Scout Gang Shows yet before the war his considerable reputation had been built on working with chorus lines of long-legged showgirls not boys. Trained as a dancer (he 'hoofed' in the West End and on Broadway with Al Jolson) he became a choreographer and producer with nineteen Broadway and thirty-four West End shows to his credit. The story of how the RAF Gang Shows came into being goes back to well before the war. In the early Thirties, as a result of his life-long involvement with the Scout movement, Reader was asked to take over the production of the annual Scout show. Changing the name to the Gang Show, his productions became the most popular amateur shows in the recent history of the stage. In 1937 the Gang became the first amateurs to appear in a Royal Variety Performance when they joined Gracie Fields, Max Miller and the Crazy Gang on the bill at the London Palladium and they later went on to star in a film. On the committee running the Gang Shows at the time was Major Archie Boyle who worked for the RAF. Impressed by Reader's work, Boyle invited him to undertake similar productions with the apprentices at RAF Halton.

By 1938 Boyle had become Deputy Director of Intelligence for the RAF and he realized that, when the war came, if ever he wanted a man who

Seated centre is Ralph Reader, on his left is Harry Trachy, who gained a considerable reputation as a female impersonater; on his right, George Cameron, who was one of the original Gang Show members who accompanied Reader on the ENSA tour in France.

could pass freely round any RAF station in the world without questions being asked and who would probably know someone there from either the Scouts or Halton, that man was Reader. Reader was offered a job in RAF Intelligence, underwent his basic training and emerged a Pilot Officer in the reserve.

'That was in July, 1939,' recalls Reader. 'When the war came I finished a show at the Coventry Hippodrome on the Saturday night and was in uniform the next day. My first job was to go to Harrow to lecture new officers about Intelligence.

In July 1940 the first unit of the Gang Show posed in front of their soon-to-be-famous back cloth. Left to right, Jack Beet, Jack Healy, Murray Browne (at the piano), Ralph Reader, George Cameron, Bill Dickie, Bill Sutton and Eric Christmas.

After about three weeks Boyle called me to his office and said he wanted me to go to France on a job (planes were being sabotaged and we wanted to find out who was behind it.) "We're going to send you over in a complete cover with ENSA," he said. "I'm going to ring up Basil Dean and ask him if he'd like to use you." Which he did. I got together about nine or ten people and started to rehearse a show. We'd only been rehearsing for three days when I had a call to go and see Boyle. "I can't send you to France with those men," he said. When I protested that he didn't know them he said he wanted the names of ten blokes who'd been in the Scout Gang Shows. "But they're not in the Services," I said. "They're all in Civvy Street." "Give me the names," he replied. I gave him the names of ten fellows and he got them all in about eight weeks.'

The show Reader produced, called *Ralph Reader and the Ten Blokes*, sailed to France at the end of November, 1939, with Leslie Henson and Sir Seymour Hicks, as part of the first official ENSA contingent to visit the BEF. The reason Boyle had objected to Reader's original cast was that he did not want any connection between the show and the RAF. After a hectic eight week tour of the front lines the show returned to England and disbanded. The cast returned to civilian life while Reader continued his rounds of RAF stations lecturing on security, keeping his eyes open for the subversive literature that was beginning to appear in camps and helping to produce as many shows and concert parties as he could.

The idea of the Gang Show did not end there. Senior officers at the Air Ministry, especially Lord Tedder, were quick to appreciate the advantages of using Reader in a dual role. More entertainment was needed and Reader was the ideal man to provide it whilst continuing his work for Intelligence. It was not a job he could manage easily on his own and three members of the party that toured France, who had since joined the RAF –

Jack Healy, Jack Beet and George Cameron – were posted to London to help him. Reader decided that the best way to utilize their services was to form an RAF Gang Show which would tour the country performing, and at the same time, help out with local productions. Other ex-Scouts from the ENSA tour were located, persuaded to join the RAF and posted to Reader's new unit. In July, 1940 the first RAF Gang Show took to the road. 'We travelled in a camouflaged Packard towing a trailer full of props,' recalls Jack Healy. 'What I remember best about that tour was that we spent most of our time doing seemingly pointless things like kicking footballs into haystacks and pretending to hunt for them while searching for arms that were supposed to be hidden there. We never found a thing.'

'There was a definite intention at one time,' says Bill Sutton, one of the group that had been persuaded to join up, 'that we should be used as Intelligence officers because we had a first class opportunity to go to places and talk to people, particularly our own troops. Although one or two of us went on an Intelligence course the idea never developed largely, I think, because we were far better entertainers and producers than we were intelligence operators. Apart from France in the early days of the war, we did little more than produce confidential reports based mainly on the general morale of the airmen. We certainly weren't spies. Our work was mainly inward-looking. The Air Ministry was very concerned about morale on remote stations and in places like the Hebrides where there were long postings because they were considered to be home postings. What we did was report on that morale.'

The idea of using the Gang Show as cover for a troupe of agents to scour the world may have been abandoned when it was realized the entertainment side of their work was just as important but Reader continued throughout the war to lecture on security wherever he went and send regular reports to London of what he found on his travels. As the number of units increased, and they spread to every theatre of war, he would appear mysteriously for a few days to see how things were going then vanish. The bulk of his work consisted in keeping his eyes and ears open and informing London of the moods he found. The only time the pages of the *Boy's Own Paper* came to life was on the ENSA-sponsored trip to France. Reader was staying at the Lion d'Or hotel in Reims when he noticed a man enter, check in his hat, toss down a

drink and leave without speaking to anyone. 'I felt foolish harbouring my suspicions,' he says, 'but at that time everything looked suspicious. When I saw the same routine repeated a couple of days later I decided to report it. Much later I learnt that my tip-off had led to a local spy-ring being uncovered. The man was passing information to the hat-check girl in his hat-band and she was passing it on to the Germans. She was shot as a spy.'

For the first six months the Gang Show was attached to the Air Ministry in London. However, the enthusiastic reception given to the show wherever it went combined with Reader's determination to do more and tour further afield led to the setting up of an official Gang Show establishment under Air Force Welfare, at Houghton House in Holborn. A small theatre was built in a lecture hall of what is now part of the London School of Economics where Reader could rehearse

Frank Havenhand and Dudley Jones stand behind Bill Dickie and some one else whilst rehearsing for the Gang Show in Drury Lane before going on tour.

and the first performance was given for an invited audience from the Air Ministry. In January, 1941 Reader was given the go-ahead to increase the number of units to three. He had already noted some of the men he wanted for the new units on his travels but to make sure no one talented slipped through the net he travelled the country looking at RAF concert parties and holding auditions. Among those who joined the new Establishment were Douglas Robinson (who later found fame as Cardew 'The Cad' Robinson and had been running his own shows at RAF Uxbridge), Reg Dixon, Joe Baldwin, Dudley Jones and Albert J Locke (who later produced the popular TV show, *Sunday Night At The London Palladium*).

The format of an RAF Gang Show closely followed that of the Scout shows. 'They consisted of a great deal of Ralph's material from Scout shows before the war,' recalls Dudley Jones, 'in the way of musical numbers like "Crest Of A Wave" and a good many sketches. We all had to join in and take part in these. As time went on Ralph wrote many topical pieces about the RAF so that one appeared as, say, a group captain in a two-hander with a terrible little erk, as we used to call the scruffy little recruits. In between Ralph's material we did our own acts. The members of the first RAF Gang Show had all been Scouts and were mostly amateurs. The increase in the number of units brought in professionals who had their

Bill Dickie, Joe Baldwin and George Cameron posed in front of the rest of the members of Gang Show unit 2. This was the first unit to go to Gibraltar, West Africa and subsequently did a tour in the Middle East, appearing in the Sudan and Egypt. They then followed the Allies in the Italian invasion in 1943.

'Le Ballet Rumpus' was a sketch in Gang Unit No. 5 (that's Cardew Robinson on the left). During the rest of the war and early post war years the Gang Shows perpetuated a tradition of entertainment which has survived to the present in recent British T.V. series such as It Ain't Half Hot Mum.

own acts. I sang ballads like "I'll Walk Beside You" and arias from *Pagliacci*. A good many people, like Cardew Robinson, wrote their own stuff. I was present in a hut when Cardew the cad of the school was born. After Cardew had invented the name for that creature with the long scarf, for nights on end, he was reading out new verses he'd written, asking us what we thought of them. We used to send him up. "Terrible," we would all groan, "Terrible!" And Reg Dixon wrote "Confidentially", his peace-time signature tune, at odd moments in RAF huts.'

Reader's own contribution was immense. Not only did he produce or have a hand in the production of every show, he wrote 163 original songs, 123 sketches, countless short gags and devised seventy-one production numbers. He remained a father-figure to his men, travelling the world several times to see how they were getting on and inspiring the intense loyalty a commander receives when he's prepared to fight any battle for those under his care. He kept close control of his units by never permitting the Establishment to become too large; its total strength, even at the end of the war, never exceeded 200.

In spite of the commonly-held belief that airmen were a special breed the RAF was not entirely free of the bullet-headed automaton who comprehended only regulations and longed to make life difficult for entertainers; nor of envy from people who felt artists in uniform had it easy and were in some way swinging the lead.

'It was always a good idea to give the show as soon as possible after arriving,' says Dudley Jones, 'otherwise the airmen would ask, "Who are these chaps who stay in bed until ten in the morning?" As soon as we arrived, as a rule, we would be taken to wherever we were doing the show and we'd spend the next hour working. Jobs were apportioned. Certain people always had to see that the backcloth was up and the lights in; others found the dressing-rooms and put out the costumes. We always toured with an iron because certain drag costumes always needed pressing and somebody did that. We each had our jobs to do. Then we would put on a show lasting a good two hours. After the show, whatever the complaints or grouses about us before, everything was all right. It was like appearing on television today: people would come up and say, "I saw you last night. It was marvellous." As a rule we tore the audience up; they used to stand and cheer.'

Cardew Robinson agrees. 'Particularly if we did a show for the authorities as soon as we arrived we were often allowed to get away with breaking small regulations. I remember at one camp one of the Gang, a very pretty boy with shoulder-length blond hair, was going out of the main gate. The sentry stopped him and asked where he was going. "To the village," said this boy. The sentry couldn't believe the length of his hair, he had his uniform on as well, so he said, "And what do you do?", meaning his job. "I'm a character lady," replied the boy and he flounced off!'

The speed of the productions left little time between sketches for an artist, who had to play several roles, to change. Bill Dickie, appearing in a cod can-can line in front of an audience that included many high-ranking officers, had changed so quickly that he had forgotten his underpants. In Italy, Harry Trachy was making a lightning change in the back of a lorry parked next to the stage as a dressing-room when the lorry was driven away. The Gang Shows never had mixed casts. When women eventually joined the Establishment it was to form separate WAAF units. Being all-male, female roles in sketches were played by men including Harry Trachy and Dick Emery.

People who saw Emery during the war remember particularly his female impersonations. Many of the characters he has since made famous on television were born on the back of an RAF truck. 'I thought he was marvellous and so did most people,' says Queenie Isaacs, a member of one of the WAAF Gang Shows. 'The first time I saw him was in a sketch called "Geraldine", written by Ralph Reader. It was the forerunner of the "Boy Friend", "Anyone for tennis?" kind of thing. Len Lowe played the handsome hero, Harry Trachy was the slinky vamp, Cardew Robinson the solicitor and Dick was Geraldine, a big bosomed, Mandy character at which he was wonderful. Another sketch he did was "Sweethearts of the Forces". Jack Healy had a white face and was deadpan, with a flat chest. Dick had the

big bosom. They just stood there looking at one another which was hysterically funny. Then Dick said, in that voice, "I'm the stand-in for the buffers at Victoria Station", which brought the house down.'

A typical Gang Show consisted of ten men under a flight sergeant. When a new unit was formed a senior member of an existing company would take over as flight sergeant in charge. In 1941 there were three units; by the end of 1942, six; by the end of 1943, ten. By the end of the war in 1945 there were fifteen home-based units, including two all-WAAF shows, and ten overseas modelled on Gang Show lines and produced by Gang Show members. The steady increase in numbers meant other young performers, with little or no experience, joined the Gang, including Tony Hancock (who specialized in an act as a green faced ghoul), Graham Stark, David Lodge, Norrie Paramor and Peter Sellers. Ralph Reader well remembers the first time he met Peter Sellers.

'I was on this station where there had been a notice on the board inviting anyone interested in joining the Gang Shows to contact me and Peter did. "What do you do?" I asked him. "Play the drums," he replied. "Anything else?" "Well, I can do some bits of *ITMA*." I told him to come to the Naafi the following morning and I would hear what he could do. The next day I went down to the

Gang Show regulars Bill Wilkie, Ron Colin, Peter Sellers and Harry Herring in one of the many comedy sketches which brought laughter to British troops in the vast theatre of war.

Cardew Robinson and Dudley Jones personified the appeal the Gang Shows had for the armed forces. It was the combination of the ludicrous and incongruous in sketches, costumes, personality, physique and good humoured unflappability.

Naafi and as I walked in I heard myself singing 'Riding along on the crest of a wave' even worse than I sing it. I walked up the steps on to the stage and there was Peter Sellers entertaining six airmen by giving an impression of me! As soon as I stepped on the stage the airmen, naturally, stood to attention. Sellers hadn't seen me and carried on until he realized something was up. He stopped and turned round. "Well," he said, "are you thirsty or do I get jankers?"'

By the time Sellers joined the Gang Shows, units were playing in Iceland, Gibraltar, West Africa, North Africa, Italy and India as well as throughout the British Isles and Northern Ireland. In 1943 George Cameron had taken his unit (with Joe Baldwin, Billy Wells and Albert J Locke) on a tour that included Gibraltar, Morocco, West Africa, the Sudan, Egypt and Italy, and Jack Beet had led the first Gang Show visit to India. Sellers was sent to join Gang Show Number 10 which after a tour of Scotland, the Hebrides, the Orkney Islands and Iceland, was bound for Bombay. In charge of the party was Dudley Jones.

'Peter used to play the drums in our five-piece

band and also take part in sketches. He also had his own solo spot which was an imitation of the entire cast of *ITMA*. His act lasted about four or five minutes and was a brilliant cameo of all the voices from that radio show. It was on that trip that he discovered one of the voices he used to use with Spike Milligan in *The Goon Show*. Indian trains had to be seen to be believed. You cannot conceive that so many people could get on one train. They were not just in it, they were on it; on the roof, hanging on the sides. Even if you had a reserved coach, which we were supposed to have for those long journeys, you had to go to great lengths to prevent the carriage being flooded with Indians. Any station we stopped at, even in the middle of nowhere where there was nothing to be seen for miles, as soon as we stopped, from the bowels of the earth, there would appear four million people with tea things, cakes, the lot. Peter and Ben Novak, who did an acrobatic act, discovered after a very short time that the way to prevent our carriage being taken over was to stand on the steps carrying on a terrible quarrel in what sounded like Hindi. It was, in fact, absolute codswollop – neither of them spoke a word of it. But the four million Indians stood and gazed in wonder and no one ever tried to get into our carriage.'

When the show reached Bombay it was hailed as 'the best of its kind in the last twenty years.' They played to enthusiastic audiences everywhere. 'Two hours of laughter,' reported a Calcutta paper, doubting whether any other show to visit the city had made a packed house laugh as much. 'There were only ten of them, every one of them with a reputation on the Music Hall stage at home and some who, I feel sure, will fill a big place in the entertainment world of the post war years. Not a minute of boredom, not a second when we were not filled with admiration for the all-round talent of this happy group.' The reporter may have been confused in thinking that Dudley Jones's three seasons of Shakespeare in Regent's Park qualified him as a star of Music Hall but he was right about the future. His opinion was shared by the critic of the Bombay *Sunday Standard* who concluded his review: 'The "baby" of the show is Peter Sellers, aged 19, the boy-drummer and impressionist. A big future lies before him.'

Before them all in 1944 lay nine months of gruelling travel across 30,000 miles of India, Ceylon, Assam and Burma. 'It is regrettable but true,' wrote a contemporary who had watched the

Gang Show unit 10 was renowned for its arduous and extensive tour of the Hebrides, the Orkney Islands, Iceland, Ceylon, Assam, Burma and throughout India. The overland journeys by van, lorry and train were exhausting but wherever the unit appeared it was lively, funny and brought laughter to many battle-weary troops.

Gang at work, 'that a tendency towards Welfare and entertainment activities is still towards derision, neglect – and even hostility by a great many Servicemen, officers and airmen alike. They consider such activities a scrounge. I would like very much to grab one of these sceptics in each hand and drag them by the hair into a Gang Show dressing-room – just to show them what hard work really is. The stage is never unoccupied for a second and each member averages about a dozen appearances; and in that number of appearances he has probably ten full changes to make – costume *and* make-up. The speed on and off the stage is breakneck. Add to this the fact that most of the shows are one night stands, and that as soon as a performance is finished they must pack up and leave for another show elsewhere – and you gain a fair notion of just what sort of scrounge entertaining is.'

With hundreds of miles between engagements which had to be covered on the ground, never by air, problems from illness and the heat, which made make-up run and shirts stick to the back so that quick changes became a nightmare, life for a company touring in India was anything but easy. 'There were times when we nearly went on strike,'

recalls Dudley Jones. 'They would muck us about with transport arrangements, then, after we'd travelled 2,000 miles, there would be no one to meet us or who even knew we were coming. We would arrive dead on our feet and falling asleep but I had to present myself to the Entertainments Officer and we had to do a show the same night. And people got sick more easily in India. At one point I had four out of my ten men ill so I was constantly revising the running order: "You do so-and-so's bit, cut that, you do something else."'

When the Gang arrived at a venue on time there was rarely a theatre in which to perform. 'We had one performance outside Calcutta stopped by "natural action"' continues Jones. 'There was a Naffi being built but it hadn't been finished and there was only one 100-watt bulb there, so, with great ingenuity, the airmen had rigged up a stage for us in an open plane bay on the airfield two miles away. It was, in fact, a boxing ring with the posts removed. We arrived there in daylight to put up our Gang Show backcloth then returned half-an-hour before the show was due to start. We never minded playing in the open air. The temperature was about eighty-five, even at night, which was ideal. There were a great many men

DIRECT FROM LONDON !

First Public Appearance In Calcutta !

From FRIDAY, December 1st
To THURSDAY, December 7th
DAILY AT 10-30 A.M. ONLY

Laughs! Laughs!! and more Laughs ! ! !

R. A. F. WELFARE
proudly presents

"THE GANG SHOW"
No. 10

A Ralph Reader Prodn
With

DUDLEY JONES. GENE PATTON
WALLY SPARKS. HARRY KANE
LES OSBORNE. PETER SELLERS
BILL WILLKIE. G. F. X. TAYLOR
BEN NOVAK. MAURICE ARNOLD

You've heard them on the B.B.C.— now you can see and hear them
at the

NEW EMPIRE

Allied Forces As. 8 each.
Officers & Civilians Rs. 2 each.

'There were only ten of them, every one of them with a reputation on the Music Hall stage at home, and some who, I feel sure, will fill a big place in the entertainment world of the post war years.'

there sitting on planks on oil drums. The moment we switched on the lights there was an invasion by every insect in India – not one moth but four million – Praying Mantises, every sort of mosquito and little greenfly. Within two minutes of switching on the lights the Gang Show letters, which were two feet high, were obscured and the insects were so thick in the footlights we were literally shovelling them up. By this time the audience had gathered and they shone headlights from cars and lorries to increase the light on the stage but we had to give up. We were covered from head to foot in creeping things and when you opened your mouth they flew in. Right up to the time of the show we

were trying to deal with them but we just couldn't cope. In the end we had to retire to the half-finished Naafi, with its 100-watt bulb, and do the show there, which meant transporting everything and everybody two miles down the road.'

It was virtually impossible for an entertainer on tour ever to escape his public. In barracks, messes, hotels, billets, on trains, boats and planes, he was always on show, expected to put on an act even if it was only talking to the men. During their nine month tour of India, Gang Show 10 received only two separate weeks of leave during which they followed tradition and took to the hills to escape from the heat. 'Needless to say we had to put on shows at the rest camp,' say Jones. 'At one we performed in a little church hall, a brick building without glass windows. All it had were holes in the walls – you didn't need proper windows in that climate. We were performing to a packed hall with Indians sitting in all the window openings when a cloud came by and quite literally passed through the hall. One moment everything was bright, the next we were in a dense fog and couldn't see a thing. A few minutes later it cleared and we could continue. It was extraordinary.'

As the war progressed many people in the RAF in Britain began to wonder if similar use couldn't be made of the talent in the WAAF. Reader resisted all attempts to make him incorporate girls into his existing Gang Shows and instead suggested an all-girl unit. The Air Ministry was suitably horrified at the thought of a dozen of its girls touring RAF Stations and Army camps. 'I felt the fellows needed to see some girls,' explains Reader, 'and we had some very talented and lovely ones in the WAAF. Eventually the Air Ministry gave in and said I could have them provided there was a WAAF officer appointed to look after them. The only one we ever had to look after was the officer! She would be taken to the Mess and would get sloshed every night, and always the girls had to put her to bed. They themselves were two hundred per cent.'

The first WAAF Gang Show was formed in June, 1944 as an experiment. Reader held auditions and selected eleven girls for whom he devised and wrote an entire show. Two months after D-Day, the girls set out for France and caked in dust gave their first performance in a Normandy field half-an-hour after landing much to the surprise of the audience who had no idea a WAAF Gang Show existed let alone would be playing for them. There were no microphones and, in the open air, the men

In June 1944 the first of the WAAF Gang Shows had a successful tryout in Houghton House in Holborn before touring Normandy, two months after D Day. Like the members of the RAF Gang Shows, of which this was a female version, every one in the company had to be versatile, agile, quick witted and spontaneous.

couldn't hear what was being said on stage but they didn't care; they were happy just looking. From there the unit went on a tour of France and Belgium. A despatch rider who passed their truck was so startled he fell off into a ditch.

As an experiment the first WAAF Gang Show was wildly successful and in December a second unit was formed from more than 500 applicants. Among the successful ones was Queenie Isaacs, an amateur entertainer who had been appearing in RAF shows in Blackpool prior to her call-up. 'The format of our shows followed that of the male Gang Shows exactly. I'll never forget the first time the boys heard us singing "Crest Of A Wave" – they nearly died! After the opening chorus we sang "How Do You Do? It is so nice of you to come" and

each of us took a bow. Then we sang a little song, four of us did a number called "The Flags Are Flying" and we did sketches including one called "By Candle-Light" in which we were dressed in our nighties. There were individual spots and then a big finale, a pageant about England with Peace, Plenty, Justice and so on, dressed in sheets and looking hideous.'

Most of the time the girls looked far from hideous. They wore gorgeous clothes and the shows were beautifully presented. Looking back they were probably too antiseptic and coy for some tastes, with ankle-length gowns and choreography that was more sedate than Folies Bergère. There was little leg or naughtiness. But at the time there was little criticism of either the

Ralph Reader also devised all the sketches, such as 'Pageant' seen here, for the WAAF Gang Shows Nos. 1 and 2. Unlike the male shows, which became the testing ground for some now famous stars such as Tony Hancock, Dick Emery and Peter Sellers, virtually none of the members of the WAAF shows gained any theatrical reputation.

shows or the girls from men who had not seen or talked to an English girl for two or three years.

'The only criticism we ever heard,' says Queenie Isaacs, 'was when we used to land on a station in our lorries, very tired and very dirty. The officers would take one look at us, say "Yuk!" and tell us there would be a party in the Sergeants' Mess afterwards. Then, when we came on stage dressed to kill – because money was no object for all our clothes – it suddenly changed to "Officers' Mess afterwards". The boys would then complain that it was only the officers who ever saw us. Unfortunately, we had to go where we were told.'

The Gang Shows became a uniquely RAF property. RAF Stations throughout Britain, the Middle East and India tried to create Gangs out of

their own concert parties or form new ones along Gang Show lines. Whenever Reader stopped off in a foreign country he did his best to advise or produce local RAF talent in the Gang Show tradition. He even managed to get some of his scripts into a German POW camp for the airmen there to put on a production. In 1944, in response to the complaints about lack of entertainment in India, RAF Welfare sent Bill Sutton, a founder member of the Gang Shows who had moved out of performing into administration, and musician Norrie Paramor out to India with orders to start six local Gang Show units. A movement which had started in 1940 as cover for Ralph Reader to travel the world and report on morale in RAF camps had, by 1944, turned full circle and become one of

Ralph Reader stopping off at Castel Benito in Italy on one of his customary flying trips to visit his troupes in the field.

the most important props of that morale. That the Gangs always gave full value was due as much to the standards Reader set as to the pride of the performers. 'Their visits,' a station commander remarked, 'were anticipated just as eagerly, if not more so, as when we announced that Vivian van Damm would be bringing down some girls from the Windmill.' No matter where a unit was or what the conditions were, Reader insisted on full make-up, full costume, one hundred percent effort and the Gang Show backcloth, a light blue cloth with the legend 'Gang Show'. 'Wherever we played,' remembers Cardew Robinson, 'whether it was the Alhambra, Bradford, or in a Wadi somewhere in the desert, Ralph always insisted we must put up that backcloth and, do you know, I don't think there was a single performance when we didn't have it up. If that's what Ralph wanted, we did it.' Particularly in the desert, away from the public gaze, Reader expected standards to be maintained. It was then, he knew, a slick, professional show would have its greatest impact. Cliff Henry, dressed in white tie, tails and top hat, was waiting to do his act for fifty men in a Wadi in North Africa. He decided to answer the call of nature at the top of the Wadi, out sight of the audience, at the moment a jeep drove past. At the sight of this figure, clad in evening dress, emerging from nowhere and irrigating the desert, the jeep slowed down, drove close to Henry, then shot away, none of the occupants saying a word. The RAF Gang Shows certainly left their mark on the fighting man!

CHAPTER FIVE

BRITAIN UNDER SIEGE

The Battle of Britain began on the morning of 13 August, 1940, when more than 200 German planes set off for the southern coast of England to begin Operation Eagle, the Luftwaffe's attempt to destroy the RAF in the air and on the ground. Forty-five German planes were destroyed that day for the loss of thirteen RAF. A week later the whole of Britain was declared a Defence Area as the skies of Kent, Sussex and Essex filled with aerial combat. Workers in the fields and in the towns, schoolchildren in class, stopped to watch the dog-fights. Newspaper placards carried hastily scrawled scores — 167 for 33 — as if the battle was a new sport. Artists in London theatres ran up to the roof to watch the fights overhead.

On 24 August two German pilots made a mistake that was to alter the course of the war. Time and again Hitler had stressed that London should not be touched by the Luftwaffe's bombs. That night the two pilots, lost and harassed by RAF fighters, decided to jettison their bombs into what they thought were the marshes of the Thames estuary rather than return to base with a full load and face embarrassing questions. The first bombs fell in the heart of the City at one o'clock in the morning. When Goering heard the news he was furious. The pilots were swiftly traced and transferred to an infantry division. But the mistake had been made and was to have an important result. The following day the order went out to Bomber Command, 'Bomb Berlin.' That evening the RAF made its first raid on the German capital. Although the damage was slight, Hitler was in-

censed. He had boasted that the RAF could never get through to Berlin and now they had. He had lost face. Furiously he ordered the Luftwaffe to raze every British city to the ground. The Blitz was under way.

On 7 September 400 German bombers, escorted by 600 fighters, made their first ordered raid on London. It was the start of fifty-seven consecutive nights of bombing and an agony that was to last for nine months. The switching of the attack from airfields to cities proved to be a turning-point for the hard-pressed RAF. For the first time since the Battle of Britain began the week's losses in Spitfires and Hurricanes were exceeded by the production of new machines. The Blitz was a deliberate attempt to destroy civilian morale and became a part of folklore before it was over. The tales of heroism and courage, the stories of the night before (the 'bomb' story became the latest way to bore your friends) and accounts of the humour of London's citizens became part of legend as did the myth that every Cockney dug from the rubble came up with a wise-crack on his or her lips. Laughter did play an important part in helping people survive a basically horrific situation; the British secret weapon was said to be a sense of humour.

Although what was happening in commercial theatres in the big cities was not, strictly speaking, troop entertainment (though troops were in the audiences), it warrants a separate chapter because, especially in London, the public found itself in the front line of battle for the first time. As Anna Neagle remarks, 'There was no difference between

The Windmill Theatre in the heart of London's Soho played continually throught the war. Even during the height of the Blitz there were continuous performances of the 139th edition of Revudeville from 11.15 in the morning to 9.15 at night.

playing for the Forces and playing for the general public. Everybody was in the same boat and entertainment meant so much to us all. To play in any theatre before any audience was a thrill because there was such spirit and everyone was hungry for something to lift them out of their ordinary difficulties.'

All London theatres felt the impact of the bombing and every one, with the exception of the Windmill ('We Never Closed') was shut at some time between September, 1940 and May, 1941 when the raids finished. The Royal Court in Sloane Square was damaged and closed when a bomb fell on the underground station next door, and did not reopen until 1952. The London Casino, Duke of York's and Phoenix were damaged by bomb blasts. The audience for *Top of the World* at the Palladium was showered with glass when the doors were blown in and the theatre was closed when a land-mine was discovered on the roof. At the Saville, *Up and Doing*, with Binnie Hale, Stanley Holloway and Patricia Burke,

closed after four bombs fell nearby. *Applesauce*, starring Max Miller, Doris Hare and Vera Lynn, which had opened on 24 August at the Holborn Empire was closed three weeks later by a time-bomb. Before the show could reopen the theatre was reduced to a heap of rubble by a direct hit. Five minutes before midnight on 15 October a 500-pounder hit Drury Lane, passed through each of the galleries in turn and exploded in the pit. Incendiaries raining in afterwards burnt out the orchestra stalls. David Garrick's mirror, a full-length Georgian pier-glass in a gilded frame, which had been hanging in the wings for 170 years, was untouched: the buckled safety curtain had taken the force of the blast. The auditorium was a mess but the offices were still habitable and mostly untouched. The following day it was business as usual for ENSA. A direct hit on the Rialto cinema passed through into the Cafe de Paris below killing several customers, band-leader 'Snake Hips' Johnson and the manager who, a few days earlier,

All that remained of the Holborn Empire after receiving a direct hit in a Blitz night raid in September 1940; fortunately the theatre was empty and there were no casualities.

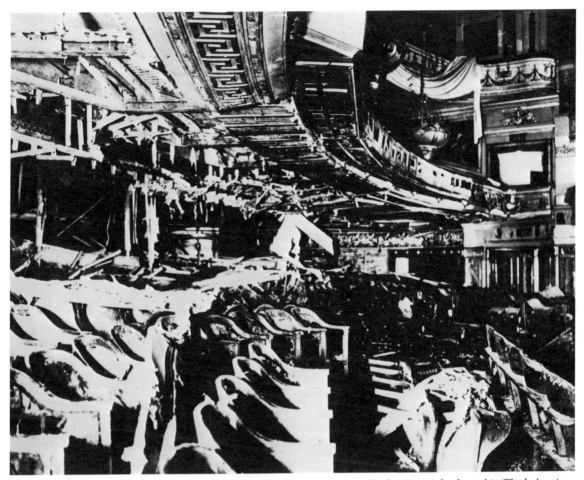

Just before midnight 15th October 1940, the Theatre Royal Drury Lane was the victim of a direct hit. The balconies were severely damaged and the orchestra pits burned out. Although some ENSA staff were sleeping on the premises at the time, fortunately for all, no one was killed or even seriously injured.

had tried to book Florence Desmond for the cabaret telling her the club was 'as safe as the Bank of England.' On 10 May, 1941, London received its final and heaviest raid. 2,200 fires burned in the metropolis that night and a record 1,436 died. The War Office, Parliament, Westminster Abbey, the Tower, the Mint and the British Museum were among the buildings damaged. Queen's Hall in Langham Place, home of Sir Henry Wood's Promenade Concerts, received a direct hit and was totally destroyed.

During the Blitz the Government made no attempt to close theatres and cinemas. Having learned the value of laughter and diversion, it was not going to repeat the mistakes of September 1939. The times of performances were brought forward to the afternoon or very early evening to give the public and performers time to get home before the raids began. The only regulation imposed was that, to avoid the streets being filled with milling crowds, once a raid started audiences should stay where they were until the All Clear. Elisabeth Welch was appearing at the Haymarket at the height of the raids.

'Whoever was on stage when the sirens went had to stop and say to the audience if anybody wanted to leave they could. We had to do this because some people were air raid wardens or ambulance drivers and had to be on duty. The houselights would come up and you would hear seats banging as people got up. Then the lights would go down and we would carry on with the show, praying we wouldn't be hit.'

Tommy Trinder was in *Top of the World* at the

Palladium. 'Apart from those who had to, not a soul used to leave. I think everybody had the idea that it couldn't happen to them.' If a performance finished before the All Clear sounded the artists would sit on the stage chatting to the audience or leading them in community singing. Occasionally members of the public would be invited on stage to do their party piece. At one theatre the cast were astonished when the star's dresser ran through a full repertoire of Music Hall songs, belting them out as if she had been on stage all her life. Some nights, artists and audience were in the theatre until four in the morning. Because of this habit of staying on, Tommy Trinder earned himself a probably never to be broken record, of playing the most West End theatres in one night.

'After one show at the Palladium George Black asked me to go down to the Hippodrome to help entertain the audience that was still there. I was then talking with Bud Flanagan about how many theatres it would be possible to do in a night and decided to have a go. Bud lent me a steel helmet with Police written on it and I set off in my little MG which I had to drive without lights since there was a raid on. Altogether I played in seventeen-theatres, stopping at the stage door and asking if they wanted me to do a ten minute spot. I was hoping to do twenty but the All Clear went after the Seventeenth.'

The men, women and children who suffered the Blitz discovered a new solidarity absent during the war up until then. However there was another side to the bombings which didn't make the papers. There was real terror and confusion, and many fled the towns and cities in a phenomenon known as 'trekking'. In the west, people trekked to Dartmoor, curling up on the wet moors to sleep; from London they trekked to Epping Forest. There was, nevertheless, little absenteeism from work. People made the effort to get to work partly because the raids gave it a new importance, partly because they knew friends would worry if they didn't show up. An aircraft factory worker recalled, 'You would see men staggering at their work from lack of sleep, snatching a ten minute doze in the canteen over their food, and still, when knocking off time came, going off with a cheerful, "See yer in the morning, boys!"' The cheerfulness of the Blitz was certainly not a myth and those who stayed in the cities had good reason to be proud. Entertainment was an essential part of the way of life. 'At no time during the war,' says Florence Desmond, 'can I ever remember a performance

Another typical publicity/propaganda photograph from the early days of the war. It fostered that spirit of preparedness and mocking good humour that prevailed throughout the dark days and nights.

being stopped because of an air-raid.' It was only in the grim light of morning when a theatre was discovered to be unsafe or no longer able to meet the London County Council fire regulations (the safety curtain had to be lowered at least once every performance) that a show was taken off. At the height of the Blitz, all London theatres closed with the exception of the Windmill where *Revudeville* (139th edition) entered its ninth year, playing from 11.15 am until 9.15 pm. Although bombs and incendiaries fell close to the theatre and a member of the stage crew was killed, there was never any question of Vivian van Damm shutting up shop. Most of the company lived at the theatre where the lounge was turned into a communal dormitory for the girls. The closures, once again, affected musicians, chorus lines and little-known entertainers. More than 3,000 musicians were out of work in the capital and ENSA was roundly condemned for 'its pitifully inadequate help'. The solution, for some, was to leave London. For others, it was a series of concerts arranged by ENSA and CEMA in the shelters and Underground stations which became home for so many Londoners during the Blitz.

Shelters produced a way of life all their own. In street shelters designed for a three or four hour occupation conditions became disgusting after a raid of ten to fourteen hours, but a sense of community developed. On nights when raids were not too heavy, shelter-crawling took the place of the peacetime pub-crawl and many were outraged at the frankness of the petting that went on. Before the war the Government had refused to consider using Underground stations as shelters for fear that the population would never come up once it had discovered the safety of a deep shelter. Londoners took the matter into their own hands and invaded seventy-nine Underground stations. The Government's fears were ill-founded; very few of the 60,000 who sheltered in the tubes stayed

down there for weeks on end. Fifteen miles of the tube system were designated shelters and it was there that the out-of-work musicians and entertainers went to play for the crowds queuing to get in or sleeping on the platforms. At the Government's request ENSA started a regular shelter service and broadcast the first concert from the Aldwych (with George Formby and Geraldo.) The BBC also broadcast *In Town Tonight* from a shelter, talking to those people who had been unable to get home for the night. In spite of the usual complaints (from shelter marshals who objected to the over-crowding a concert produced, and the public who preferred to sleep)the concerts were widely enjoyed.

The value of entertainment was brought home to Richard Hearne when he was appearing in *Shepherd's Pie* at the Prince's Theatre. 'During the heaviest raids the show closed for a few days. I arrived one day to find I was the only person there – no one had told me it had been cancelled. When we reopened the manager of the cigar department of Dunhill, who after a raid had been found in the

Many Underground stations, like this one, the Aldwych, became shelters during the nightime raids. Londoners were given shows by voluntary and organized groups of entertainers.

69

shop ruins searching for lighters, was brought to the show by two friends. He'd been badly affected by the bombing. His mind had gone and he was deteriorating fast. After the performance his friends brought him round to my dressing-room. "Mr Hearne," he said, "you have saved my life. I now want to live." That was the power of laughter.'

Theatre staff during 1940–41 were trained fire-fighters and plane spotters. During performances they would take turns to do duty on the theatre roof. A stage carpenter saved one theatre while the show was on when he smothered two incendiaries. At Drury Lane fire watchers hurled many incendiaries into the street below. Male members of the show at the Windmill included three Home Guard, two auxiliary firemen and fourteen ambulance men, while at Drury Lane, W MacQueen Pope was the ARP Warden. 'I was the Home Guard sergeant and we used to have quite a few up and downers,' remembers Eric Tissington who ran ENSA's routing section. 'As soon as a raid started Pope would come into our office (a converted dressing-room) and say, "All downstairs into the shelter." Well, I was very busy and my girls, who were typing and filing, were quite happy to stay – we put on tin hats and got ready to stand behind the pillars – so we stayed. "I'm the Air Raid Warden. I order you downstairs," he would say. "And I'm the Home Guard sergeant. We're staying put," I would reply. We always stayed.'

There was little serious drama on the West End stage. Edith Evans gave successful daytime poetry recitals at Wyndham's but during the Blitz audiences mostly wanted to laugh, not be made to think. The most popular shows were Variety, revue and farce. Edith Evans, again at Wyndham's, starred in a Farjeon revue, *Diversion*, with Dorothy Dickson, Bernard Miles, Peter Ustinov and a young actor making his West End début, Dirk Bogarde. *Diversion*, Ustinov recalled, 'was to do for the dressed what the Windmill was doing for the undressed.' Nudity and knickers seem to have been the formula for success in the theatre of 1941, provided, of course, the nude did not move. Fear of the censor was still greater than fear of the German bombs. In spite of the dangers of theatre-going during the Blitz, all the theatres, when open, did good business. When bombs closed a production the management would send it on tour until it was safe to return or the theatre had been patched up. Theatres out of town which had once been only number three dates suddenly became attractive venues for glittering West End productions.

But London was not the only target for the German bombers. All the industrial conurbations suffered their share of hardship. Liverpool, Plymouth, Coventry, Southampton, Humberside, Clydebank, Glasgow and Belfast all had massive raids. In Clydebank only seven of the town's 12,000 homes escaped damage. And when the Luftwaffe was ordered to bomb Britain's historic cities in an attempt to destroy buildings of tourist interest and the pride of the inhabitants, Canterbury, Exeter, Norwich and Bath suffered too. On 15 November the most devastating raids of the war began on Coventry. For five days its citizens took a pounding which brought them close to the edge of endurance. 50,000 homes, 500 shops and the cathedral were destroyed. The theatre went in the first raid. Other provincial theatres suffered. Birmingham Repertory Theatre had a history of closing, reopening and closing. When *Up and Doing* closed at the Saville the cast was sent to Manchester. 'The management decided we would do it out of town,' recalls Patricia Burke. 'In fact, since it was nearly Christmas, it was decided that we should put on a pantomime using the same cast. We all travelled to Manchester and were there only three days when they started to bomb Manchester.'

Under such circumstances civilians had as much right to expect to see the best entertainment as troops in the field. Basil Dean agreed and at the request of the Ministry of Labour, ENSA put on additional concerts and performances in shelters, Underground stations, refuges for the homeless and factories involved with essential war-work.

This increase in work, coupled with a growing demand for companies to visit troops overseas in the Middle East, placed a new burden on ENSA. With commercial theatres in full swing ENSA was desperate for new faces and stepped up auditions. Among the thousands of would-be performers who flocked to Drury Lane (on average seventy a day were auditioned) was sixteen-year-old Paula Baird, a conjuror who was to become the first woman to win the coveted Magic Circle Silver Wand.

Pushed to the limit ENSA was happy to accept any offer of professional help, often without vetting it properly. John Carlsen was an Entertainments Officer in the Midlands when the Original Cardini from the London Palladium was billed to give a show at one of his ack-ack sites.

Hugh Lloyd was one of the unknowns who gained his first professional experience appearing in front of an audience with ENSA. The first company he joined was so bad that it folded after three days. But Lloyd was one of the lucky ones: he joined George Thomas's Globe Trotters and stayed with them until the end of the war.

'At that time Cardini was the greatest silent magician in the world. I had seen him at the Palladium before the war. I was under the impression he was in America so I went along to this ENSA concert very pleased. When "Cardini" appeared, out came this plump Midlander who had a very good magic act but certainly was not the Original Cardini from the London Palladium. I phoned the ENSA area representative the next day and told him that although this man was good he should not be billed as the Original Cardini, which he wasn't. I knew because I'd seen him. "Well," said the ENSA man, crossly, "the chap you saw at the Palladium must have been an impostor!"'

Although ENSA continued to attract criticism and be the butt of jokes ('What kind of jokes did our ancestors enjoy?' asks a historian. Hasn't he seen an ENSA show?) the Government recognized the value of its work and in March, 1941 issued a report recommending the Treasury to take over financing its work from Naafi. At the end of May, ENSA officially ceased to exist when it became the Department of National Service Entertainment, a branch of the civil service, with Dean as Director. In practice the name ENSA continued to appear on all playbills and posters.

Although the preference during the Blitz was for lighter entertainment, a subtle and growing change could be detected. With the call-up of older age-groups and a broadening of tastes in the men who went to make up the services there came an increasing demand for different types of diversion. This was self-evident in the popularity of Dame Myra Hess's lunchtime concerts at the National Gallery and the success of the Old Vic tour of Wales (sponsored by CEMA). 'We played to troops, steelworkers and miners in the villages,' Dame Sybil Thorndike recounted. 'We didn't take sets, just a screen, but we played in costume. We took *Macbeth* which we did in the Prince Charlie period with Lewis (Casson, her husband) playing Macbeth as Hitler. When we told CEMA we intended taking *Macbeth* they said "Oh, poor Welshmen!", but the audiences loved it; they were wonderful. We opened during an air-raid – we had lots of raids on the tour – and none of the audience

This is an **THE**
E.N.S.A.
SHOW

LANCHESTER MARIONETTE THEATRE

(Waldo and Muriel Lanchester from Malvern)

VARIETY
UNDER-WATER BALLET
GRAND CIRCUS

This is the Show that went to Buckingham Palace and the
Paris International Exhibition
The Most Famous Marionette Theatre travelling the Country
Don't Miss It !!   Something Quite Different ! !

**THESE SHOWS HAVE BEEN ARRANGED
ESPECIALLY FOR YOUR ENTERTAINMENT
AND YOUR FULL SUPPORT IS REQUESTED**

ever left. We tried out Shaw's *Candida* as well but we had cut it. They thought it was frivolous.'

During the first eighteen months of its existence ENSA had been forced to modify its ideas of what constituted ideal troop entertainment. Dean, with his theatrical background, had always pressed for more erudite fare than non-stop variety but had been baulked by those on his committees who thought they knew best. Several factors helped change their minds: the criticism of all but the best variety shows, the lack of talented singers and dancers and the growing need, discovered in the adversity of the Blitz, for entertainment of more lasting value. That a symphony orchestra should prove as popular as a dance band came as a surprise. An all-girl revue such as *Nine Till Six* was obviously well-received. What was totally unexpected (particularly after the initial disasters with drama) was the reaction to Repertory companies touring plays, to John Trevor with his one-man adaptations of Shakespeare and the

The Lanchester Marionette theatre was extremely popular with troops from the earliest days of war. Their audiences, many completely unsophisticated and ignorant of live theatre, believed utterly in what they saw and only barely realized that the puppets were not real people.

CERTIFICATE

A2464

CERTIFIED that the holder of this Certificate :—

(a) Mrs. Miss (b) WILCOX. FLORENCE. M.

(c) Who is employed as E·N·S·A· ARTISTE.

is authorised to follow the Armed Forces of the Crown, and is entitled in the event of capture by the enemy to be treated as a prisoner of war under the provisions of Article 81 of the International Convention Relative to the Treatment of Prisoners of War.

For the purposes of such treatment (a) her status is equivalent to that of an

(a) Officer Other rank in the British Army with the rank of

(d) LIEUT.'

(a) delete words not applicable
(b) fill in full name of holder
(c) fill in type of employment
(d) fill in equivalent military rank for type of employment

..........(Signature)

D.D.A.W.S. (E)

Florence Margery Robertson married Herbert Wilcox and was known to the public as Anna Neagle. From her earliest days as a Cochran young lady to her theatrical and cinema careers she was always very popular. Despite her reputation, the directors of ENSA at first thought she would not go down well with military audiences except as a musical comedy performer. They were proved dead wrong when the troops cheered her whether singing, dancing or acting in a serious scene from one of her past successes.

Mystery Plays, even to marionette shows such as the Lanchester's.

The Lanchester Marionettes was a small, go-anywhere, Category D show. Waldo and Muriel Lanchester had offered their services to ENSA at the outbreak of war and been refused on the grounds that the men wouldn't want to watch Punch and Judy. Their performances bore no resemblance to seaside puppets. They included musical items, sketches and an underwater ballet danced to the music of *Swan Lake*. After two years touring under their own steam ENSA adopted them.

'At first,' says Waldo Lanchester, 'the troops used to be suspicious. We would sometimes start a performance with only the Entertainments Officer in the hall waiting to go off to the bar to tell the others if we were any good. Soon after we had started the hall would fill up and we rarely ended without a sizeable audience and an apology. We found it was often better to keep quiet about our connection with ENSA. We arrived at one camp to find the Entertainments Officer had organized a coach to take the men into the neighbouring town and there were none left to watch us. And in the winter, when it was freezing, it was impossible to get the men out of their warm billets into a draughty hall.

Once in, audiences were fascinated by the marionettes and how they worked. 'The Lanchester Marionettes gave us a charming show,' wrote an officer in his report to Drury Lane, 'which was clearly much appreciated and enjoyed. Being the type of entertainment with which most soldiers are unacquainted it would be advisable to advertise it more beforehand. We only received two posters an hour or two before the performance.'

'After a performance,' says Waldo Lanchester, 'I had to go in front of the stage with one of the marionettes to show them how they worked. Even so some didn't think of them as puppets but as real people. At one camp where we played in the middle of winter a soldier was concerned lest the swimmers in the Underwater Ballet should catch cold and at another, the cook appeared with some extra-small sausage rolls he'd spent the afternoon baking "especially for the little people." '

Even an established star like Anna Neagle was not expected to be a wild hit. ENSA wanted her to appear in a show of excerpts from musicals but her husband, Herbert Wilcox, devised something completely different.

'The first half,' Dame Anna recalls,' 'had Billy Milton, Mae Coffey, who was an opera singer, and an actor reciting scenes from Shakespeare, a lovely

Anna Neagle has always been appreciated by her colleagues for her readiness to co-operate in whatever venture she was involved. It was typical of her to sign autographs, pose with the boys and proudly sport her ENSA uniform intact. There were other stars who were too vain to subject themselves to the anonymity of a uniform. They wouldn't accept the practicality of Basil Dean's thinking. They would not understand that by wearing the uniform, if captured they were protected by the Geneva Conventions; if caught in mufti by the enemy they could be shot as spies.

ballet dancer and her partner doing swing-time, semi-ballroom dancing and me doing a couple of musical comedy numbers. The second half was taken up with one act from the Housman Play, *Victoria Regina*, and ended with Mae Coffey singing "Rule Britannia". We did a final rehearsal at Drury Lane and they said it was not really the sort of show they wanted. They didn't want the play at all but Herbert banked on it because of the experience we'd had in Canada doing plays for audiences which included a lot of RAF boys.'

Billy Milton, who played the piano in the show and acted as compere, remembers the dress rehearsal at Drury Lane. 'I heard Frank Collins say, "Anna Neagle? She'll be no good for the troops at all. Going down to Salisbury Plain? Oh no, they won't like her." Herbert came to me quietly on stage and said, "Don't bother to do your piano acts. Anna's just going to walk through her pieces." We took special lighting with us and opened on a Monday at Bulford Camp. And the reception Anna got! It raised the roof. Every bigwig at Drury Lane said, "My god, what a surprise!" Then they couldn't work her hard enough.'

Concentrated raids on Britain finished in August, 1941 and apart from intermittent attacks the bombings did not start again until June, 1944 when the V-1s and V-2s, the doodle-bugs, began to rain on London. In the intervening years Britain remained on the alert expecting either an invasion or a renewal of the bombing. Until the end of 1944 no one was safe. In June, 1943 Stubby Kaye and his USO troupe, touring American camps, were dive-bombed by an ME109. Before going on to give a show they lay in a ditch while their truck was destroyed. In the spring of 1944 James Cagney had a performance interrupted by a dogfight overhead. Cagney and the audience dived into the nearest shelter as the fuel tank from the German plane crashed through the theatre roof. Throughout the Blitz the commercial theatre did a roaring business and Army Welfare, deciding ENSA could no longer cope with demand, set itself up in direct opposition. ENSA struggled on, suffering the brickbats, receiving little praise. Once the Blitz was over Dean decided to pay his own tribute to the bravery and heroism of London's citizens. He mounted a spectacular pageant on the steps of St Paul's Cathedral with a script by Clemence Dane and bands from the Household Cavalry and the Brigade of Guards. The bands and several massed choirs were conducted by Sir Henry Wood. Edith Evans, Sybil Thorndike, Marius Goring, Robert Speaight and Leslie Howard were among the artists who took part. It was broadcast in Britain and in the States. It was a triumphant, uplifting experience for all who took part, saw the performance or listened to it on radio. The next day ENSA received a complaint that it had blocked London's traffic.

CHAPTER SIX

THE BANDS PLAY ON

'Many of the people who came to see our show,' says Terry-Thomas of the Stars in Battledress light music sextet which he compered, 'had never heard our sort of music before, the light, pop classics. At the end of a show there was always a feeling of exhilaration. They found it uplifing as if to say, "Look at me, I have listened to classical music and enjoyed it." '

This change was gradual. Music may have had charms to soothe a savage breast, according to Congreve, but as far as the Military Authorities were concerned it meant only the skirl of pipes, the rattle of drums and the beat of a military band stirring the heart to action. Possibly because the Services understood music's military role and music was universally popular, musicians were more immediately acceptable than any other uniformed entertainer. If a man entered the barracks gates carrying an instrument that could be used in a military band he was welcomed with open arms. Should he play the violin, double bass or cello, however, that was a different matter. He would be consigned to the workshops or put on potato peeling, jobs in which he could utilize his skill with his hands. That is unless he were fortunate enough to join the RAF and be posted to Uxbridge.

Uxbridge was the home of the Central Band of the RAF under its Director of Music, Wing Commander Rudolph O'Donnell. O'Donnell, a musician of distinction, was interested in all forms of music. His ambition was for the RAF to produce the best of all music both on and off parade. His own particular hobby was the RAF Symphony Orchestra (a body which became official only because it existed) made up from Central Band personnel and string players he had managed to have posted to Uxbridge. Among the orchestra's ranks were some of the great instrumentalists of symphonic music. Playing violins were Harry Blech, David Martin, Frederick Grinke, Max Salpeter and Leonard Hirsch. Playing the French horns were Dennis Brain and Norman del Mar.

One of the many popular musicians who benefited from O'Donnell's presence at Uxbridge was trombonist George Chisholm. Early in 1940 he was playing with Ambrose's band at Kilburn when the band was fronted by an unknown singer named Vera Lynn. 'Seven of us decided to volunteer,' he recalls. 'We thought that if we were to have any chance of playing music at all the best thing to do would be to get in and see if we could form the nucleus of a band which would see us through our service. Suddenly, Ambrose found himself seven men short as Tommy McQuater, Jock Cummings, Andy McDermid, Sid Colin, Marty Craig, Harry Lewis (who'd just become engaged to Vera Lynn) and myself rolled up to Uxbridge and volunteered.' Having signed on, they turned to leave. 'Where do you think you're going?' asked the sergeant. They explained that they were booked to appear at Kilburn that night. The CO was called in and gave them a week's leave to complete the engagement; then it was into uniform.

'I and the other trombone player did our practising in the ablutions,' says Chisholm, 'where

George Chisholm (playing on the trombone) said that they decided on the name Squadronaires quite by chance, 'When we were all in our usual inebriated state. Not only did we think it had a nice romantic sound, we thought that, after the war, when our children asked What did you do in the war, daddy?, we could say "I was a Squadronaire"'

the acoustics were marvellous. It was out of most people's way, except for the odd visitor who came in to spend a penny. Sometimes they would say, "Ooo, that's good," and stay. We kept our eyes open for any other musicians and managed to get hold of fourteen to form what was later to be called The Squadronaires.'

The Squadronaires were never officially bandsmen and their music-making came second to being airmen. Rehearsals and concerts had to take place during off-duty hours while the day was filled with heaving coal, sweeping leaves, whitewashing stones and cutting grass. 'One day,' remembers Chisholm, 'when we were rehearsing, an officer walked in just as we were told to go back to bar five. He was horrified that Jimmy Miller, an airman, had said this to a sergeant and a corporal and stopped us until Jimmy had been given three stripes. Only then was he allowed to say, "One, two, three."'

Largely due to O'Donnell the RAF's attitude towards music was always the most enlightened. It was realized that a man who could not be fitted into a military band still had an important role to play entertaining his fellow airmen. Professional musicians were encouraged to choose the RAF as their service and stations were urged to form dance bands.

Sam Costa, a member of the BBC Variety Repertory company, was yet another musician who discovered he could continue to play if he volunteered. He had started life as a pianist and had just begun to make a name for himself as a crooner. His days in the RAF were to change the direction of his career once more, as John Arnatt recalls:

'The RAF always had five-piece bands and I knew the saxophonist in one. He invited me to join them as compere, which I did although I was in the Army. We worked on several stations and on one of them was Sam Costa, then billed as "Radio's Romeo of Song". He was dying to try comedy and I remember we all agreed to let him try a gag in the show. His very first gag was to come on stage and say, "I have a special notice. An AC2 with his own knife and fork would like to meet another AC2 with his own steak and kidney pudding." It's a good gag if done properly and it went down very well.'

So Sam Costa started telling jokes and building up the routines he used later in such shows as *Much Binding-In-The-Marsh*. Not every musician managed to change his tune so successfully. Reg Beard played the double-bass in Costa's band. 'He also wanted to be a comic,' says Costa, 'and one day, during a Naafi show, he said to me, "Tell me a joke, something I can go out with and make the fellows laugh." I told him a terrible joke, but one we liked very much at the time: "What did the brassiere say to the hat? You go on ahead and I'll give the other two a lift." We thought that was very funny in those days. Reggie screamed with laughter, thought it was marvellous and went out. "Say, fellers, what did the brassiere say to the hat? You go on ahead and I'll come on later." Silence. He came off grumbling. "You rotten swine," he moaned. "You told me that was funny." '

Notwithstanding the War Office directive of April 1940 that entertainment should be cut back by fifty per cent to allow men more time for training, by mid-year the Services were acutely aware of the need for musicians. Pianists were wanted to accompany singers, violinists to play on a variety bill, bands to give concerts or play for dances. Anyone who knew which way up to hold an instrument was given a chance and the most unlikely combinations emerged. The RAF Salon Orchestra, which played light classics and later toured India and the Far East, was just such a mixture. Conductor was organist George Boyd; violinist Al Goldstein had played with Alfred Rhodes's Tzigane Orchestra, Cyril Gooden, a schoolmaster, was a member of the Whitby Spa Orchestra; cellist Arthur Alexander had played with the Bournemouth Symphony, Walter Hague with the Manchester Symphony and Warrington Musical Society; Sidney Ellison was principal trumpet of the London Philharmonic and Nat Berlin was a member of Jack Hylton's band; Eric Weston, the pianist, was an accountant.

Sir Adrian Boult found himself conducting in possibly the most unusual concert of his career in Bristol. 'It was at a birthday party for the local Home Guard. Henry Hall asked me if I would like to conduct his band and I agreed. 'Tiger Rag' was chosen and when I asked for a score so that I could study the work, which I didn't know, they looked at me askance. Eventually they found me a spare trumpet part which was no use except to tell me the time. I knew that dance band leaders danced about while beating time, so, without rehearsal, off I danced into "Tiger Rag". I could recognize from the music that the piece had a beginning and a middle then reverted to the first section for the finish. As soon as the last section started I leant over to the pianist, who was nearest to me, and asked him how long to go. "About thirty bars," he replied. I carefully counted thirty bars, then threw myself into the air with a twiddle of the baton, as I'd seen Henry Hall do. I will never know how but as I hit the stage the band stopped dead to riotous applause. We had actually finished together! That finished my one-and-only attempt to conduct a dance band.'

Musicians in uniform prided themselves on being different from their fellow Servicemen.

'We were a race apart,' admits George Chisholm. 'We had longer hair than most and our habits were definitely different from the fellows who had short back-and-sides, boils on the neck and a cold water shower at five every morning. They couldn't quite make us out. But the band was always accepted by the run-of-the-mill airman. He'd sit down and listen to a concert anytime. But amongst some of the sticky-type officers, some of whom never accepted us because we were popular and they weren't, there was a terrible jealousy. It was very difficult at first. We were the lowest of the low. We used to turn up at places and say we were the band, and they'd say, "So what?" We were nothing until it was necessary to have a dance and then, "We'll get those chaps to play." Suddenly we were important.'

All men appreciated a live band in the Mess, none more than officers. Since one of the few ways an ordinary Serviceman could get his own back on the hierarchy was by refusing to play for it, officers went out of their way to patronize musicians. A good band was not only in great demand within its own unit, it was requested everywhere, so that CO's considered them status symbols. The RAOC had the Blue Rockets led by Eric Robinson, Balloon Command had the Sky Rockets under Paul Fenhoulet, the Navy had George Crowe's Bluegrass Boys, Tubby Hayes formed The Napoleons, Geoff Love formed a

At the time of his call up, it was widely rumoured that Glenn Miller was reluctant to give up his career as the conductor of the world's most popular dance band. The U.S. Air Force immediately reformed his band in uniform to send them on tour and to Europe as the band of the American Expeditionary Force. Known as General Eisenhower's 'personal band' Miller's trip to Newbury in Berkshire caused more excitement in the town than King George VI's visit.

Greenjackets band show. When Stars in Battledress started it was quick to utilize the talents of Nat Gonella, Michael Flome (who was killed in France) and Sid Millward. When the War Office decided, in March, 1941, to relieve ENSA of being the sole provider of entertainment to the Army, provision was made for units to set up dance bands and money was allocated for the purchase of musical instruments. The culmination of the dance band movement was the formation of the three famous bands of the Allied Expeditionary Force – the Canadian Band under Robert Farnon, the American Band under the legendary Glenn Miller and the British Band under ex-Military Policeman George Melachrino. One of the most famous of the uniformed bands, and one which continued after the war, was the RAF's Squadronaires.

Dance bands were always popular entertainment as ENSA had recognized in 1939 when Jack Hylton and Geraldo were co-opted on to the

committee advising on popular music. Among the earliest parties to visit the BEF in France had been the bands of Hylton, Joe Loss, Ambrose, Jack Payne and Billy Cotton. Many of the service bands, both British and American, even those set up through the initiative and enthusiasm of individuals, became full-time entertainments and started touring. The band with which Sam Costa appeared was sent to Iceland.

'There's always a know-all on a camp and this one came up to us and said, "Do you know where you're going? Iceland!" We all groaned. That was like hell. Then we remembered the date – April first All Fools Day – so we said "What a funny joke!" Some joke. That afternoon we found out we were going to Iceland and they needed entertainment there, they really did. We played every night and most afternoons. Outside Reykjavik there were some terrible little posts, way out in the back of beyond. At one station we went

Touring in Iceland frequently became an endurance test for the troupes who were sent out to bring light relief to those men stationed in lonely and remote outposts.

Another funny thing; Iceland is the Land of the Midnight Sun and it doesn't get dark in summer. It was maddening. We would go to bed at one in the morning and it was like a grey day in England. I wrote to my wife and said it's terrible here; we can't sleep because it's light all the time. In her next letter she wrote back and asked why don't you pull the curtains? This, in a Nissen hut which had never seen curtains in its life!'

George Chisholm remembers when the Squadronaires started to tour.

'We were asked to do a Sunday concert for charity in Newcastle. The Air Council said it would be all right as long as we did a week at a nearby camp, so we were posted to Long Benton which was a balloon centre and nothing else. We drove up in this old truck, all the way from Uxbridge, and arrived at about three in the morning. It was pouring with rain and nobody was about. We wandered around until eventually some guy appeared. We said we were the band and back came the inevitable reply, "So what? What are you doing here?" We said we were supposed to be doing a week there but he didn't know anything about it and put us in an unused hut to sleep. There were palliasses in there, ringing wet, which had

to, we were told there were just twenty fellows there and we thought, how awful for them. When we got there, there were about ten fellows and ten girls all in evening dress, having an absolute ball. We were sorry for those guys and there they were having a wonderful time! So we played and had a great time. After about half-an-hour we found out it wasn't ten fellows and ten girls, it was twenty fellows with ten of them in their best dresses!

In the best tradition of 'troupers', the Squadronaires took things as they came. Ronnie Aldrich joined this popular group some time after it was formed and continued with the group as Ronnie Aldrich and the Squadronaires until many years after the war.

obviously never been used but we were the worse for drink so in we went. Tommy McQuater, who was the corporal, suddenly thought that in the morning, which was only a couple of hours away, some idiot would come banging on the door and tell us to get on parade, so we took out the light bulb and drifted into a drunken stupor. Sure enough, the station WO, who had been in the service all his life, came round. He'd always gone through the same routine and got it fixed in his head: I put my hand on the handle, I open the door, I kick the place down and I shout, "Wakey, wakey! On the floor! Out of bed!" He got to our hut, bashed the door open, kicked, banged and shouted, smashed the light switch down and, of course, there was no bulb. It penetrates his head there's something wrong with the light so he still shouts out. From one of the beds comes the voice of Tommy McGrath, "Bugger off!" There's total darkness, it's raining and he can't see anybody. Nobody has ever spoken to him like that in his life. "Who was that?" "Joe Stalin," replies Tommy. And this idiot, instead of thinking I'm being had, thought, it's a name, I'll ask his number. "What's your number?" By this time we were all breaking up and there were mutterings of "Piss off", "Bugger Off", and so on. Suddenly he thought, they'd never dare speak to me like that unless they were officers. He apologized, went away and never came near the hut again.'

Service bandsmen playing for civilians were the cause of a major row. Early in 1942 the long-simmering feud between ENSA and the military came to a head. Jealous that so many artists were in uniform and that ENSA shows were being unfavourably compared with Service productions, ENSA looked for a way of getting its own back. On 19 February, Evelyn Walkden, Labour MP for Doncaster, asked the Secretary of State for War about uniformed musicians appearing in commercial ventures. 'They bring discredit to the Army,' he said. 'They disturb morale and create discontent in depots because fellow soldiers say you have only to be part of somebody's jazz band and you were excused everything.' This was, Mr Walkden concluded, a grave misuse of man-power and the Minister should convert these Toy Soldiers into real soldiers without delay. Toy Soldiers – the phrase had a nice easy ring to it and the press seized on it as if they had been attacking ENSA itself. Certainly there was a case to be answered amongst musicians stationed near London, especially those in the Army. Every night the

toilets of Piccadilly Circus would be full of men changing out of uniform into evening dress before hurrying off, instrument case under arm, to an engagement in a band somewhere. It was said, with some justification, that if a general walked into any London theatre in uniform half the orchestra would be on its feet standing to attention. The effect of this attack was not to release serving men to ENSA, as had been hoped, but to make bands wary of playing any concert which charged admission at the door. Since these were almost entirely for charity, only war charities really suffered.

Dance bands by no means had a monopoly of the sort of music troops wanted to hear. Dunkirk and the Blitz united the country in a way the Phoney War had completely failed to do. It was no longer them and us against the enemy, but the British against the Germans. Hitler's greatest mistake during the Blitz, according to Liberal politician Clement Davies, was to bomb Buckingham Palace. 'If only the Germans had had the sense not to bomb west of London Bridge there might have been a revolution in this country. As it is they have smashed about Bond Street and Park Lane and readjusted the balance.' The realization that the Nation was fighting for survival brought about a new-felt spirituality requiring a suitable form of expression, which, to a considerable extent, was found in the works of the great composers. Music that previously was considered 'not for us' was discovered to have meaning. This does not mean everyone forsook jazz and dance bands to listen to Sir Adrian Boult, just that artists and programmes previously considered to have no place in troop entertainment became increasingly popular. 'Slowly I began to realize – all too slowly, my critics will say,' wrote Dean, 'that the simplest entertainments were failing to meet the spiritual challenge of the hour. Changes would have to be made even though they might cause a rumpus inside the organization.' And cause a rumpus they did. When Dean proposed giving music a more prominent place in ENSA's programmes someone remarked that the troops were getting plenty, what about the Bands Division? Trying hard to escape from the rather frightening image of classical music, Dean proposed calling the new concerts Good Music. Advisers were appointed to each Command, responsible for finding out what programmes the troops wanted and distributing records. By the end of 1945 there were 3,000 record clubs in the Services.

The first Good Music concert was given in Aldershot in October, 1940 by Maggie Teyte, Eileen Joyce, Nancy Evans and Alfred Cave. The response was so good that the visit was extended to last a week. Before long there were seven Good Music parties on tour. John Foskett was at RAF Halton when he saw that one, including Maggie Teyte, Parry Jones, Eileen Joyce and Ivor Newton, had been booked into the theatre.

'I must admit I thought, they must be joking, it will be a disaster. But I was proved wrong. It attracted an audience of between 500 and 700 for every performance and we even lit the show, probably the first time a classical concert has ever had a lighting plot. I still remember Eileen Joyce playing "Jesu, Joy of Man's Desiring" on the grand piano, stage drapes lit deep purple and a pale blue spot playing on her and the piano. She looked quite ethereal. The show was very well received and I'm sure led the way for many young airmen and airwomen to a deeper love of good music.'

ENSA was more fortunate with its classical musicians than with other artists. Because the demand for 'good' music was not so great, top artists could invariably be found to fill a bill and whereas a comic on his own for an hour would be struggling, it was no new experience for a soloist to give a two hour recital. Virtually every leading musician did at least one ENSA tour.

The newness of concert-going for many meant audiences frequently breaking concert hall etiquette by applauding between movements (a reaction none of the artists seemed to have minded). Many of the men were unsure of the names of the works. Harriet Cohen was asked to play Beethoven's Unfinished Concerto and a singer was asked for Faust's 'Oh, what a frozen hand you've got.' Symphonies, concertos, operatic arias, chamber music – no attempt was made to play down to audiences. Programming remained as it would have been in peacetime. When Maggie Teyte, who had studied in Paris with Debussy, gave a recital at Aldershot she was thrilled to receive a note signed by twenty soldiers asking for his songs. Eva Turner, possibly the greatest Turandot this country has ever produced, was astonished to be asked to sing the 'Liebestod' from *Tristan*, with only piano accompaniment. There was none of the hostility towards German music in the Second World War that existed in 1914–18, so Beethoven, Wagner and Richard Strauss featured prominently alongside more obscure and comparatively 'difficult' works. Boult included the first

symphony of William Walton in concerts for the RAF and works by Vaughan Williams, Bruckner, Sibelius, Bax, Rawsthorne, Rubbra (the last two were in the Army) and Moeran were performed regularly.

Much of the success of a concert depended on the overture with which it began. If it caught the attention, the audience would stay. If it bored them, they would leave in droves. Sir John Barbirolli and the Halle Orchestra performed for an audience that had never heard a symphony concert before. He later told Basil Dean it was one of the most moving he had ever given. In May, 1943 Sir Adrian Boult and the BBC Symphony Orchestra gave the first ENSA symphony concert for the Army at Aldershot. Boult was delighted, and surprised, to be told that the record box-office income, held previously by Gracie Fields, had been beaten by 1/9d. The following week the orchestra played for the Navy at Portsmouth. After the last night of the week's engagement an old rating, who had missed not a note of rehearsals or performances, and who had never been to a concert before, turned to Walter Legge who was in charge of ENSA's Good Music section. 'God,' he exclaimed, 'it's worse than women or drink the way it gets you!'

It was musicians such as Sir Adrian Boult and Yehudi Menuhin who proved to the authorities that good music was not only for the longhaired minority but in fact that it satisfied a universal craving.

In September 1943 Sir Adrian Boult, under the auspices of ENSA, took the BBC Symphony Orchestra to St. Athan's RAF station in Wales. Nightly he conducted the musicians for a week to crowded audiences in the local cinema. Among the pieces he played was the brilliant and difficult Symphony No. 1 by William Walton.

'They were so attentive and appreciative,' Sir Adrian Boult says. 'I remember sitting at the back of a concert we gave for the RAF at St Athan. Albert Coates was conducting and before the performance started the hall was full of smoke, with nearly everyone smoking cigarettes. Once the music began they were so still it was a great shock to the eye to see someone lift a cigarette to his mouth. By the interval the entire hall was clear. Then, of course, everyone lit up again and the hall was full. During the second half the same thing happened – they were so still the hall cleared completely.'

The availability of big orchestras was limited by their other work broadcasting, giving factory concerts (under the auspices of ENSA and CEMA) and bread-and-butter performances to make enough money to keep going. ENSA music advisers such as Richard Austen in Northern Command and Harold Grey in Western Command attempted to fill the gap by forming orchestras from Services' personnel but these were confined to large garrison towns and relied on troops staying put. They were never an entirely satisfactory alternative. The ideal music group was a small, highly mobile party or an individual performer needing little in the way of facilities. Solomon, Pouishnoff, Eileen Joyce, Moura Lympany, Louis Kentner and Maggie Teyte all went out to give recitals on their own and small groups, of no more than half-a-dozen artists, were sent on the normal ENSA circuit. One such party, led by Dennis Noble, was the first Good Music unit to visit the Middle East, as an experiment. An open letter to Basil Dean, published in *Trunk Call*, the paper of Paiforce, the Army stationed in Iraq and Persia, told ENSA what the men thought.

'I must admit that for a long time I have been one of your severest critics, but now I think it is time we all took our hats off and let go three hearty cheers for ENSA. Last night I saw what was announced as an ENSA "Experiment" – six opera stars, namely Miriam Licette, Nancy Evans, Dennis Noble, Walter Widdop, Alfred Cave and Ivor Newton. I wish you could have been at that show, Mr Dean. Swing fans, opera enthusiasts and chaps with no certain preference either way, all stood and applauded for nearly five minutes at the end until Mr Dennis Noble had to call for silence. This is the sort of show we want. We are not very fond of "blue" shows. Just because we are in the Army and a long way from home, we do not want any lowering of moral standards. Yes, I know we laugh at and cheer these shows; we have a good time and appreciate the work the artists put in for our entertainment, but it does not take much to make us chaps laugh in these times. It is when we stand up and cheer that you must begin to take notice.'

When the Good Music Party appeared at the RAF base on the island of Muharrag, in the Persian Gulf, it was to give the first-ever concert there. Not even the oldest inhabitant could recall seeing a piano on the island before. The hall of bamboo and palm fronds in which the artists performed was hung with notices that read 'Please bring your own seat' and 'The rule for this concert is hats off and boots on'.

Occasionally a Good Music party did have problems with an audience as Cyril Hunt of the medical corps recalls:

'I went along to see a "show" which turned out to be an ENSA Good Music Party at the hospital where I was stationed in North Africa. There was a large audience of patients and staff simply because there was nothing else to do. For most of the audience it was deadly dull with the members of the troupe playing and singing popular classics. They soon began to supply the missing "blue" element when asked to join in some well-known Irish songs by a very good-looking blonde. There were wolf-whistles and snide remarks shouted at the platform. Then, on to the stage stepped a very tall, plain young woman with a harp. There was a sudden and complete silence. The lady seated herself, drew the harp to her shoulder and after a few very nervous preliminary chords played a tinkling wisp of a piece. There was not a sound, not even a cough from the audience throughout the playing during which the harpist became more and more nervous. Daintily she plucked the last ethereal chord and there was a pause in which the silence could be felt. Then crashed out the most tumultuous applause. She was obviously astonished. A happy smile appeared on her face,

she rose and bowed to the audience who renewed their applause. She sat down, took up her harp and began an encore which was something the audience had not wanted. They had overdone their politeness. But the applause had done something to the harpist. It had mistakenly given her the confidence she lacked. For the next hour she played as only a fine performer can and the troops loved it and wouldn't let her go.'

One of the greatest and most popular classical artists to appear for ENSA (and he appeared in every theatre of war) was pianist Solomon. Not only was he a consummate performer he was much-loved as a man. Bill Walsh, stationed on the island of Malta, was present when Solomon demonstrated his wide-ranging repertoire.

'After the recital Solomon came up to the Sergeants' Mess and at about two in the morning gave another recital, of all the barrack room ballads, from Wee Nell to the Great Wheel. He finished by challenging any pianist present to play a short composition he had with him. Three people had a go but none of them made it since two notes had to be struck in the middle of the keyboard while the player's hands were fully extended left and right. Solomon then demonstrated how the notes should be played – with his nose.'

Not once did Solomon have a moment of temperament, an argument or a disagreement in circumstances which would have tried a saint. On an occasion when he was booked to appear in place of an indisposed Dennis Noble he arrived to find Noble recovered, waiting to go on. Without a moment's hesitation he sat down at the upright and accompanied him. Once when he tried a piano before a recital several notes were missing. There was no problem, he assured the Entertainments Officer – he would just play round them.

Another pianist who made many tours for ENSA was Russian virtuoso, Pouishnoff. In Algiers, staying at the Hotel Arletti, arrangements were made for him to have his own room rather than for him to share with a stranger. The GI on the desk kept an anxious eye open for his celebrated guest to tell him his room had been changed. A distinguished, white-haired gentleman entered. 'Pouishnoff?' the American asked. 'Certainly not,' replied the man. 'I'm staying the night and pushing off in the morning.'

ENSA did not have the Good Music field entirely to itself. Realizing that there was a need for more serious music than even Eugene Pini's sextet was providing, Stars in Battledress decided

Solomon, the international virtuoso pianist, whose recordings of the Beethoven Sonatas are not only still available but are among the most brilliant ever performed, proved that such music was not 'caviare for the general'. He played wherever he could and whenever, on grand pianos, and duff uprights. He entertained, as here in Catterick, January 1943, not only with the Classics but accompanied singsongs and barrack room ballads in the Mess.

to set up a chamber music group. Composer Edmund Rubbra, serving in Wales with the Royal Artillery, was asked to lead it. He was joined by cellist William Pleeth from the Signals and violinist Joshua Glazier from the Service Corps to form the trio which was later to become very familiar on concert platforms and radio.

'We were called the Army Classical Music Group, a part of the Central Pool of Artists,' says Edmund Rubbra. 'As soon as we had rehearsed a repertoire of piano trios we went out to Chester where we gave our first concert. Then we went all over the place, up as far as the Orkneys and finally, in 1945, over to Germany. As time went on our trio became a quartet with the addition of Charles Kahn, a viola player, then a quintet with flautist Joseph Slater, and finally we got a singer, Sam Rabin.'

Rabin, Manchester-born of Russian ancestry, had trained as an artist. A fine athlete, he represented Great Britain in the Olympics and had

wrestled professionally. He was heard singing in an Army concert party and invited to join Freddie Frinton's Stars in Battledress unit to provide a vocal interlude.

'I was with them for a year and hated it,' he recalls. 'I felt if I ever heard a comic crack another joke I would go mad. Then I heard about the Classical Music Group, auditioned at the War Office and was accepted. I was singing operatic arias and *lieder* – the usual concert repertoire. Edmund Rubbra used to ask audiences not to applaud between movements, to wait until the work was finished. I used to go on and say: "Please applaud as much as you like between songs."'

'Sam was a marvellous singer,' continues Rubbra, 'with one of those very deep Russian bass voices. And very temperamental. He hated the idea of an audience being paraded for a concert, which often used to happen. When Sam got to know the men had been marched in he would come on the platform and say, "If any soldiers are here because they've been forced to come then I'm not going to sing." And he wouldn't.'

Rubbra was promoted to sergeant to run the group but everywhere they went an officer travelled with them. 'He would insist on introducing us even though he had a stutter. One famous remark of his, after giving biographical details of us all, was, "In short, every member of this group is at the top of the tree in various string combinations." He never realized how ridiculous this was.

'We went everywhere by lorry on which we took our own piano. We removed the legs so that we could sit on top. If the camp we were playing in had a good piano available we didn't bother to unpack ours because it was a bit of a business; we had to do it on our own in sight of the audience. We had to lift it on to the platform, get under it, put the legs on, screw the pedals on and so on. We went to a camp near Liverpool and were confronted by quite a good stage with a very big piano on it, meticulously covered by a cloth and locked. The sergeant in charge of the key duly came, took the cloth off and unlocked it. When I tried it there were at least ten keys that didn't work at all. They wouldn't go down; they were stuck with damp. It was impossible to play. The officer in charge

turned to the sergeant, "Why did you tell me this piano was all right for a concert?" "It was this morning, sir," the sergeant replied. "Only six notes didn't work."

'We were very much a minority interest and only supposed to play to those people who really wanted to hear us, but some Entertainments Officers took it upon themselves to get as large an audience as possible. Once we were advertised as Ed Rub and his 7-Piece Band, making no comment on the fact that we were a classical music group. The audience came in, overflowing, and when I got up to announce a Haydn piano trio there was a terrific stamping out.'

Dress for a performance by the Army Classical Music Group was an especially tailored, navy blue dress uniform with brass buttons up to the neck, which helped make the evening more of an occasion than if the group had worn battledress. Often it was assumed the moment a performer donned uniform he doffed his talent. Soldier actors, fresh from an appearance in the West End, would be told they were quite good and asked if they had ever acted before. Temperamental civilian starlets would refuse to take direction from a man in uniform because he was a Service-

Members of the Army Classical Music Group Chamber Ensemble of the Stars in Battledress were led by Sergeant Edmund Rubbra. The Group included William Pleath, standing on Rubbra's right, and Sam Rabin on his left.

man and they were the professionals, even though he may have directed the original London production. Reginald Kilbey, famous before the war for his regular broadcasts with the Albert Sandler Trio, was playing the cello with the British Band of the AEF after he left Stars in Battledress.

'The Band contained a lot of famous and very fine musicians. We gave a concert with Richard Tauber and Moura Lympany as soloists. Moura Lympany played the scherzo from Saint-Saëns' Piano Concerto and Richard Tauber sang Massenet's *Elegy*. This begins with a cello solo which I played. Afterwards Moura Lympany came up to me and said, "You played that solo beautifully." I said, "Thank you very much." Then she asked me if I had ever thought of taking up the cello professionally. Well, we were all in battledress and little hats so she wasn't to know. I didn't want to embarrass her so I said I hadn't, that it had always seemed much too chancy.'

The increasing popularity of classical music meant increasing opportunities for uniformed musicians throughout the world to play in trios, quartets, small orchestras playing light classics or give solo recitals. In Cairo the Director of the Egyptian State Broadcasting Orchestra, a motley collection of international refugees, decided to turn his musicians into a symphony orchestra. He invited Hugo Rignold, a renowned jazz violinist with Jack Hylton's band, who was with the RAF in Egypt, to become the leader and to recruit some Services personnel.

'Because HQ thought this was a good idea,' he remembered, 'an order went out requesting CO's to make returns of any bodies they had hanging around who had been professional musicians. They were sent to me, I sorted them out and got the people I wanted posted to Cairo or nearby so that we could rehearse and make it a proper symphony orchestra in our spare time. We had no real problem with instruments because anyone who had been a professional musician usually had theirs with them. I had my violin but while I was in the desert I played so very little that I left it with friends in Cairo. Part of my job in RAF Welfare, to which I was posted out of the desert after an operation, was obtaining accoutrements for games and instruments for people who wanted to form unit bands in the desert. If they wanted a fiddle or a banjo or whatever they would apply to us. So we knew where instruments were.'

The first concert given by the new Cairo Symphony Orchestra was conducted by Major Anthony Lewis (now Sir Anthony, Principal of the Royal Academy of Music). After two further concerts as leader (at one of which he played the violin part in Beethoven's Triple Concerto with Lt Gerald Gover (piano) and Meyer Reininger (cello) who had been recruited from a night-club) Rignold was able to realize a life-long ambition.

'I suddenly found this world of symphonic musicians not so awe-inspiring as I had expected, so I said to the Director that it was not unusual to invite the leader of an orchestra to conduct the odd concert: would he consider it? I had been full of enthusiasm for the whole project of forming the orchestra and the Director was pleased with the work I had done so he said yes.'

Hugo Rignold, who was later to become musical director of the Royal Ballet and principal conductor of the City of Birmingham Symphony Orchestra, made his début in front of a symphony orchestra in March, 1943, in a programme that included Weber's *Oberon* Overture, Mendelssohn's *Italian* Symphony and the Schumann Piano Concerto, with WAAF Officer Nancy Weir as soloist. Invited back for a second concert he decided to perform Schubert's Unfinished Symphony. Richard Capell, music critic of the *Daily Telegraph* and an authority on Schubert, was in Cairo and offered to review the concert for the *Egyptian Mail*. He wrote of Rignold: 'He has the roots of the matter in him and the end of the concert left one feeling full of interest in his future, should circumstances develop his experience.' Encouraged, Rignold turned his back on the leader's desk and took up the baton full-time. At his next concert Capell wrote, 'Rignold can surely, if he wishes, make a name for himself as a conductor.'

He could not have had a tougher training ground. Even when ENSA took over running and part-financing the orchestra after the fighting in North Africa had finished (changing the name to the Middle East Symphony Orchestra) it remained part-time. 'Normal working hours for the Services in Cairo,' Rignold recalled, 'were from eight until one, then four-thirty until eight, so we were free to rehearse in the afternoon, in the heat of the sun, for two or three days a week. Although the musicians were all former professionals, the orchestra had an amateur status and had to be run that way. When we got to rehearsal, the man with the key hadn't turned up so we were locked out of the hall. When we got in there were no stands or the music had gone missing. But because we all

Squadron Leader Hugo Rignold successfully commandeered musicians and instruments wherever he found them to form a Symphony Orchestra in Cairo in March 1943. This was his debut as a conductor.

wanted to play and wanted to give a good performance, we managed. We gave approximately a concert a week throughout the Cairo area, which could mean anything up to a hundred miles away along the Canal.'

Soloists were either musicians in the Forces (Nancy Weir, Gerald Gover) or guests such as the Palestinian pianist, Pnina Salzman. Half the orchestra were drawn from the Services, mostly the RAF; the other half came from a variety of European and Arab countries and Rignold's major problem was communication. He talked to three of the first violins in French, to some of the second violins in Arabic. Three players spoke only Italian and, fortunately for Rignold, the Rumanian cellist and an Austrian could understand his German, as could the Greek flautist who passed on instructions to the clarinettist in an Arabic dialect Rignold had not found time to learn. The rest understood English.

Programmes were governed by the availability of sheet music and the size of the orchestra. 'We used to have the help of King Farouk's State Bodyguard Band when we needed extra brass or woodwind players,' said Rignold. 'It was always very difficult to get the entire orchestra to rehearse at the same time because of postings, duties and so on. At one final rehearsal I thought at last, we've got a full orchestra! I really thought we had. But someone said the second bassoon and the tuba player were missing. "Where the hell are they?" I said. There were wild gesticulations from other members of the Royal Band to explain that they were outside. It was sundown and they were down on their knees, praying. Things were always happening. When we toured down the Canal all the instruments would go in a truck and we would go in a coach. Frequently we would arrive and the instruments wouldn't. At another final rehearsal, miles from Cairo, the soloist in the piano concerto

came on to the platform, took his bow, opened the piano lid and there was no keyboard. The Cairo firm supplying us with pianos had loaded the first one they saw, the lightest, on to the lorry without checking it had its workings. Luckily there was an old upright there used for dances so the Chopin F Minor Concerto was played on that.'

Another Serviceman who seized the opportunities that went his way was accountant George Mitchell. Posted to the Pay Corps in Finsbury Circus, Mitchell, who had been learning the piano, was dragged into the Mess to accompany singsongs. The musical evenings became a regular feature of Mess life and since some of the ATS girls were quite good, he decided to form a choir.

'I found eight girls and eight boys and we formed a sort of Glee Club which went down very well. One of the boys had been a dancer and when we decided to do something different with the choir – just standing, singing, seemed rather boring – I asked him to devise a routine for everyone and we put together a half-hour show of popular songs and dancing.' Mitchell's group became known as the Royal Army Pay Corps Swing Choir and built up quite a reputation touring and broadcasting on Services' radio. After the war the nucleus of the choir stayed together, keeping the successful song and dance format they had used in the Army, and changed their name to the George Mitchell Minstrels.

For the performer in the right place at the right time the war had its advantages.

CHAPTER SEVEN

ENTERTAINMENT AFLOAT

For the Service with the most advanced thinking in areas of welfare, the Royal Navy had a surprisingly ambivalent attitude towards live entertainment. As early as the 1920's a box of contraceptives would be left at the head of the gangway for sailors going ashore and, in common with the other Services, the Navy commandeered brothels in foreign ports. The reasons were neither liberalism nor social conscience but expedience. Contraceptives cut down on pox and freed sailors for their duties: running brothels allowed regular medical inspections and prevented infiltration by Axis agents. Yet when it came to simple pleasures like a variety show or a play, official thinking was non-committal. If someone wanted to put on an entertainment, good luck to him. If no one did, it didn't matter. The importance of entertainment dawned slowly and no moves were made towards setting up an official Naval live entertainment establishment until the war was almost over.

This attitude is easy to understand. The problems of organizing permanent entertainment for the Navy were immense. At sea the tight routine and lack of space in all but the largest ships made formal entertainment impracticable and when a ship reached port the last thing a sailor wanted, the Sea Lords reasoned, was to watch a ballet, even supposing a ballet was available and the port knew the ship would be arriving. Afloat, Sod's Opera, as home-grown entertainments were called, was consigned to the dog watches, the matelot's free time, and consisted of a few jokes, a sing-song or card tricks. Ashore, the sailors were left to fend for

themselves. Only the largest bases appointed Entertainments Officers and even there, with populations tending to be peripatetic (sailors between postings or off on leave), it was difficult to produce shows on a regular basis. The Entertainments Officer was left to his own devices and had to rely on bringing in artists and productions rather than producing his own. For this he needed contacts in show business for, until the end of 1941, ENSA parties were forbidden to visit naval establishments. In 1939 the Navy had opted to take its Naafi profits separately and since it wasn't paying for ENSA's work, it didn't qualify to receive shows. Individual ENSA companies, once on the road and away from the administrative glare of London, would break the directive as often as possible but such a system was inevitably haphazard and unsatisfactory. Of those artists who did perform for the sailors from the earliest days one stands head-and-shoulders above the rest: Evelyn Laye, darling of the West End musical stage. In 1939, after the first scare of bombings had subsided and the theatres reopened, she was in Scotland for the try-out of a new Cochran revue and was invited to lunch in Edinburgh.

'I was sitting next to Lord Inverclyde,' she recalls. 'He worked a lot for Merchant Navy charities and wanted me to go to Glasgow for a Sunday concert. "I have my price," I found myself saying to him. "Yes?" he said. "How much do you want?" "It's not money I'm after," I replied. "I want to go to Scapa Flow." "Impossible!" he said. "Then I can't come back to Glasgow with you," I told him. I really had no idea what I was talking

Throughout the duration, the Royal Navy ships had little room which could be assigned to entertainments. Morale on board ship for the men and the troops they carried was frequently maintained by diversions that were impromptu and perforce performed on deck and only in fair weather.

about but I had this feeling in my bones that they were in desperate need of entertainment up there.'

Although she had never visited Scapa Flow, the vast natural anchorage in the Orkney Islands, some second sense, or possibly the stories of Scapa's loneliness told her by a former boyfriend who was there during the First World War, had convinced Evelyn Laye that she had to visit there. And she was right. Scapa, a home posting, was a windswept, desolate place, far from towns and entertainment. Men were stationed there for months on end with little to break the monotony. Although, when Scapa eventually became part of the ENSA circuit, an old salt looked up from his paper and growled at a pretty girl accordionist, 'It used to be quiet around here,' the majority found the solitude unbearable. Strings were pulled and arrangements made for her and four of the Cochran company (Doris Hare, Martyn Green, Cliff Mollison and Gordon Whelan) to fly up for a

single concert. The day before they were due to leave the admiral on Scapa phoned her.

' "What do you want to come up here for?" he asked. When I told him I had this funny feeling he was in need of entertainment, he said, "This is no place for a woman." I assured him I wouldn't be any trouble and he asked if I'd been vetted. I told him we all had – our backgrounds, our parents and our grandparents had all been thoroughly investigated before permission had been granted. "I'll call you back on this one," he said. "If I haven't phoned by five in the morning you can come." He hadn't phoned by five so we started off for the airfield. The weather was so bad that ours was the only plane up that day and they gave us all brown paper bags. I've never known a trip like it. "We're passing Inverness," the pilot said. "I don't care," I replied, "I'm going to pass more than Inverness in a moment." It was awful. Finally the pilot said he was very sorry but he couldn't go on.

It was so bumpy we would have to turn back. "Look," I said, "we've been sick for the past five hours, we can't turn back. There's a crack of blue sky over there. Make for it." We made for it, there was more blue and on we went.'

'We landed at Kirkwall,' remembers Doris Hare. 'Just before we arrived we both did up our faces. Boo (Laye) was wearing a very pretty little hat which she'd put on especially to greet the Navy. When we got off the plane there were about four admirals there to meet us. As I got out the wind took my skirt up over my head and the admirals had to hold me and my dress down. Then Boo, that beautiful, wonderful lady, made a full musical entrance and everything blew off! Her hat disappeared back to Edinburgh, her hair went straight up and she had to be held down, too.'

The party transferred to the island of Hoy where they were to give the concert. Recovered from her air-sickness, Evelyn Laye went to get changed:

'"Ah, yes, Miss Laye's luggage," they said and that went down the line from the admiral to the flag lieutenant to the small fry. Eventually a terribly white, shaky young man came back and whispered into an ear. And so on back up the line until the admiral turned to me and said, "I'm very sorry; all your luggage has been left on the plane."'

'I used to wear a little black dress,' continues Doris Hare, 'with a lot of fringe on it, which wiggled when I wiggled. That, my little box of make-up and my songs were all I had and I was carrying them with me. But Boo had suitcases full of wonderful dresses, all her make-up, lots of magazines and other wonderful things she was taking up for the boys. And they'd all gone back to Edinburgh! We were taken to our dressing-room – a lean-to with a terrible old rusty bed to sit on, a bit of broken mirror, and my cheap bit of old make-up for this beautiful star. She went to the corner, looked in the piece of mirror and said, "I've come all this way and I'm going to have to sing to the sailors with a face I've been sick in!" We did the show in a huge hangar, literally hung with sailors. They'd been waiting for us for three hours and

Evelyn Laye had a particular spot in her heart for the plight of the men of Scapa Flow. She is seen here on one of her trips in 1942 with Will Hay, Bud Flanagan and Chesney Allen.

were all grimy covered with dirt in their duffel coats. The reception was unbelievable. I sang some rather *risqué* songs (now, of course, they'd be like hymns) and told a few gags, Boo did a conjuring act with Cliff Mollison and then she sang, songs like *Only A Glass Of Champagne*. She finished with *I'll See You Again*, Noël Coward's song, and there wasn't a dry eye in the house. Never, never in her life has she sung it better; she couldn't have sung it better. It was marvellous and magical. The place fell in.'

'It was fantastic,' agrees Evelyn Laye. 'There are nights which you remember with love and gratitude. I have great gratitude for that night. We went to a lot of trouble to get there but we were repaid a thousandfold. I know it sounds slushy, but it's true.'

The evening was not just one of the most memorable in the long, memorable career of Evelyn Laye. It meant more to the men at Scapa than would have seemed possible. They were suffering appalling weather and acute home-sickness; they felt forgotten, many suicidal. Then the star of the West End theatre had appeared before them. 'If this woman can come up here with her friends to see us and stick it for five hours in the air,' the admiral told them in his speech of thanks, 'you can stick it for a bit longer.'

Evelyn Laye had found her war work but it wasn't to be easy. In spite of the success of that first visit the Sea Lords had reservations about supporting a venture run by a woman. It took all her charm and a lot of her own money to convince them she was serious. Back in London she gave Sunday concerts to raise the money to send a second party of Beatrice Lillie, Tommy Trinder, Douglas Byng, Norman Hackforth and Hugh French. Their Lordships finally succumbed and, as well as their blessing, gave her £9,000 from Home Fleet funds to organize star parties to visit Scapa. The money reached her on her birthday. 'I wrote back and said thank you very much but it's not enough.' But it was a start even if Basil Dean viewed her efforts with deep suspicion.

The Germans were also doing their best to relieve the boredom of life at Scapa. Each evening, at the same time, a plane would pass over the fleet and drop a bomb into the Flow. These raids were considered to be no more than interesting diversions and the officers of one ship requested a later dinner because by the time they returned from watching the show their meat was cold. Tommy Trinder, who opened every performance by putting

his head through the curtains and saying his catch-phrase, 'You lucky people!', remembers that no one told them about the raids.

'We were unpacking and getting ready for the show and hadn't heard any warning. At the time the performance was due to start I dashed on stage, stuck my head through the curtains and – there was no one there, except for one very old boy who just sat and looked at me. I was tongue-tied. We'd actually seen the audience going in! "There's a raid on," he said finally. "They're out on the guns." We had to wait for them to come back before we could start. It was a memorable trip to visit Scapa. Dougie Byng, in particular, was a riot with his type of entertainment. He would come out dressed as an ATS officer and be talking to an Army officer. "It's no good your boys chasing our girls, Major. Oh, no. Our girls have got it here." And he'd tap his forehead with a finger. "It doesn't matter where your girls have got it," the Major replied, "my boys will find it."'

A star visit to the Orkney Islands remained a special occasion. Most of the time, if there was to be any entertainment it had to be provided by the men themselves. Actor-manager Arthur Lane was an ordinary seaman when posted to Scapa. During the bleak mid-winter months before ENSA shows found their way north and star parties were infrequent, he organized sing-songs and variety shows on the mess deck of his ship, *King George V*, flagship of the Fleet. They were small-scale and designed to keep him and his fellow ratings amused. But because Lane was a professional, word of him soon spread. Early in 1941 the C-in-C, Home Fleet, sent for him and told him that since all leave was being cancelled (the *Tirpitz* was expected to sail at any time) he wanted him to organize some sort of entertainment. On Flota, Lane took over the Playhouse (a derelict building left from the previous war) and got together a company from his ship to put on *Scapa Nights*, a Palladium-style revue. Apart from actor Robert Eddison and musician Bobby Pagan the cast were amateurs. 'Although most of them were regular sailors' says Lane, 'they were very good and my life as producer was very easy since they were all stage-struck. They thought the whole idea was very glamorous.'

It took two months to get the show ready. On the very night of the dress rehearsal the *Tirpitz* sailed, 'Action Stations' sounded and the cast of *Scapa Nights* had to run for their ship still wearing make-up. For another two months *King George V*

The theatre at Flota, for some reason, was practically never used, and almost all the star visits, such as this act with Chesney Allen, Will Hay and Bud Flanagan were presented in halls, hangars and Messes.

patrolled the waters off Iceland and only when it returned did the curtain go up on the show. For three nights they played to men from the *Rodney*, *Prince of Wales*, *Renown*, *Victorious* and US battleships *Tuscalusa* and *Wichita*. In between his naval duties Lane was asked to produce a second revue, *Hello Flota*, and then decided to stage the old melodrama, *Sweeney Todd*. 'This was a great success but fraught with difficulties. For the first time, in order to get the best cast possible, I chose men from the entire fleet. And, of course, the inevitable happened. Just as we were starting to get somewhere with a scene, a ship would sail and I would lose an essential member of the cast. In particular we had some talented boys from the *Prince of Wales*. She left us for the Far East and was later sunk off Singapore.'

The situation at Scapa was repeated at Naval establishments throughout Britain. A sailor would have an opportunity to watch or take part in a performance only if there was a keen amateur or professional on the base who was prepared and able to give up his time to put on a production. The possibility was less remote for a man drafted to one of the traditional homes of the Navy, such as Portsmouth, Plymouth or Rosyth. These were accessible to touring companies and local amateurs and limited attempts were made to mount productions. Among the amateurs doing what they could for naval entertainment was Vera Harley, a member of the YWCA staff attached to the joint YM/YWCA club at *HMS Heron*, the Royal Naval Air Station, Yeovilton. She had spent the early part of the war touring ack-ack batteries along the Thames estuary with her own show, *The Highway Gang*. Arriving at Yeovilton she organized poetry readings and entertainments and, eventually, a revue. Called *Fresh Herons* this was so popular that it became the ship's official concert party, with a new production every month. She also took part in the occasional play with actors who were at Yeovilton on a course and

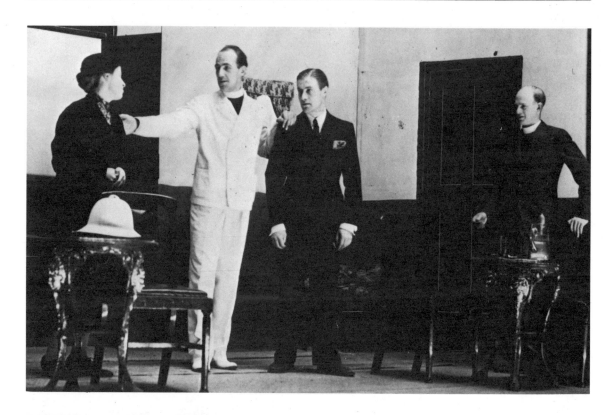

Vera Harley, attached to the joint YMCA and YWCA at the R. N. Air Station in Yeovilton, organized plays, concert parties and poetry readings for the men stationed there. She also performed from time to time, as seen in the photograph above, with Michael Hordern in a production of Outward Bound. *The couple below were doing dramatized renderings of classical English poetry.*

knew how long they would be staying, among them Michael Hordern and Douglas Storm, both training to be Fighter Direction Officers. This was a job for which actors were considered ideal since they had the voice control to be able to combat poor radio talkback when in contact with pilots. Plays were, however, a rarity and most actors, if they found themselves on stage, were more likely to be singing or dancing.

Entertainments Officers, whose early efforts had met with indifference in most cases, if not actual hostility, were later encouraged to do all they could and were delighted to receive any offers of help. Ronnie Hill was in his office at Portsmouth when there was a knock on the door. 'In walked this marine who looked at me and said, "I am the Great Casson." He told me he was a hypnotist and asked me if I would like him to do a show in the

94

theatre. I thought this was a wonderful idea but could foresee terrible dangers when he began asking for sick-bay attendants to be on duty. Anyway, the commodore gave permission for the performance and Casson gave a most remarkable show.

'At that time I had a bunch of lads who looked after the theatre, swept it, kept it clean and so on. They also slept in it because it was better than some accommodation in barracks. They liked this because they didn't have to pay any attention to the bugles at six in the morning and could get up at about eleven. Whenever I complained that this wasn't on they took no notice. It transpired that Casson, literally by clicking his fingers, could put one of these lads, a highly persuadable Irishman, into a trance. One night Casson asked me if there was anything I wanted him to tell Paddy to do. I said, "Yes. I want you to arrange for him to wake up at six o'clock every morning for a week and get the others up." It wasn't at all popular but it worked!'

Revues and Variety were, of necessity, the staple diet of naval entertainment put on by the Navy. Programmes were easier to put on, could disguise a paucity of talent and, if half the company had to sail on the day of the performance, the running order could be changed, unlike a play which would have to be postponed.

'If I was doing a revue myself', says Hill, 'I would do it entirely with our own bunch. I never bothered to get in anyone else because it was too difficult with rehearsals which had to be in the evening when most people were free. But for other shows – straight Variety – I could usually find enough talent to put on a programme and invite a big star to come down and top the bill, people like Phyllis Robins, Kay Cavendish, Edward Cooper, Brian Michie or Douglas Byng.'

Entertainments Officer for the Plymouth area was composer Vivian Ellis. His domain covered the Naval establishments of Plymouth, Devon and Cornwall where many fishing villages had a naval presence. Sailors within reach of Plymouth were ferried to the performances by bus. Shows were then broken down into small units and taken on tour for the rest. This happened, on average, every three months, the interval between new productions. The mobile units did not play just to sailors as Charles Sadler who worked with Ellis recalls:

'We played to audiences with civilians in, people who worked on the bases or helped the Navy in some way. Needless to say the touring shows were not always as slick as they might have been and on one occasion when there was a long scene change I was sent out front to do a cod conjuring act to fill in time. I picked on an old boy in the front row. "I expect you'd be surprised if I produced a rabbit from your pocket," I said. "Yes," he replied in his broad Devon accent, "I would, 'cos I've got a ferret in there." And he really had! He pulled out a live ferret! By the time the audience had stopped laughing the show was ready to go on and, thankfully, I escaped.'

In 1943 the situation in all Naval establishments, particularly in the West Country and the North, improved dramatically. Instead of having to plead with artists to visit them, Entertainments Officers were inundated with requests from stars desperate to play Devonport or Rosyth. This change of heart was brought about by renewed bombing in London and the Home Counties. Entertainers who had previously seen no reason to leave the metropolis or who couldn't find the time, were, overnight, free and anxious to tour the regions even if it meant travelling with ENSA. This exodus of artists, coming as it did soon after the establishment of the Army's Central Pool of Artists and the RAF Gang Show, both of which instructed its units to play for all services, meant the Navy found itself well-off for touring productions.

Overseas, senior Naval officers were becoming increasingly concerned that their men, especially those who had been at sea for long periods in small ships, were missing out on organized entertainment. It was no longer sufficient to rely on the occasional production being around when a ship put in to port and ENSA area organizers were asked, and sometimes ordered, to make shows available. This was not always as simple as it might seem largely due to the reluctance of the Navy to inform anyone outside the service where ships were or when they might be expected. Nigel Patrick found this to be one of his greatest headaches when he was running ENSA in Naples.

'I could never find out where Naval units were, when ships were coming or going. I was continually being ticked off for not providing enough entertainment for the Navy. I pointed out that it was very difficult to do this when I never knew if ships were coming in and couldn't be told because of security. The way I managed to get round this was to have a private code with an officer friend attached to Navy House. He would send me a signal, all highly unofficial of course, whereby if a ship was due in, Pigeon One meant a big show was

ENSA PICTURE NEWS

ISSUED FORTNIGHT

| No. 20 | FREE PRINTS available to NEWSPAPERS and MAGAZINES on application to:— PUBLIC RELATIONS DIVISION, THEATRE ROYAL, DRURY LANE, LONDON, W.C.2. | Phone: TEMPLE B 1575 |

THEY ALL LAUGH WITH ENSA

The candid camera catches the Services "off guard . . ."

ENSA provides entertainment of all types, from Symphonic music and Shakespeare to song-and-dance shows. But one thing all services have in common; they enjoy a laugh, In these photographs, taken at random among services audiences at ENSA shows, the accent is on laughter .... the King leading the way.

The King was paying a visit to the Home Fleet when this ENSA show was given ashore. More than one officer laughed "'til he cried."

[OVE

required within forty-eight hours; Pigeon Two, a small one; and so on. Of course, it was always possible the ship didn't arrive on the day it was supposed to but at least something was ready if it did. I spent a lot of time working out false destinations then switching shows at the last moment.'

Such a system relied on a concert party being in the locality at the right time which was not always the case, though the major Mediterranean ports tended to become area headquarters from which ENSA parties were controlled and could generally manage to find a show of sorts. Many of the larger ships appointed Entertainments Officers to liaise with shore and put on some sort of entertainment while at sea. Generally it was a quiz – What sort of books did Zane Grey write? Twenty-eight days solitary for the first man who says dirty! – a few jokes – The captain met a new recruit. "So you're the new recruit, eh? I suppose it's the same old story; the fool of the family goes to sea?" "Oh, no,

sir. That's all changed since you joined up." – or a sing-song. Michael Hordern gained a considerable reputation in the wardroom of *HMS Illustrious* for his rendering of 'I have a little Pussy, It's so pretty, Oh, so small.'

A ship the size of *Illustrious*, with hangars and flight deck, had room to build a stage and was able to progress from the messdeck sing-song to a production which could be more ambitious than a succession of turns. 'We can have more and better ship's concerts in future,' wrote the Entertainments Officer in the ship's paper. 'A new open-air stage that can very easily be rigged is being contrived using the boxing ring, some cloth bought in Durban and the Bosun's brains. With such an arrangement it will be possible also to invite other ships' shows over here, thereby proving to ourselves how much better *we* are! We'll get going pretty soon so let us know if you are a rising star. We can use you!'

In September, 1944, when the war in Europe

Robert Eddison and Michael Hordern were both serving on board HMS Illustrious *when they put on a show called* Illustrations. *As in the case of productions put together by professionals in the forces, this was a revue partly assembled from memories of bits from West End shows.*

was entering its last phase, the Admiralty finally decided that the Royal Navy could no longer rely on ENSA being in every port or ships putting on occasional entertainments but should have its own official productions. What gave rise to this decision after so long was the turning of attention to the Far East. The war with Japan was expected to last a further two years at least, with the Japanese fighting fiercely to retain every Pacific island. It would be a long hard struggle before the Allies could take Japan itself and a British presence in the Far East was considered vital to safeguard our interests in any subsequent peace negotiations. As soon as men and ships could be spared from the European war they were despatched to the Far East.

It was pointed out to the Admiralty that under the conditions of war envisaged, with ships and men far from regular ports, it would be impossible for concert parties to visit them. If entertainment was desirable it would have to come from within the Navy itself. The Admiralty agreed and plans were made for the building of two Amenity ships which would be attached to the Fleet Train, each containing a laundry, brewery, bars, cinemas, shops, rest rooms, games rooms, a chapel and a theatre – everything considered essential for the

sailors' welfare. In the Pacific the Americans had already learned the value of the Fleet Train, a flotilla of vessels to which fighting ships, far from home, could return for refuelling, repairs, ammunition, medical attention and rest. The Admiralty, hampered by not having one in the Indian Ocean, had decided to follow suit.

Two ex-Blue Funnel Line ships named the *Agememnon* and the *Menestheus* that had already been converted to minesweepers were chosen to become the new Amenity ships and were ordered to the Pacific coast of Canada for a complete refit. Merchant seamen from the Blue Funnel Line would be responsible for running the ships, the Naafi for the catering, bars and shops, and the Navy for the entertainment and administration to provide it. Each ship was to have an entertainment company of fifty-five, including officers, ratings and bandsmen from the Royal Marines. The entertainment section of Naval Welfare Services in London, run by Kim Peacock (the first 'Paul Temple'), Harold Warrender and Jon Pertwee, was detailed to find the artists. They chose Ronnie Hill to produce the show to go on board the *Menestheus*.

'It took a terribly long time for them to get it moving,' Hill recalls. 'Then we had this period of

The Menestheus *was truly an amenity ship designed to bring entertainment to the sailors in the Pacific. It not only had a theatre, cinema and chapel but also cafeterias, buffets, bars, stores, tailors, cobblers and the only floating brewery in the world.*

Ronnie Hill, on the dais (wearing trousers), produced Pacific Showboat *for the* Menestheus *in the tradition of lavish West End revues, complete with glamorous gowns and scenery changes as well as chorus and dance routines, which can be glimpsed at in this picture of the finale of the show.*

extraordinary auditions. A signal was sent out to the Home Fleet saying anyone who wanted to volunteer for this thing should apply. By this time I had fixed a director, Hedley Briggs. He was extremely well-known for his production work with the Farjeon revues just before the war and was also a designer, character actor and a well-known dancer, being one of the original Sadler's Wells Company. We both came up to London for these auditions and there were hundreds of them: hundreds of impersonators, hundreds of Bing Crosbys. It was rather shattering because the talent was pretty terrible and a lot of people came along because they thought they would get on to a soft number. Eventually we got a company together – all men since we were not allowed to have women – and we all went away and waited. Suddenly we got a date to start rehearsals in London about two months later. Having said we must have this chap and that chap, we would find he had been drafted out to Singapore or something. A great deal of time, in fact, and the country's money was spent flying members of our cast back to us.'

The shows were all-male because it was assumed that the Amenity ships would be going into the firing line and it was planned that the productions should be broken down into small units to visit men who could not get to the ships. Although the Admiralty expressed no concern for Wrens being bombed on shore it drew the line at it happening afloat.

In June, 1945, *Pacific Showboat*, the first official Naval show of the war, was launched at the Lyric Theatre, Hammersmith. Produced by Ronnie Hill, designed and directed by Hedley Briggs, the musical director was Bobby Pagan and in the cast were John Hewer and Peter Hawkins.

'It was a sensation,' says Hill. 'People fought for tickets, especially the queers who were mad about us – all those men in drag, though none of our drag performers made any attempt to look like women. We had put together a revue. I wrote a good deal of it and we got material from people like Herbert Farjeon, Geoffrey Wright, who was also in the Navy, and Nicholas Phipps – all well-known revue writers of the time. A scenic artist had been brought in, two really magnificent pianists and an

"TOKIO EXPRESS"

PROGRAMME

OVERTURE: The "Oceanaires" Theatre Orchestra of S.S. "Agamemnon"

under the direction of Mr. K. A. McLean, Bandmaster (W.O.), L.R.A.M., R.M.

At the Pianos: Frank Gordon and Norman Whitehead

1. "HEY THERE" (Arthur Lane and Bobby Pagan)

The Working Party: Michael Jacobson, John Taylor, Leonard Meredith, Roy Marriott.

The Crusher: Artie Mayne.

The Ship's Company: Robert Sinclair, Cliff Clayton, Ricky Johnson, Phil Barker, Dave Smith, Michael Mills.

The Wrens: Bobby Fletcher, Geoffrey Riley, Douglas Mills, Ray Powell.

1st Officer, W.R.N.S.: Tommie Rose.

2. ARTHUR LANE introduces
3. BILLY FARDOE and his Music
4. CLIFF CLAYTON AND RICKY JOHNSON. Fools rush in
5. THE INTOXICATION OF THE WALTZ

The Dancers: Bobby Fletcher, Geoffrey Riley, Douglas Mills, Ray Powell.

The Showgirls: Leonard Meredith, Michael Jacobson, Billy Fardoe.

The Singer: John Taylor.

6. AFTER THE SHOW (Nicholas Phipps)

(a) The Girl - Bobby Fletcher
The Man - Michael Mills
(b) The Man - Michael Jacobson
The Girl - Tommie Rose
(c) The Diplomat - Artie Mayne
The Duchess - Arthur Lane

7. GEOFFREY RILEY
8. "I WANT TO APPEAR AS A MAN" - - Tommie Rose
9. BOBBY SINCLAIR and his Magic
10. DOUGLAS MILLS' TWINKLING FEET
11. EVACUEES (by permission of Firth Shepherd)

The Vicar - Artie Mayne
His Wife - Tommie Rose
Mr. Custard - Michael Jacobson
Sydney - Cliff Clayton
Arthur - Arthur Lane
Jack - Ricky Johnson
Mum - Michael Mills

12. A ROMANY RHAPSODY

INTERVAL (5 Minutes)

13. "HEY, GOOD LOOKIN'"

The Girl: Bobby Fletcher.
The Boy: Artie Mayne.
The Dancers: Michael Jacobson, John Taylor, Leonard Meredith, Roy Marriott, Phil Barker, Bobby Fletcher, Dave Smith, Ray Powell, Douglas Mills, Geoffrey Riley.

14. MOMENTES MUSICALES (by permission of Firth Shepherd)

(a) Piano - Norman Whitehead
Sousaphone - Arthur Lane
Violincello - Cliff Clayton
The Singer - Ricky Johnson
(b) Violin - David Smith

15. THE DEEP SOUTH

The Dancer - Douglas Mills
The Singer - Roy Marriott

16. CLIFF CLAYTON AND RICKY JOHNSON AGAIN
17. SIX HANDS IN HARMONY

Norman Whitehead, Frank Gordon, Leon Young.

18. RED PEPPERS (by permission of Noel Coward)

George Pepper - Arthur Lane
Lily Pepper - Tommie Rose
Alf (the Call Boy) - Michael Mills
Bert Bentley - Arty Mayne
Mr. Edwards - Michael Jacobson
Mabel Grace - Bobby Fletcher

19. PHIL BARKER IN BANJOMANIA
20. WE SAY GOODNIGHT

(a) The Fleet's Lit Up
The Singer: Roy Marriott
(b) This is Our Dream of England (Jacobson and Gordon)
The Company

GOD SAVE THE KING

THE COMPANY:

O. A. G. Riley, P./O. F. E. Davies, L./Sea. M. D. Jacobson, L./Sea. E. R. Marriott, L./Sea. L. Meredith, A. B. T. L. Fletcher, Wtr. E. C. Rose, Ldg. Wmn. H. Eades, A.M. (O) W. Fardoe, Tel. D. R. Smith, Stores Asst. G. R. Sinclair, Stwd. P. S. Barker, A/B. G. D. Clayton, A./B. J. A. Taylor, A/B. A. Mayne, A. B. R. E. Powell, A/B. D. Mills, Ord. Sea. F. W. Johnson, Cook P. Cliff.

THE ORCHESTRA:

Conductor: Mr. K. A. McLean, L.R.A.M., R.M., Bandmaster R. A. Hobbs, Band Corporal L. E. S. Young, Band Corporal J. H. Jemmett, Band Corporal A. E. Pottle. Musicians A. W. Jolliffe, T. Hunter, I. R. Evans, R. J. Swales, J. Graham, M. E. Nicholls, R. L. Rainey, E. Mills, V. M. Wilson, J. C. Harrison, Peter Worsfold, N. C. Price, S. Artis, D. Brown, E. T. Hemmingway, A. R. Moore, N. Scurlock.

The programme for Tokyo Express *fully illustrates the lavishness and variety that went into the preparation on, and production of, the Music Hall presentation designed for the* Agamemnon.

American dancer from the Palladium to arrange our choreography.'

Two weeks after *Pacific Showboat*, the second show, called *Tokyo Express* and destined for the *Agamemnon*, moved into the Lyric for its try-out. Welfare Services at the Admiralty had experienced some difficulty in finding Arthur Lane, the man they wanted to produce it. Quite by chance Jon Pertwee had run across him in a bar and told him to report to head office. His second-in-command was Michael Mills, the television producer who in peacetime had been pounding coconuts in the BBC Drama Department's sound effects.

'When they sent me the signal to report to London,' says Mills, 'I was at sea and didn't get it for a month. Then they said they were very sorry but as they hadn't heard from me they had filled the post. I was bitterly disappointed and could see only two years of Jap-bashing in front of me. However, the gentleman they got in my place was a little odd. When they had the first morning's rehearsal he got the Marine band and those great,

hairy matelots, who had just come off their ships, doing calisthenics and reciting to music. When Arthur Lane walked in and found them reciting "Ode To A Nightingale" to piano accompaniment he thought he'd got a nutter. He was quickly removed and they sent for me. Just in time. I had already been issued with my tropical kit and was about to leave for the Far East.'

Mills became stage director of *Tokyo Express*, making occasional appearances in production numbers. Norman Whitehead was the musical director and among the musicians were Leon Young and Signaller Terry Sandford who had been awarded the DSM in the Crete campaign, played the piano and after the war changed his name to Russ Conway.

Like *Pacific Showboat*, *Tokyo Express* was produced on the revue formula of sketches and musical numbers. If Hill's production leaned towards West End sophistication, Lane's deliberately went for the other end of the market.

'Arthur had the common touch in that he knew exactly what the Navy wanted,' explains Michael

Mills. 'The show was always extremely popular. There was a banjo player who played old plantation songs with which the audience would join in and he always finished with "Stars and Stripes" It was a colourful show with lots of sets and the band, with five brass, five saxes and a rhythm section, which used to lift the roof off. The general feeling used to be, "Oh, it's the Navy, it will be tatty." But it wasn't. It was a bloody good show of a rather brash music hall style. The only time we were ever sent up was when we did the opening number and there used to be some whistles for the men dressed as girls. I remember standing next to a large stoker at the back of one of the theatres and he had obviously come from the bar. He was standing with a pint in his hand, cheering and carrying on. Either his eyesight wasn't very good or it was far enough back because he suddenly turned to me and said, "Cor, I don't half fancy that bint! I'd like to give her a basinfull!" He was talking about one of the ratings!'

After the opening weeks at the Lyric both shows were sent on a tour of British Naval establishments since neither ship was ready. By this time the war in Europe had finished and a further tour of Holland and Germany was arranged to fill in time. That over, the ships still hadn't been completed so they were sent on a second tour of Britain and Northern Ireland before it was decided they should travel separately to the east coast of Canada and make their way slowly across to Vancouver to join their ships. Before either company had got very far an event took place which had never entered the Admiralty's calculations. On 6 August, 1945 the bomb was dropped on Hiroshima and within days the Pacific war was over. It was decided that the *Tokyo Express* company should complete its tour of Canada, raising money for charity, before being repatriated for demob.

'We got as far as Vancouver, took one look at the *Agamemnon* and then returned home,' remembers Michael Mills. 'We travelled every-

Boys and 'girls' in the final line up of Tokyo Express *with Tommy Rose facing the microphone and Michael Mills, the sailor on the left, who stage managed the show itself and has subsequently become the television producer of the British comedy series* Some Mothers do Have 'Em.

101

where in Canada by train and the bane of my life was the Royal Marines Band. They were always late. This train had steam up and was waiting to leave. All the men were on board except for the Marines who'd gone off down the main street to get a drink. I was walking up and down the platform, holding the train, praying it wasn't going to leave twenty-five Marines behind, muttering, "Where are those effing Marines?" A voice behind me – it was Maclean the bandmaster, an impeccable man, absolutely correct in every possible way – said, "*Royal* effing Marines, if you please, Mr Mills. *Royal* effing Marines."'

Pacific Showboat was detailed to go ahead and join the *Menestheus* and sail slowly across the Pacific entertaining the remnants of the British Fleet.

'We reached Vancouver,' says Ronnie Hill, 'and were met by the RN Officer in charge. I was enormously excited and said, "When can we go and see the ship?" "Oh," he said, "no hurry." It was two days before he took me down to the shipyards where the conversion was taking place. The riveters were still in. There was no thought of leaving Canada for at least four months.' For the next few weeks the company hung around British Columbia sightseeing, playing the occasional show, losing half-a-dozen men to demob and searching frantically for replacements. Finally they were allowed on board.

'The ship was the sort of thing one hears about civic theatres today,' says Hill. 'Hundreds of thousands of pounds are spent equipping a town with a civic theatre and then they don't consult the people who are going to use it. When we got on board we found it was practically unworkable. For a start the stage was so highly polished, like a ballroom floor, that you had only to walk on it to fall over. There were a lot of things wrong with the lighting, there was no rake on the auditorium floor and no space in the wings.'

The problems were rectified as far as possible and the *Menestheus* finally set sail, with both brewery and *Pacific Showboat* working, in Feb-

ruary, 1946. As an experiment in entertainment it was a failure due mainly to the fact that the ship was too late arriving on the scene. Potential audiences were so widely scattered that the show played only to those it could find. That meant mostly in ports where there were other attractions. The men, too, on both sides of the footlights, were at the end of a long, hard war and were anxious to throw off their uniforms and return home. There was no real planning to the journey. The most memorable shows, according to Hill, were those for POW's released from Japanese camps. For the remainder of the seventy days they were on board the *Showboat* company received mixed reactions. 'In Kure,' recalls Hill, 'we were virtually playing to the same ships day after day for twenty-eight performances. The first two or three were a sensation with the theatre packed. Then, after some had seen the show two or three times, they would, without exception, head for the bar and we were doing a show to maybe fifty people, in a theatre seating 350. Officialdom took over and the men were detailed: Party A to the canteen, Party B to the theatre. So we got our audience back by compulsion. They attended, they laughed and were quite good, except we noticed they began to leave before the end. First of all they would go during the item before the finale; then during the one before that until half-way through the second act we would be losing ninety per cent of the audience straight to the bar.'

The bar was the most successful feature of the *Menestheus*, beating even the canteen where the most popular item on the menu in the Pacific was egg and chips. During the six months of its brewing life the brewery on board sold over a quarter of a million pints. A report forwarded to the Admiralty noted that although the beer was brewed from sea-water the brewery was 'a distinct success, both as regards quantity and quality.'

In June, 1946, nearly a year after the war had finished, the *Menestheus* turned for home and put an end to the Royal Navy's one and only attempt at official live entertainment.

CHAPTER EIGHT

THINKING ABOUT THE WAR
THE ABCA PLAY UNIT

O ne of the most interesting of developments in troop entertainment came with the formation, half-way through the war, of a Play Unit by ABCA, the Army Bureau of Current Affairs.

The Bureau had had its genesis in the aftermath of Dunkirk. Searching for methods to combat the lowering of morale due to that humiliating withdrawal the Adjutant General, Sir Ronald Forbes Adam, came up with the idea of holding weekly seminars on current affairs. Before his appointment to Adjutant General he had tried an experiment with his officers in Northern Command of discussions with the men based on events in the daily papers. He wanted to extend this type of discussion to the entire Army. He wanted the purpose of the conflict with Hitler brought into the open. During the 1914–18 war the soldiery had never been allowed to question what it was doing nor why, but this time Adam wanted it to be different. He wanted troops to talk about the war, to discuss the reasons for it, to know how they were governed and what they were risking their lives to defend. He approached William Emrys Williams, a leading figure in adult education (later Sir William, a founder and Secretary-General of the Arts Council), to become the civilian head of the Army Bureau of Current Affairs, the organization which would run these discussions.

ABCA was a part of Army Education, training men to lead discussions during the compulsory ABCA half-hour, preparing information leaflets and providing an administrative back-up to the scheme. It was worthwhile work but hardly caught the imagination. Williams began to wonder what else he could do to put over current affairs in a more lively way. It was his idea to use drama. Out of this unlikely background came the ABCA Play Unit; unlikely because the concept of presenting current affairs could have produced worthy but boring plays. Instead, the ABCA Play Unit produced some of the most exciting experimental theatre seen in Britain over the past few decades. In attitude and achievement the Unit symbolized the Brave New World feeling of the nation at the time; that here, at last, was the war to end all wars; that the old order really would change and Britain would become a land fit for everyone to live in. Although it produced only six plays during its three year life, the Unit constantly broke new ground in subject matter and methods of stage presentation. There were few stage techniques (ironically still hailed as innovatory when they appear today) that the Unit did not employ. But just as the ideals for which the Unit stood began to crumble when Hitler was defeated and people began to realize little had changed and the bright future was nothing but a dream, so the ABCA Play Unit faded away at the end of the war.

Williams may have decided that he wanted to dramatize current affairs but he had no idea of how to achieve it. In 1943 he was visiting a training course for ABCA officers run by Michael MacOwan, an education officer with London District Ack-Ack who had been running the Westminster Theatre before the war.

'Bill Williams came up to me and said, "I know you. I used to come to your theatre." "That's nice," I replied, "but those are far off days." "You're just the chap I need," he went on. "I've been thinking about how we could dramatize ABCA. I think we could make plays out of it. I don't know how but you think about it." And that's how it started. I was very busy running my courses for London Ack-Ack and I did think about it but not very much. Bill kept ringing me and asking if I had had any ideas and I'd say I had but they were taking time to develop. Then he started pushing and pushing. About that time I met Stephen Murray who had a small unit of actors working for London District Theatre. Stephen was very worried because his unit was not established and he thought it was going to be wound up. I told him about William's idea and suggested that if we could come up with something it might be a way of getting his unit established. I didn't know where we were going to start or what it might lead to. I only had a vague idea that we might do something along the lines of the American Federal Theatre producing *Living Newspapers.*'

The *Living Newspaper* was a terse, unbiased presentation of issues of the day evolved by the Federal Theatre, a nationwide project started in 1936 to give work to needy professionals. The success of the *Living Newspapers*, which attracted wide audiences most of whom had never been to the theatre, led to the Federal Theatre's downfall. It was closed on political grounds in June, 1939.

'MacOwan told me he was getting the scripts written,' recalls Stephen Murray. 'Time went by and nothing happened so I decided to write the first one myself. It was called *United We Stand*. The idea was to draw a parallel between Abraham Lincoln holding the United States together under pressure of secession and nobody holding together the League of Nations. It was twenty minutes long and very fast-moving with lots of scenes and light changes. There were eighty light cues and sixty sound cues. As we didn't have tape in those days everything had to be done from disc. I had no idea whether it would work but we rehearsed furiously, night after night, until we were ready to try it out.'

The play was performed at a gunsite during one of the regular afternoon ABCA half-hours. The men were marched in expecting a lecture and had no idea they were about to see a play. 'It went off like a fire-cracker,' says Murray. 'It had the most startling reception. It was one of the most fantastic experiences I have ever had. Those very tough people stood up and cheered.'

'It was a very good play,' says MacOwan. 'There were bits of scenes from Drinkwater's play *Abraham Lincoln* interspersed with bits Stephen had written and he had put it all together very cunningly indeed. There were loudspeakers round the hall and numerous light changes; everything was very electric. It was totally new in this country. Joan Littlewood had been putting on documentary pieces in Town Halls in the 1930s but to my knowledge there had never been anything quite like this. It was an entirely new way of putting on entertainment and it hit hard. The audience loved it.'

The technique Murray employed, which was used by later ABCA writers, owed less to the stage than it did to the cinema, with its use of short, pithy scenes, cross-cutting between time and place, lights and music. Since the play had to be adapted to a variety of stages, scenery was kept to an absolute minimum. Most of the action took place in front of black curtains so the audience was forced to use its imagination to fill in details of the set.

The Unit immediately booked the play in to another gunsite and MacOwan excitedly phoned Williams at the War Office. 'I said, "You've kept bothering me about this ABCA idea, well a friend of mine has put together a piece. Would you like to come and see it?" He came and brought the Adjutant General with him, which was a bit of a shock. The performance went just as well. Again the troops loved it. The Adjutant General was like a dog with two tails. He kept saying, "This is marvellous, this is marvellous. We must have this throughout the Army. Every unit must have a company like this." I explained that we had been about six months dreaming up those twenty minutes and that both Stephen and I were professionals; I couldn't see how it could be extended to every unit in the Army. "Oh," he said, "run short courses and train people how to do it." We just smiled and agreed.' Even when the ABCA Play Unit became an established feature of Army life it never grew to more than two units.

After the try-out before the Adjutant General, MacOwan was summoned to the War Office and given the go-ahead to set up the new Unit. He took Stephen Murray with him but before the Unit could start work an interval came in the shape of a new play written especially for the Army by J B Priestley. MacOwan's department was ordered to produce it in a no-expense spared production. *Desert Highway* opened at the Garrison Theatre in

Desert Highway with Emlyn James, John Wyse, George Cooper, Stephen Murray and Stanley Rose, was written expressly for the British army by J. B. Priestley as a play that was meant not only to entertain the men but to stimulate them.

Salisbury at the end of 1943, moved to the Theatre Royal, Bristol, and then went on a tour of army camps and commercial theatres, raising funds for charity, before starting a three month season at the Playhouse, Northumberland Avenue, on 10 February, 1944. MacOwan directed, Stephen Murray played the lead and top actors in the Army, such as John Wyse and Emlyn James, were brought in, mostly from Stars in Battledress. From the Playhouse, *Desert Highway* again went on tour. After leaving the cast, his part being taken over by James Donald, Murray was commissioned into the ABCA Play Unit, the nucleus of the company being drawn from his London District Theatre Unit.

The first 'official' ABCA production, in the summer of 1944, was *What's Wrong With The Germans?* The play opened with an officer coming in front of the curtains to announce that the performance had been cancelled; in its place would be a discussion of the German character. This was a carefully scripted pastiche of an officer leading an ABCA discussion and was so convincingly played by Brian Oulton that at one camp he was offered a glass of water by an officer in the front row. At the end of Oulton's opening speech another member of the company, planted in the audience, stood up and began to tell of the German family with which he had been billeted after the First World War. The curtains opened to reveal the family and the soldier left the audience to take part in the action. During one scene the son, a Social Democrat, addressed the audience about his beliefs. His speech was interrupted by Nazi storm-troopers bursting in, truncheons at the ready. 'It really was quite frightening,' recalls MacOwan. 'It gave the audience the feeling of what it was like to live in a police state where a perfectly peaceful meeting could be suddenly broken up by armed men. The storm-troopers seized the speaker and beat him up. While that was happening Stephen, as the Nazi chief, entered from the back of the hall, climbed on to the stage and proceeded to deliver a Nazi address, finishing with screams of "Seig Heil!" He was absolutely magnificent and completely terrifying. At one place, where the audience was very young, I thought there was going to be a riot. They screamed, they yelled, they booed and were about to get up on the stage to get Stephen. It was the most astonishing piece of audience partici-pation I have ever seen.'

Audience participation was what the ABCA plays intended. They were short (none lasted more than forty minutes) and were written to provoke thought and discussion. 'Their object,' according to official documents, 'is to dramatize a subject of immediate interest, to present a certain amount of information and then to indicate different points of view about it. The plays are not propagandist for they are designed to encourage thought and discussion by giving an airing on the stage to the opinions, hopes and fears of the audience.' A performance had to stand on its own. There was no official discussion time in the hall immediately afterwards but if later the men didn't talk about it or the ideas it had raised, the play was considered to have failed. The scripts themselves were the product of heated discussion between MacOwan, occasionally Stephen Murray, and the three writers MacOwan engaged, Bridget Boland, Jack Lindsay and Ted Willis.

'We wrote very much as a committee,' says Bridget Boland. 'No play was written entirely by one person.' At script meetings in the War Office, MacOwan took the chair and all four would play out alloted political roles: MacOwan was the liberal, Boland the true-blue Tory, Willis the grass-roots socialist and Lindsay the communist. 'We could have handled the material very care-fully, not offending anyone,' says Boland, 'but we thought that would be a bore. The whole point of ABCA was to start discussions, to start the soldier thinking for himself. After the play we wanted them to go away and talk – and if *we* didn't start an argument *they* weren't going to. We worked on the principle that if it doesn't annoy somebody, it's a bore, cut it out. Find something that is going to annoy somebody, the object being to annoy everybody equally.'

Jack Lindsay, an Australian writer who was in the Army, was, in fact, an ardent left-winger, and Ted Willis, the only civilian in the trio of writers, had been writing left-wing documentaries, based on the *Living Newspaper* format, for the amateur Unity Theatre. Bridget Boland who was in the ATS and came from a family of Irish Liberal politicians was first engaged to write film scripts.

'It was Bill Williams's idea that we should start making ABCA films and Bridget, who was a successful film writer – she did the script for *Gaslight* – was sent to us,' recalls MacOwan. 'When she turned up and I told her we did plays, she said, "I don't know anything about that; I'm here to write films." I said, "All right, but since you're with us you'd better find out a bit about what we do. There's a dress rehearsal of a show on this afternoon. Buzz along and see it." So Bridget went off to see the rehearsal at the YMCA in Tottenham Court Road, where we did all our productions, and came back terrifically excited. "When do I start writing the next one?" she said. We never did make any films.'

The ABCA plays utilized every conceivable style and method of presentation – factual epi-sodes, fantasy, cartoon, sound effects, lighting and poetry. It was the poetic element in particular which formed the basis of the difference between the work of ABCA and the Federal Theatre's *Living Newspaper* which used only straight documentation. Poetry, either as verse or height-ened prose, was provided by Jack Lindsay who had used it successfully in his mass declamations written during the Spanish Civil War. 'It was essential, of course,' he says, 'that the troops should not feel they were being got at, that they should not be suspicious because it was poetry. To my great relief it was quite clear that they didn't suspect they were hearing poetry. The poetic passages got over as straight emotional statements against which they never reacted.'

The Great Swap, or *Lend Lease* as it was more popularly known, written by Willis and Lindsay, explained the thinking behind and workings of lend lease. The next play, *The Japanese Way*, was perhaps the most successful of all the ABCA productions. Written by Bridget Boland and Jack

Whereas the Russians had sessions of political indoctrination for their fighting forces, the British, unlike the other Allies, put on topical plays designed to bring current affairs and debate to the men. None of the Allies did as much as the British to raise controversial issues and foster discussion of the problems of the day.

Lindsay in 1945, as attention was turning to the Far East, it examined the upbringing of a Japanese sniper from the time of his birth to the moment when he came face-to-face with the Allied troops he had to kill. André van Gyseghem played the Japanese soldier.

'The play began with two Australians waiting to pick off the sniper,' he says. 'They were discussing what it was that makes a man act as the Japanese did, what there was behind the Japanese way of life that makes a man not care twopence for life but give everything to the State. Over this came my words, sometimes in verse but mostly in a highly dramatized prose. We then showed the sniper's life – growing up, becoming a school-boy, at university – showing how the State gradually took over until he ended up in the tree shooting Australians. It was very exciting theatre with a strong message.'

Margaret Courtney played the Japanese mother. 'We were due to perform in a church hall at the top of a hill in North Wales. It was terrible

weather, icy cold, and our lorries kept sliding back down the hill. Eventually we had to leave them and manhandle every single prop, light, pole, bit of wood and all the skips up to the hall. By the time we got them up we were so late that we didn't have time for a final check. Near the beginning of the play I was discovered, baby in my arms, on a thrust rostrum singing a lullaby with just a spotlight on me. It had always worked well but this time, because we didn't have time, I had to go on without checking the rostrum or the spot. I wasn't worried; we'd done it so many times before I knew roughly where I was. I knelt down on the rostrum in the dark, clutching the doll I used as the baby, waiting for my cue when I suddenly thought I'm not far enough forward. I shuffled forward with this tight kimono on and the baby in my arms and went straight off the edge of the rostrum! The spotlight came up and I was discovered in the front row on the knee of a brigadier, my wig over my eyes, the knitting needles I wore in my hair up my nose, still clutching the doll. I sang the lullaby from his knee and afterwards, in the Mess, everyone said what a good idea it was!'

By May, 1945, the war in Europe was over and thoughts were turning to demob and the kind of world soldiers hoped to return to. Ted Willis tried to reflect this in *Where Do We Go From Here?*, written with the assistance of Boland and Lindsay.

'There was a tremendous feeling towards the end of the war,' says Willis, 'of "We've won! We've won for the second time in twenty-five years. Is it going to be the same?" There was a fear that there would be mass unemployment again, that we would repeat the mistakes of the 1920s. Soldiers were uncertain what they were going back to. Young men who, in a perverse way, had found fulfilment in the Army which they'd never found before were facing the prospect of returning to clerking jobs, shop assistant jobs and dull factory jobs, without even the certainty that those jobs would be there for them. There was a militancy amongst soldiers which was fixed very much on the idea of what had happened in 1918 and the determination that it wasn't going to happen again.'

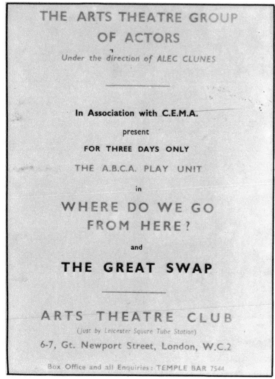

THE ARTS THEATRE GROUP
OF ACTORS

Under the direction of ALEC CLUNES

In Association with C.E.M.A.

present

FOR THREE DAYS ONLY

THE A.B.C.A. PLAY UNIT

in

WHERE DO WE GO
FROM HERE?

and

THE GREAT SWAP

ARTS THEATRE CLUB
(just by Leicester Square Tube Station)
6-7, Gt. Newport Street, London, W.C.2

Box Office and all Enquiries : TEMPLE BAR 7544

The special season, given in London before going on to Germany, that the ABCA play unit gave was enthusiastically received by a star studded audience.

Where Do We Go From Here? was concerned primarily with concepts of freedom. The Beveridge plan had just come out and the play started with the premise that some sort of social welfare was necessary. The questions it posed were, how much and how far should it be allowed to infringe upon personal liberty?, – questions which are still being asked today, more than thirty years later. It was a remarkable piece, a hard-hitting social documentary written long before such plays became fashionable. It was also entertaining and extremely popular, having the advantage of playing before audiences which were passionately concerned with the subject. It also broke new ground by being one of the first plays on the British stage written by and for the working class in that it hadn't been written by someone with no experience of the life he was describing or who was using working class dialogue simply for comic effect. It was a disturbing play for the authorities since it challenged the divine right of politicans to decide what was good for the people they governed. One of the most surprising aspects of the Play Unit was that it was always allowed to operate without censorship. The ideas expressed in the plays were often far from comfortable for reactionary generals but, probably because Sir Ronald Forbes Adam took a personal interest in his creation, no one ever censored a single script.

By the time *Where Do We Go From Here?* was produced the Unit was beginning to change. The original company played a three day season at the Arts Theatre to show the theatrical profession the sort of work they had been doing and then went to Germany, in August, 1945, for a three month tour, ending with a performance at the Marigny Theatre, Paris, on 24 November. Michael MacOwan left the War Office and Bridget Boland took over running the Unit. She wrote the next and last of the ABCA plays, *The Bomb's All Yours*, a few weeks after Hiroshima and Nagasaki. 'This was the least good of the productions,' she says. 'For one thing it was the nearest to being written by one person – I wrote practically all of it myself – and that was a bad thing. But also it wasn't really a subject about which there was an awful lot to discuss. None of us realized, I certainly didn't, that we had entered the atomic age. We had no idea what an enormous subject we were dealing with.' The play was performed by a second ABCA Play Unit under the direction of André van Gyseghem, and taken on a CEMA tour of England and Wales. Stephen Murray's company returned from France

Where Do We Go From Here? *(above) was a boldly outspoken and true-to-life play about the problems to be faced at the end of the war.* Othello, *in which Alan Badel played the Moor, was, on the other hand, a much condensed version of a classic.*

and Murray left the Unit as did many other artists who had been with it since the beginning. Among the newcomers picked to take their places were Michael Langham, an ex-POW, and Alan Badel, a twenty-three year old from the 6th Airborne Division. Van Gyseghem's Unit, scheduled to visit the United States (a visit that was cancelled because of expense though there were rumours in the company that the Unit would be politically unacceptable) was rerouted to the Middle East. They took three productions: *The Bomb's All Yours, Where Do We Go From Here?* and, as a radical departure from custom, a truncated version of *Othello* in which Alan Badel played Othello and van Gyseghem, Iago. It was the least successful ABCA tour. Members of the company fell ill and performances had to be cancelled; there was friction between artists who, along with the audiences watching them, were more concerned with getting out of the Army than theorizing about

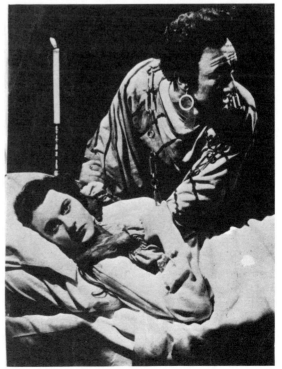

When, in 1945, the bombing of Hiroshima inspired the ABCA play unit production of The Bomb's All Yours *the issues exploded by that horror were still not clearly defined and certainly the future implications were completely clouded by the enormity of the event.*

the world they wished to inhabit. The mood which spawned ABCA had passed. Many of those involved with the Play Unit in the early days hoped a way might be found for an ABCA-type company, producing ABCA-type plays, to continue after the war. The idea was reluctantly abandonded as MacOwan explains, 'I personally came to the conclusion, though I don't think everybody agreed with me, that it would not work because we had started to split up as a Nation. Political differences were becoming more marked. We no longer had a coalition government for instance. We had a government and an opposition. Political divisions were becoming sharper; there was no longer that common ground. During the war the one thing that united the whole Nation was that we'd got to win the blinking war. That man Hitler had to be stopped whatever anyone's political views; that was the overriding thing. While you had that, you had a common chord in your audience which could be struck. That unity no longer existed after the war and I felt it would

be very difficult to make satisfactory ABCA plays after the war.' Jack Lindsay did make an attempt to carry the ABCA-style into some of his later work but it was not successful. ABCA had served its purpose. That purpose is best summed up by Ted Willis talking about *Where Do We Go From Here?*

'It didn't answer any questions, it just posed them. I think its greatest quality was the fact that it involved the soldiers and I know that when we moved on they went on discussing the play. Long after the show broke up you'd see groups of soldiers standing together, sitting together, discussing. And you can't ask any more of theatre than that people should carry on discussing. I've never believed that it's the job of the dramatist to answer problems. But if he can pose them challengingly and invitingly and leave people talking, he's done a fantastic job. In all the experience I've ever had with the theatre, the most satisfying was *Where Do We Go From Here?*'

CHAPTER NINE

ENTER UNCLE SAM

In 1939 the American public took little notice of what was happening in Europe. For some, the adventurous and the unemployed, the war came as a heaven-sent opportunity and a steady stream of young Americans, eager to join the Canadian or British Forces, crossed the border with Canada. But the majority gave it no more than a passing thought. It was not their war, it was an ocean away and the outcome would have little effect on their lives.

That September the most immediate concern was felt by the British community in Hollywood. Should they rush back to 'do their bit' or wait until they were ordered to return home? A deputation was sent to Washington to see the Ambassador. His advice was to stay put and help keep the British way of life before the American people; there was no need for them to return to Britain which had more than enough men to cope.

In May, 1940 Belgium fell, then Holland, followed by Dunkirk. The Hollywood exiles became increasingly restive. In August the *Sunday Dispatch* launched an attack on them, accusing them of ducking their responsibilities and ignoring their country in its hour of greatest need. J B Priestley repeated the attack in one of his Sunday morning *Postscript* broadcasts which had been introduced to counter Lord Haw-Haw's propaganda. Alarmed by the accusations, which he felt could do nothing but harm to Britain's cause, the consul in Hollywood called a meeting at which he asked all British actors, actresses and directors to sign a letter offering their services and indicating a willingness to return to Britain as soon as required. These letters were taken to Washington to the Ambassador by a deputation led by Cary Grant, Laurence Olivier and Herbert Wilcox, the film director husband of Anna Neagle. The Ambassador told them to report back to their colleagues that everyone should continue working but must make themselves available for public appearances to raise funds for the various war charities that were springing up, among them the British Red Cross, Bundles for Britain, the Committee To Defend America By Aiding The Allies and the British War Relief Association (the President of the West Coast Division was Basil Rathbone). Their efforts were to be co-ordinated by the consuls' Advisory Committee of which Ronald Colman, Basil Rathbone, Herbert Marshall, Cedric Hardwicke and Brian Aherne were members. One of the committee's first tasks was to raise money to provide ambulances which were in short supply in Britain. It was not just British stars who worked for these charities. Several American actors, in particular Edward G Robinson who had escaped from oppression in Rumania and had no wish to see it engulfing the rest of Europe, did all they could to help with time and huge sums of money. Others, like Carole Lombard, refused to be become involved. The war, she declared, was wrong and she would have nothing to do with it.

But if America would not go to war she could not escape the war coming to her. The concern felt by the British exiles was being echoed at the highest governmental levels where pressure was increasing for the States to give more than verbal support to her beleagured allies. In mid-1940,

Joseph Kennedy, the American Ambassador in London, was sending pessimistic reports to Washington about Britain's prospects. Britain, he declared, was finished. Nothing could save her. To send arms or money would be to throw them away. President Roosevelt, distrusting Kennedy's judgement, sent his personal envoy to find out the truth. The envoy reported back: Kennedy, although primarily concerned for his stocks and shares, was correct; the British were finished, they were up to their necks in serious trouble but, he added, they won't admit it and never will; they will never be beaten. He advised the President to send every dollar and all the military aid he could spare.

Roosevelt's response was swift and decisive. In June a shipment of half-a-million First World War rifles, 80,000 machine guns and 900 ancient field guns, was on its way across the Atlantic, followed by fifty obsolete but serviceable destroyers, the fifty ships 'that saved the world'. Lend Lease, the system of supplying military equipment in return for trade concessions, territorial rights or other materials, had begun, to be confirmed in December when Congress passed the Lend Lease Act. It was obvious to all but the most blinkered American that it was no longer a question of would the United States enter the war but when?

Towards the end of 1940 the heads of the YMCA, the YWCA, the National Catholic Community Services, the National Jewish Welfare Board, the Salvation Army and the National Travellers Aid Association, agencies that had worked together during the 1914–18 war, met in Washington to work out a common strategy to put into action when that moment arrived. Their purpose was to formulate ways of catering for the spiritual and moral welfare of the Armed Forces by the provision of clubs and social centres. A working party, set up under the chairmanship of Walter Hoving, tried to discuss its ideas with the Chiefs of Staff but met with little enthusiasm. The Federal Security Agency had plans for its own welfare programme as did the War Department. Neither wanted a civilian organization muscling in on its territory. After weeks of conferences and controversies nothing had been decided. The stalemate was broken by the President. He told a meeting of the Joint Chiefs of Staff how he wanted welfare operations run: the private organizations, represented by Hoving, would handle on-leave recreation while the government agencies would provide the buildings, which should have a common name.

The name chosen for the new organization, when it filed for incorporation on 4 February, 1941, was the United Service Organizations for National Defence, later shortened to the United Service Organizations Inc. USO, as it became known, had been born. But its birth didn't mean

The first national fund-raising campaign for USO got underway when General George C. Marshall (of Marshall Plan fame) unveiled the poster in New York's Times Square on 2nd June 1941 illustrating President Roosevelt's slogan appealing to Americans to support the organization.

Thomas E. Dewey who later became Governor of New York headed the first fund raising campaign for USO, seen here shaking hands with the first president of USO Walter Hoving (on the left). He is surrounded by government officials and representatives of the six founder organizations of the USO.

the way was clear for work to start. Like ENSA in Britain (and many of the events in USO's history paralleled those in ENSA's) USO was met with indifference, obstruction and hostility. No one seemed clear on what the exact function of the new organization was to be and as a public-funded body (it never received official financial backing) there was a pressing need for money. A public relations committee was formed which, headed by Thomas E Dewey, an ardent supporter of USO, raised sixteen million dollars in the first year. By August not one of the promised 360 buildings was ready. The delay was brought to President Roosevelt's attention and 300 men of the Army Corps of Engineers were set to work. Eight weeks later, on 28 November, the first two USO clubs built with federal funds were opened.

Early in 1941 the first peacetime draft in American history had started. Young men entered an Army ill-equipped to receive them. They had to train with broomsticks for a war everyone assured them they would never have to fight. They were looked upon, not as men preparing to defend their country, but as losers in a national lottery. Towns and cities to which they were sent treated them with a mixture of indifference and annoyance, and there was little for them to do off-duty. Professional drama and vaudeville companies, amateur societies and individuals did what little they could to entertain troops in their localities. In February, at the request of a student friend from UCLA who had been inducted into the Army, Joe E Brown paid an unofficial visit to Anchorage, Alaska, that lasted three months and took him to the Aleutians. Jack Benny accepted an invitation to play for Servicemen in California and started a series of camp tours that were to continue throughout the war. In Hollywood a committee was set up to finance and present stage and screen stars throughout California. Pepsodent, the sponsors of Bob Hope's radio show, came up with the idea of presenting the show each week from a different camp, starting at March Field, California, where Hope appeared for the Army Air Force. Not only did troops get to see some of the top acts as Hope's guests, the sales of Pepsodent rocketed. In Ohio, the professor of a university drama department announced his plan to entertain the forces with plays and variety put on by performers in the ranks. In New York, the Friends of New York Soldiers and Sailors organized concert parties which were sufficiently successful for the group to change its name (at the request of the War Department) to the Citizens' Committee for the Army and Navy and for its groups to travel further afield. During the summer of 1941 seven shows played to three million men all over the continent from Newfoundland in the east, where Larry Adler, the harmonica player, took a small party, as far west as the Rockies.

It was a casual and careless way of providing entertainment. Stars went out if someone they knew was on a base to invite them and if they could find time. Soldiers stationed further afield than California or who knew no one in Hollywood went without.

It became increasingly clear that USO had neglected to plan for one important area of welfare: live entertainment. During 1941 the Army had built 186 theatres on Army and Navy bases but with no organization and experience to run them they remained dark and empty. USO decided to take matters into its own hands. Rather than continue giving grants to amateur and professional companies to tour the Forces, it would organize all entertainment itself. As soon as the Hollywood committee, responsible for presenting stars in California, heard of the proposal it was worried. It knew that amateurs, however well-intentioned, running a nation-wide entertainment service could produce untold problems. Members of the committee flew to Washington for a meeting with Hoving. He agreed that a separate body, with its own board and administration, drawn from the profession, should be set up to cover the entertainment service. On 30 October, 1941, under the chairmanship of Abe Lastfogel, USO Camp

Shows Inc. was formed. There was no rush to join USO by artists desperate for work as there had been with ENSA in Britain. All the theatres, dance halls, night clubs, restaurants and places of entertainment were open and doing good business. However, there were enough people prepared to accept USO's rates (one third of what an artist would earn for a commercial engagement; stars to give their services free but have all expenses paid), who saw a tour with USO as a way of doing something for the country, for work to start immediately. Concert parties (the only type of entertainment USO wanted for some time) began to play in camps across the States and on 1 November the first overseas unit climbed aboard a B-18 transport plane, christened 'The Flying Showboat', to begin a 13,000 mile tour of the Caribbean, from Puerto Rico to British Guiana. Within a matter of days, four additional units were on their way to Newfoundland and the Arctic.

Officially America was still not at war. In June, 1941, 400 technicians had been sent to Northern Ireland, followed in September by a further 600, to build air and naval bases for US Forces to guard the Atlantic shipping lanes. Technically they were employees since the British government was paying for the contract, but it was a clear stretching of neutrality even if it didn't actually break it. To avoid antagonizing the Germans and the American public the operation was carried out with the utmost secrecy on both sides. At the time an opinion poll reported that ninety-five per cent of the American population was against any involvement in the war. At the beginning of December eighty-five per cent of the population still had no wish to become involved. On 7 December the Japanese attacked Pearl Harbour and America was in.

There was a rush of Hollywood stars to visit the troops with every press agent in town claiming his client as the first. Carole Lombard turned full circle and threw herself into non-stop work selling war bonds. On 20 January on a flight back from the first war bond rally in her home town of Fort Wayne, Indiana, her plane crashed near Las Vegas and she was killed. Actors and actresses joined in selling war bonds, volunteered for USO or enrolled in Civil Defence organizations. Within a few months Hollywood had lost such stars as James Stewart, William Holden, Douglas Fairbanks Jnr, Ronald Reagan, Robert Stack, Clark Gable, Victor Mature, Robert Taylor and Dan Dailey to the services in spite of a pronounce-

At the start Bing Crosby was strangely unsure of himself as a troop performer, but he soon became tireless in touring the garrisons and hangars throughout the States and later in Europe.

ment in May, 1942 that movies were an essential industry and stars could claim deferment from the draft. The Screen Actors' Guild, sensing the public outcry, disclaimed any part in the decision. The British Consul's advisory committee gave way to the Hollywood Victory Committee, an organization to marshal and administer the talent of the film capital. Big stars wanting to entertain troops volunteered to the Victory Committee, others to USO. The two often combined forces; stars wanting to go overseas had to go through the auspices of USO.

For comics like Jack Benny and Bob Hope appearing in front of a live audience held no fears, they welcomed it. But for a film star without an act, used to working from a script, there were problems. Even a singer as popular as Bing Crosby,

who spent most of 1942 travelling the States with Jimmy van Heusen as his pianist, playing to thousands of Servicemen, found the experience daunting. Phil Silvers, then a little-known comedian, persuaded Crosby to work for USO and accompanied him on some of his trips. 'He'd been making contributions to the USO in the form of large cheques,' Silvers remembered in his autobiography. 'He wouldn't admit it, but he was a little afraid of working on stage, even with a mike, in front of a live audience. There was some subtle difference, in his mind, between entertaining a big live audience and amusing the unseen millions over the radio, even though he had an audience in the studio for the Kraft Music Hall.' Brian Aherne discovered the hard way what it was like for an actor who couldn't sing or dance to visit troops when he was sent on the first of his many tours by the Victory Committee. 'Just talk to the boys, I was told, they like to see you. After a long, overnight flight in an Army C47, I arrived very tired at a camp in Georgia. A Special Service lieutenant met me and drove me directly to a huge Mess hall, where we joined the chow line with hundreds of young soldiers. As soon as we finished eating, he rose, banged his tin dish on the table for silence, and introduced me. The noise died away for a moment as the astonished GIs, knife and fork in hand, looked up expectantly, waiting for the show to begin. I stood up and swallowed, for this is the actor's recurrent nightmare, to be up there, on stage, with no material. Somehow I found a few words to say to them about Hollywood. I apologized for not being Betty Grable or Alice Faye and I asked for questions; none came, so I sat down. It was one of my poorest performances. All afternoon I was taken round and lamely repeated myself on the drill grounds, the firing range, in the machine shops, the car pool, the hospital and every part of the installation, and when at long last I got to my bare little room at night, I took pencil and paper and cudgelled my tired brain for a joke, a story, anything to entertain, or even justify my presence ... I cursed the Hollywood Victory Committee which, with so much talent to draw upon, had not supplied me with a word of material.'

Spencer Tracy faced the same problem. Too old for service and unhappy at not participating in the war, he was at a boxing match, in 1943, when some sailors heckled him and accused him of being a draft-dodger. Lionel Barrymore suggested he should sing. When Tracy protested that he couldn't, Barrymore pointed out that half the

A concert to welcome Mexican troops to the Allied side was organized in Ensenada in 1942. Taking part in the revue were, among others, (roughly left to right) Irving Berlin (in striped suit), behind him Dick Powell, Joan Blondell, James Cagney, Jinx Falkenberg, Lupe Velez (behind microphone), Desi Arnez, Lucille Ball, Joan Bennett (black and white dress) and Hedy Lamarr (in skirt and jacket).

world would pay good money to hear him try. He did try and toured California before going to the South Pacific and Alaska for USO. After one concert, he was approached by a young GI. 'Gee, Mr Tracy,' he said, 'I'll bet you could really act if you tried. Have you ever thought of going on the stage?' Gary Cooper, off-screen a shy, private man, also overcame his fear of a live audience by singing when he went on a USO tour of the Pacific.

By April, 1942 USO Camp Shows were fully operational. Thirty-eight companies were overseas in Bermuda, Panama, Iceland and Newfoundland. One had got as far as Australia. In the States there were dozens of small units on tour. America's entry into the war brought a flood of applications from professionals and amateur entertainers anxious to break into show business. Several, including Dorothy Shay, the hill-billy singer, got their first chance through USO.

Fifty-six year old Al Jolson became the first USO star to visit a war zone when he went to Alaska early in 1942. The troops were told a great star was about to visit them and rumours swept the camp that it was Lana Turner or Dorothy Lamour. The disappointment could be heard miles away when Jolson was introduced. He started telling jokes until someone asked for a song, then another, then another. Jolson, who was going through a crisis in both his personal and professional life, had found where his audiences were. 'We gave two performances in Anchorage, each to an audience of 1,500 soldiers. Each show lasted an hour and I almost wore the knees out of my pants singing "Mammy" ', he told *Variety* on his return. But "Mammy" really got a workout the next day when Fried (Martin Fried, his pianist on the trip) and I gave nine shows, each of an hours' duration.' When news of his reception reached

116

The American Red Cross established entertainment units outside the US on its own premises. The Rainbow Corner in the heart of Piccadilly provided GIs and their guests with a place to meet and drink which was one of the most popular centres during the 'Yank invasion'. Welcome as the Americans were, they were still described as overpaid, over sexed and over here.

Washington, the War Department asked USO to arrange as many similiar tours as possible.

In August, 1942 Jolson led the first star party to Britain. With him were Merle Oberon and Allan Jenkins. The visit was not a total success. There was friction between the artists and although they were welcomed by the GIs their tight schedule left time for only two performances for British troops. After the publicity in the press preceding the visit the British were understandably disappointed and blamed Basil Dean and ENSA. The relationship between ENSA and USO was never the most harmonious. The US technicians and advance contingents of troops who had arrived in Northern Ireland in January, 1942 had been allowed to attend ENSA concerts but application was soon made to London for US forces to receive separate allocations of entertainments. This was agreed provided all shows were paid for, but the build up

of troops and billeting of American units with British ones made it impossible to segregate audiences. Dean's answer was a reverse of lend lease: US forces would receive ENSA shows if British troops could see USO entertainers. Early in the year Deanna Durbin offered to tour Britain for ENSA, an offer that was accepted and widely publicized. In February the visit was cancelled. The Hollywood press dismissed the visit as a publicity stunt staged to frighten her studio, Universal, into settling a feud over her contract; she claimed that her husband was being prevented from travelling with her; the British Embassy issued a statement defending her good faith and the American government tartly announced that there were thousands of troops at home who needed entertaining. The derision poured on Miss Durbin's head was comparable to that heaped on Gracie Fields by the British press. Deanna

Durbin, who spent most of the war touring for USO, was little more than a scapegoat for a feud that was raging between USO and the Red Cross over who should be providing overseas entertainment for US troops. Basil Dean, anxious to establish some sort of reciprocal arrangement with USO, sailed to New York in November to meet Abe Lastfogel, only to find Lastfogel had left for London. After many frustrating and unsatisfactory meetings, Dean concluded an agreement with the Americans that wherever ENSA was organizing entertainments, the US Army Special Services would act in collaboration. This never worked in practice. ENSA provided USO Camp Shows with equipment (seventy-five portable stages in 1943; one hundred and thirty-five in 1944) but British troops saw few American

entertainers. The first request for theatrical equipment received from the US Army at Drury Lane included several hundred portable stages and £5,000 worth of greasepaint. The row between USO and the Red Cross was finally settled by General Marshall, the US Chief of Staff, who decided that entertainment for US troops overseas would be provided by USO but that the Red Cross could continue to put on shows in their own clubs and hostels.

When it came to persuading the big stars to go overseas USO found it had a problem. Although many of them had gallantly offered their services earlier in the war, when USO put them to the test they were unavailable – their studios wouldn't release them; they were wanted for a radio show. Many of the most popular male stars had signed

Deanna Durbin, at the time of the war, was the highest paid movie star in the world, and like Bing Crosby, Joe E. Brown, Bob Hope and Jack Benny was tireless in visiting the troops throughout the US.

This musical adventure had its premiere in Blackpool. The woman in an otherwise all male cast was drum majorette Dorothy Gisser. Each member of the company had previously appeared in Broadway productions.

on. USO required a minimum of three months for an overseas tour to be worthwhile and few artists were prepared to sacrifice their careers for that long. One who did was Bob Hope. At the start of the war, Hope was already a star. In December, 1942 he went to entertain in Alaska, the first of four major tours, covering 200,000 miles, he was to make, which earned him the accolade from *Variety*, 'America's No 1 soldier in greasepaint.'

Two months earlier Edgar Bergen had taken Charlie MacArthur to the Aleutian Islands. On 22 December fifteen entertainers left New York by plane for the South Pacific. In February, 1943, ten performers travelled to the Middle East. By the spring of 1943 there were 119 USO units playing overseas. USO had divided its territories into four circuits. In the States there were the Victory Circuit, posts, camps and naval stations with 1500 troops or more; the Blue Circuit, for camps with

between fifteen and 1500 men, visited by five-handed shows; and the Hospital Circuit which started in March, 1944. Overseas was called the Foxhole Circuit, though the trip to Britain was renamed by the artists the Spam Circuit.

Overseas all USO shows became the responsibility of the US Army Special Services Division (Entertainment Section). USO would only supply artists for overseas service on a direct request from the War and Navy Departments. The company would be assembled in New York and given a try-out in front of local service audiences. Scripts were vetted by the Special Services Division for filth or racial jokes, and, once approved, could not be altered. Any artist who broke this ruling was subject to immediate dismissal. Once abroad the units came under the care of Special Services which provided food, accommodation, transport and audiences. All shows were free for US troops.

USO was not the sole provider of entertainment for the Services. Among the other tasks of Special Services was to produce GI shows to supplement the work of the professionals. It also helped those Army outfits which wanted to put on their own productions by supplying costumes, technical equipment, designing and building theatres and stages, and issuing a specially written manual called *At Ease*, which contained enough material for fifty shows. Many GI shows became full-time entertainments, touring the Foxhole Circuit, the most famous of which was Irving Berlin's all-male revue, *This Is The Army*. This began life on Broadway in September, 1942 giving public performances for charity and went on to tour in Britain (where it was seen by the Queen and the two Princesses), North Africa, Italy and the Pacific. Service units provided bands and orchestras and the American Red Cross produced plays with GI talent. Edward G Robinson made a visit to Britain in October, 1942 at the invitation of the Office of War Information to broadcast propaganda to Europe and entertain US Forces, giving a portrayal of Little Caesar.

'I was announced, I appeared, and the ovations were beyond anything I'd ever known,' he wrote later. 'What was I to do? No singer, I. No stand-up comic. No entertainer. Well, I'd been forewarned. What they wanted was not Edward G Robinson but Little Caesar. Accordingly, I had worked out, before I left, with the help of Jack Benny, whole idiotic routines, inevitably beginning with "Hey, youse guys," and including "Buy your beer from

Irving Berlin's highly successful revue This is the Army *was seen throughout the world theatre of the war. The veteran song writer himself (seen here with Noël Coward) always appeared in one number dressed in a facsimile of his WW1 uniform. He sang the famous 'Oh how I hate to get up in the Morning' from his own WW1 musical production* Yip Yip Yaphank.

me or else." I even took along a felt hat and a trench coat, and it didn't work very well until I remembered whole speeches from *The Racket*, a play in which I'd appeared ... I remember the opening of one of my earlier speeches at an Air Force base in the north of England. I began by saying, "I am happy to be here, the most privileged moment of my life, to see the men who are defeating Hitler." I have never laid so big a bomb in my life. I could sense the audience despising me. So that crazy actor instinct took over, and to stop the buzz of their boos and Bronx cheers, I ad-libbed, "Pipe down, you mugs, or I'll let you have it. Whaddaya hear from the mob?" There was an instant burst of high laughter and applause.' Also in Britain, Ben Lyon and Bebe Daniels, both domiciled in

London, helped form the American Overseas Artists Unit which travelled the country entertaining the forces and began to broadcast 'Stars and Stripes in Britain' coast-to-coast in the States.

Back in New York the American Theatre Wing organized plays to tour and gave away a thousand tickets a day for Broadway shows to men in uniform. A production of *Harvey*, starring Frank Fay, was sent to the Pacific. Katherine Cornell and Brian Aherne toured Italy, France and Germany in *The Barretts of Wimpole Street*. In Hollywood, in November 1942, Bette Davis and John Garfield opened the Stage Door Canteen, modelled on the one in New York. The Canteen had room for several thousand servicemen and every night served 2,000 cooked dinners, 10,000 sandwiches and enough coffee to sink a battleship. Stars like Marlene Dietrich worked long hours in the kitchen while Hedy Lamarr, John Loder, Betty

Hutton, Abbot and Costello and Judy Garland waited on table, and Betty Grable danced with soldiers and sailors. Other stars, like Dinah Shore, Bing Crosby and Frank Sinatra, dropped in to entertain. Early in 1943 the Victory Caravan set out on a three week tour of the States to raise money. On board the train were James Cagney, Cary Grant, Pat O'Brien, Laurel and Hardy, Bert Lahr, Groucho Marx, Charles Boyer, Claudette Colbert, Olivia de Havilland and Joan Bennett. The Victory Committee received complaints that a factory visit by Dorothy Lamour had slowed down production but she announced her determination to continue touring.

There was never any problem with finding entertainers willing to visit troops stationed in the States, but overseas was a different matter. Troops abroad never saw enough entertainment and it wasn't long before the same complaints that had

As one of their contributions to the war effort, Judy Garland and Marsha Hunt helped Joe Pasternak, the film producer, entertain ten members of the US Army Tank Corps on the set at the MGM Studios in Culver City.

one. Don't let yourself slip, don't try to fool a GI with a Hollywood face and very little talent; above all don't underestimate him by thinking all he wants is a leg show and dirty cracks ... Every woman back home wears a halo now and those who represent her had better keep theirs on too. I've heard a girl swear out here and sensed a roomful of men freeze for a second. Give them laughs but see that they are good laughs. Give them plays.'

In the beginning USO concentrated on small, go-anywhere variety companies that would give a 90 minute show usually directed and produced by the principal comedian, or a big star with a couple of supporting acts. As the war progressed it, too, discovered a demand for minority entertainment in music (Jascha Heifetz visited North Africa) and drama. GIs in London, making their first visit to a live theatre, pronounced themselves well pleased and announced their intention of going regularly to the 'live movies'. The big bands of Tommy Dorsey, Artie Shaw, Cab Calloway and Glenn Miller toured, along with musical shows and sports units. Joe Louis and Sugar Ray Robinson gave demonstrations mixed in with comedy routines, anglers showed how to fish, baseball stars made personal appearances. 170 artists visited hospitals in the battle zones to sketch the wounded for their families back home. Of the 5,424 salaried entertainers employed by USO during the war, 1522 were sent overseas in a total of 119 units. During its first six months, twenty-four USO Camp Shows gave 3,791 performances to audiences of two million. During 1945, over 151,000 performances were given to seventy-two million. By the end of the war USO shows had been seen by 172 million. And there still weren't enough.

After his UK concert tour, Glenn Miller took off on 15 December 1944 on a private flight to Paris to make arrangements for his band which was to follow. He never arrived.

been made about ENSA were being made about USO. The shows did not appear often enough, they were frequently of a low standard and too much material was 'blue'. 'Don't ever fool your-self, a GI wrote from New Guinea, 'that the GI audience in the S. W. Pacific, hungry for entertain-ment as it is, is not a discriminating and a smart

CHAPTER TEN

THE MIDDLE EAST

War came to the Middle East for no other reason than that two armies were there facing one another. From bases in Egypt Allied troops were guarding the Suez Canal; Italian forces were guarding their North African colonies in Libya, Cyrenaica and Tripolitania. After Dunkirk, Mussolini saw what he thought was the opportunity to pick up a few prizes for Italy and declared war on Britain. There being little strategic value in holding vast tracts of desert, the fighting began as a straightforward attempt by each side to annihilate the opposition.

The desert terrain in North Africa produced a form of warfare quite different from that on any

Christmas Day 1942. An impromptu celebration for the 8th Army in the Tripolitanian Desert.

other continent. An army could advance for mile after mile without making any significant gain and armed strikes had to be made over huge distances, far from bases and support columns. It was a highly fluid, mobile war in which the opposing forces surged backwards and forwards along the North African coast as each side gained the advantage.

Entertainment under such conditions had to be just as flexible with small, self-contained units that wouldn't get in the way but could go wherever needed. Not until May, 1943 after Rommel's forces had been defeated was it possible to organise entertainment on a large scale.

In July, 1940, the month Italy declared war, the Allied forces were being entertained by local amateurs and those Divisional and Regimental concert parties that had arrived with the first military detachments. In Palestine, where the 9th Army was garrisoned to secure the Mediterranean oil pipeline terminals, the RASC had its own concert party, *The Rascals*. Run by Gordon Turner, *The Rascals* were taken over by Naafi to play throughout Palestine and Egypt. In Cairo, Naafi also took over the routing of other Army shows: *The Muddle Easters*, *Nomads of the Nile* and *Middle East Varieties* which starred Norman 'The Mad Earl' Caley. Towards the end of 1940 two ENSA Parties, *Hello Happiness* (run by Reg

Gordon Turner, the tall man to the right, created the Rascals concert party which was one of the earliest groups to tour the remote units in the Middle East.

Lever who had taken a company on the first ENSA tour of England) and *Spotlights*, reached Cairo and gave a combined performance on 1 October, in the Opera House, before the C-in-C's of the British, Australian and New Zealand Forces. Lever then went to Palestine, *Spotlights* remaining in Egypt. For nearly a year these two companies, the Army shows and a handful of amateur concert parties were responsible for all entertainment in the Middle East.

In February 1941 Erwin Rommel arrived in Tripoli and the Germans became involved in the desert war. The armies of Generals Wavell and O'Connor, which had given the Allies virtual control of North Africa, were forced back into Egypt by the advancing Africa Korps. An area that hadn't seemed so important to ENSA and Army Welfare suddenly became vital. ENSA despatched an administration to take over from the Naafi in Cairo. Among those sent out was actor Noel Howlett who had joined ENSA as a stage manager.

'In spite of the warm welcome we were told was awaiting us,' he recalls, 'when we reached the Canal Zone no one knew we were coming and we had to make our own way to Cairo. The office there was in chaos. The major in charge wasn't the slightest bit interested in entertainment and two of the men who had been running things for him had to be sent home, one for embezzlement, the other for drunkenness.' The *Hello Happiness* company, whose whereabouts had been unknown to the office, hadn't been paid for nine months.

Stung by accusations that it had been falling down on its job, ENSA had decided to send out a star party in an effort to salvage its reputation. Sir Seymour Hicks, who, with his wife Ellaline Terriss, was on his way to lecture in South Africa for the British Council, agreed to stop over in Cairo and appear in the play *Sleeping Partners*. His co-star was to be the French singer-actress Alice Delysia. The play was never performed. When Delysia arrived on her own in Cairo the officer in charge of the ENSA office failed to meet her. Most of the time he ignored her and if they did chance to meet he was rude. He made it quite clear that she and other ENSA artists were an unwelcome intrusion. Delysia was furious. She threatened to return to London and reveal to the press and public how inefficient the Egyptian end of ENSA was. Fortunately for ENSA she didn't. Following so close on the fierce criticisms of its work in France and its chaotic endeavours to

Troops to whom her name meant nothing, hearing they were to see a top French star, groaned when a short, slightly dumpy woman walked on stage; she was not at all what they expected. Yet, within minutes, every one of the audience was in love with her.

Initially all entertainment was confined to Cairo, the Canal Zone and the fringes of the desert. Concert parties, even service ones, were kept to the rear of the action playing for the wounded and men withdrawn from the line to rest. The generals were reluctant to allow them too far forward for fear that a performance would destroy concentration. When General Montgomery took over the 8th Army in August, 1942 he would not allow women near the front lines. He felt they would be a distraction for men he was asking to commit themselves to possible death. For the first two years of the desert war not even nurses were allowed into the battle zone.

Once the 8th Army began its push west at El Alamein, in October, 1942, entertainers started to move out into the desert after it. Women, too, appeared in the most unexpected places. Travelling back down the line on leave a soldier was relieving himself in the customary manner, over the tail-gate of the truck, when a staff car, which had not caused him a second thought, went past. He found himself staring down into the faces of three grinning nurses. A party of girl singers entertaining the 4th Indian Division after the battle of El Alamein came face to face with a soldier naked in a tin tub, washing. He carried on. As far as he was concerned, women had no place on a battlefield.

Montgomery's refusal to allow women near his men until the fighting was over was due entirely to what he considered were the interests of his men. It had nothing to do with concern for the girls' safety. Indeed, they were often safer with troops in the desert than they were in Cairo and other large centres. The two dancers in one concert party were totally ignored; it was the female impersonator who attracted all the attention. An American combat unit turned down a visit from a USO all-girl troup; they had achieved a certain tranquility and had no wish to jeopardize it.

A common complaint throughout the war was that show girls were monopolized by officers and that other ranks rarely got the chance to talk to them. This inevitably led to rumours of impropriety, for the most part unfounded, according to Reg Lever. 'At a party after one show a very young

French-born Alice Delysia, who was a favourite in the West End in the years between the wars, became, for the men of the 8th Army, 'the greatest trouper of them all'.

provide a West African service, Delysia's revelations could well have killed off ENSA overseas. She was persuaded to stay by Rex Newman who had been put in charge of ENSA's Overseas Section and had flown to Cairo to try and sort out the muddle. At first she had refused to see him but his constant barrage of flowers to her hotel made her relent. Newman was severely lectured and heard ENSA torn to pieces. The offending officer was removed and Delysia agreed to stay. She topped the bill at two all-star concerts in Cairo, compered by Sir Seymour Hicks, then set off on a round of desert concerts and hospital visits that lasted for two-and-a-half years. Her ceaseless work entertaining the men she knew would one day free her homeland won her a place in the affections of all in the 8th Army who heard her.

All ENSA units were equipped with portable stages for their touring productions. This desert scene had its counterparts throughout the areas wherever members of the British forces were stationed. It was customary to put on several shows a day.

officer put his hand on the knee of one of my girls – on her suspender actually. She turned round and said, "What are you doing?" "I'm sorry," he said. "It's just that I never could resist meccano." Apart from that incident, which was really only a joke, I never had any trouble at all. We used to live out with the troops in the orange groves of Tunisia, in tents in the desert, and we never had any trouble. This was respect for the girls because it so happened I had very nice girls with me. I suppose if I'd had one or two tarty types we might have got that sort of thing, but I didn't have tarts. That's all there was to it.'

When girls appeared on stage in the desert, they did so, not as sex-symbols but as representatives of the women left behind. It meant a lot to the men to hear an English voice, to see a girl well-dressed and hear, first hand, what life in Britain was like. The most successful female entertainers were those with personality, prepared to spend time talking to the men. Artists leaving

Cairo for the first time were warned to handle the troops carefully, especially those who handed them a non-existent puppy to hold or asked them to say a few words to an invisible parrot on their shoulder. Sometimes, soldiers would just stare, nervous and tongue-tied. Once they had summoned up the courage to speak they would talk endlessly about home and produce lovingly-tattered photos of their wives and families. Dorothy Harbin, wife of conjuror Robert Harbin, remembers being asked to keep taking off her hat by a man who just wanted to recall what the movement looked like.

One thing that did upset troops was to see ENSA girls in Cairo being taken out by rich Egyptians and having a good time, because the Egyptians had the money and the soldiers didn't. Other girls upset men by consuming a week's ration of drink in an hour.

Cairo, the focal point of service administration in North Africa, untouched by the rigours of war, was filled with coffee shops, cinemas, night clubs and every hint of Eastern promise. In spite of official disapproval the city was a magnet to Allied troops. It was out in the desert, where the fighting was, that troops went without. Apart from not being allowed too far forward, entertainers had problems reaching units and staying close behind a fast and constantly moving front line. *Hello Happiness* was one of the few companies that managed to get off the beaten track.

'We had a caravan, the sides of which let down to make a little stage,' recalls Reg Lever, 'and we had black-and-white screens on either side to form wings. We also had a mini-piano which came with us everywhere and that was it. The girls lived in the caravan while the men scrounged a tent which we used to pitch alongside. The show itself was an hour-and-a-half, without interval, a good time because the men had to relieve themselves. It was non-stop variety: sketches, songs, trios, conjuring and comedy.'

Away from the safe areas of the Canal Zone performances were given during daylight. Lights at night would have attracted the attentions of the Luftwaffe. As it was some daytime shows came to a premature end when the stage was raked with machine-gun fire or the bombs started to fall. As the audience dived for cover when bombs fell close during an open air show Alice Delysia responded by waving a Union Jack at the planes and singing even louder. Jack Benny was shot at by his own side – and he wasn't even on stage!

Improvisation was the watchword for any desert performance. Felix Barker was sergeant in charge of the *Balmorals*, the concert party of the 51st Highland Division, when they arrived in the Western Desert.

'Up in the front lines, where we took the show,' he says, 'it was impossible to give a performance at night because no lights could be shown, nor during the day because of bombing. So we gave what we called Moonlight Matinees in the Wadis where the

The Balmorals concert party entertaining the Highland division in the western desert from the back of a captured German trailer. One of their most popular turns was Reginald Purdell's famous parody of Milton Hayes's poem 'The Green Eye of the Little Yellow God'.

soldiers were. We devised them purely in aural terms and they worked very well. We didn't bother with costumes or anything like that but put them on almost as if they were radio broadcasts. They showed that one didn't always have to have a proper stage and a proper theatre. The only time in the desert, before Tripoli, that we had a proper stage was on New Year's Eve, 1942. I was told that Sir Oliver Leese, the Corps Commander, was coming and the general wanted a show that would start about ten and go on until midnight, when we could all have our Hogmanay. I pointed out that this was going to be rather difficult because the Germans were still flying over and bombing anything that moved, and absolutely no lights were allowed to be shown. General Wimberly brushed this aside and said, "What is quite obviously wanted is a theatre. Build one." And, as can only happen when a general gives a command, a theatre was built, then and there, in the desert! A crater was dug in the sand and sandbags piled all around to build up the side walls. I had selected a gentle slope with a small dip in the ground and hundreds more sandbags were put in to form a semi-circle of tiered seats rather like a Greek or Roman amphitheatre. And, absolutely regardless of petrol shortages at the time, a truck was sent to Benghazi to bring back a marquee; a generator was found from goodness knows where. The marquee was thrown over the whole of this little amphitheatre and painted so that no light could get through, the generator was got to work, and we had our theatre.'

Although ENSA had started a regular Middle East service in July, 1941, with so few performers trying to entertain so many men dispersed over so large an area and continually on the move there were many troops who never saw a show during the three years of the desert war. Even a regular uniformed company, like *The Balmorals*, was unable to play continuously. Before the battle of El Alamein the group was turned into a camouflage squad, disguising ammunition as it came forward ready for the offensive.

For the majority entertainment was something provided by themselves and meant the usual joke-telling, sing-song or recitation amongst a few soldiers gathered in a circle. Only on a special occasion, such as Christmas, was an attempt made to put on a rehearsed show. Bill Stevenson was in a Signals Squadron that put on a desert perform-ance of *Dick Whittington*.

'The original script was supplied by ENSA but it was largely scrapped and adapted to meet the circumstances. Between the acts we had sketches dreamt up by members of the cast, which included the CSM. We also had a band of about eight, all Squadron members. Our theatre was a marquee, the stage being constructed from oil drums and any scroungable material. Dresses and costumes were improvised or made from anything we could lay our hands on. One excellent material was torn mosquito netting, dyed with mepachrine tablets and tea, and made up by handy needle users. We did everything by hand. The backcloths were designed and painted by a chap who'd been a theatrical designer in Civvy Street, using old tent cloth and camouflage paint. I've never seen anything since to compare with what he did. Stage lighting was constructed by Squadron engineers and used portable generators. We gave one performance and that was it.'

The humour in these desert shows mocked the Germans and laughed at the soldiers' plight. Occasionally it was vulgar but rarely was it obscene. The longer a soldier had been away from home the more nostalgic – puritanical even – his tastes became as he tried to remember the life he had left behind. Crude jokes about infidelity were worrying and not funny.

'Every show had its quota of rude jokes, of course,' remembers Roland Coombs who was a member of the *Kairotics*, an RAF concert party. 'Vulgarity, but not obscenity, was a regular feature of such entertainment. Community singing provided an opportunity for parodies of well-known songs and the only real obscenity I ever heard came from audiences at those gatherings, particularly if the Egyptian National Anthem was played. The words sung by the British soldiers left no doubt about their attitude towards the Egyptian monarch. The extraordinary thing about such a rendering was the benign way in which it was received by Egyptian onlookers. No doubt unfamiliar with English they accepted it as a genuine mark of respect. You can tell how wrong they were from this potted version ('Stanishwaya' is the Egyptian for 'wait a moment',):

> *Up your pipe King Farouk*
> *Hang your bollocks on a hook.*
> *Queen Farida is happy and gay*
> *Because she's in the family way.*
> *Stanishwaya, pull your wire,*
> *Up your pipe King Farouk.*

After El Alamein, the tide of success swept the fighting along the North African coast, away from Egypt, and ENSA set about getting its house in order to entertain troops left behind or waiting to be sent forward. A production centre was established in Cairo under scenic artist Bill Anson to prepare shows locally and assist the steady flow of companies arriving from West Africa and Britain. Many London-produced shows were considered unsuitable by Rex Newman. Shows needed to be simple and direct, with the minimum of clutter, and Newman spent much of his time re-producing. Noel Howlett, who had been managing a tour of an army production of *Night Must Fall* on the express orders of General Auchinleck, was asked to re-produce the first ENSA play to reach Cairo, with some of its cast missing. This was *George and Margaret*, in which Howlett had appeared in the West End. He became the official play producer for ENSA in the Middle East and put on twelve productions before his departure in 1945.

Much of the success, and failure, of ENSA overseas was related directly to the efficiency of local officers appointed to oversee the productions and make sure they were routed to the right places. Nigel Patrick was very critical of administration in the Canal Zone.

'I was stationed at Geneifa at the end of 1942. It was the sort of place you couldn't really see because it looked like next door. You couldn't tell where one place stopped and the other started. When I went to take up my Command, I found it consisted of a CSM and two clerks, that was all. Suddenly about a thousand bodies, who had to be sorted out and documented, would arrive from various convoys, so either one had nothing to do or one's twenty-four hours were filled with twenty-five hours work. Anyway, when things calmed down we had to try and find some way of relieving the boredom, so we got hold of ENSA. As no one knew where one placed stopped and another started, and as a show was told to go to No 5 Base Ordnance Depot with an Egyptian driver who didn't know what No 5 BOD was, other officers used to pinch the show on its way down from Cairo. As I was at the tail end of all this, we got very few shows. I got somewhat needled and complained bitterly. Having complained so much, I was told: "Join it and put it right."'

So Patrick joined ENSA administration. His first move was to double the amount of entertainment available by insisting companies play twice-nightly for units outside Cairo. The artists didn't

like it nor did the officers who had to arrange performances but since few shows lasted more than ninety minutes, it was relatively simple. To compensate the artists Patrick gave them Saturday night off. Not even a war could stop the traditional Saturday night booze-up and men either stayed in their Messes or went into Cairo; the last thing they wanted was to watch a concert party. For those who did want something more cultural than bars and brothels there were the popular 'Music for All' concerts and amateur groups.

By June, 1943 North Africa was in Allied hands and the desert war was over. Eyes turned across the Mediterranean towards Sicily and Italy. But before the strike was made at 'the soft underbelly of Europe' there was a period of preparation.

'It was quite obvious that the 8th Army was going to sit on its haunches for a bit prior to the invasion of Sicily and Italy,' says Richard Stone the agent, who had won the Military Cross at Aguila. 'I suppose because I'd been an actor and knew a bit about entertainments, I was taken to Divisional HQ, with Cecil Clarke, and we were made temporary Entertainments Officers while there was this pause in hostilities. We were based in Homs and our great asset was Leptis Magna, an enormous Roman amphitheatre with 7,000 seats, about a hundred miles outside Tripoli. We brought in Divisional concert parties, such as the *Desert Rats*, the *Balmorals* and the *Black Cats*, to play for a week at a time. Then we'd get a visiting ENSA party for two or three days. The one I remember in particular had Vivien Leigh, Leslie Henson and an all-star company. Or we'd cook up something ourselves. Microphones were quite unnecessary because the wind always blew in off the sea and you could stand on the stage and whisper, and every word would be heard by 7,000 people. We managed to get on something pretty well every night although, seating that number, we got through audiences very quickly. That lasted from two to three months.

'It was also decided that we should have a brothel in Homs. There was endless discussion as to whether it should be populated by the whores of Tripoli, whether it should be a medical or a welfare job to select these ladies, and who was going to bring them down. Eventually it was decided it should be both and I went to Tripoli on a lorry with a medical officer to collect them. I didn't have much to do with their selection which was entirely a medical job. I was only in attendance as the welfare representative! Bringing them back to Homs

Harry Brunning at the microphone in the concert party called Swingtime Follies *aboard the* Ark Royal *at Gibraltar. The production, the first to visit the Rock, went without any publicity because the Admiralty did not want to disabuse the Germans who had reported the aircraft carrier as having been sunk.*

they all wanted to have a pee, so we let them out of the lorry in the middle of nowhere. At that moment, the entire Highland Division appeared over the horizon, much to the Highland Division's glee, and we had to bundle the girls back into the lorry and beat a hasty retreat.'

For a brief spell, until the war swept them into Sicily and Italy, men who had not seen a live entertainer for three years suddenly had time, as did those who had wanted to do something but couldn't. Every available talent was recruited to help put on a show. Hospital staffs, convalescent centres, service units, and ENSA shows worked flat out to entertain. But given a moment to think, audiences began to wonder where their star favourites were and why they were not appearing.

One notable exception was *Christmas Party*, an all-star revue that flew to Gibraltar in December, 1942. Only Gordon Marsh's *Swingtime Follies* and one other ENSA show had visited the Rock before them. Organized by Hugh 'Binkie' Beaumont of

Tennant's (one management that made sure its stars played troop shows) *Christmas Party* contained 'the cream of the English Theatre': Sir John Gielgud, Dame Edith Evans, Elisabeth Welch, Jeanne de Casalis, Phyllis Stanley, Beatrice Lillie and Michael Wilding. During their four week stay they gave fifty-six performances (one on board ship to more than 2,000 men), visited hospitals and toured gun-sites talking to the men. Most shows were given in the island's Rock Theatre. When the curtains opened on the first performance, Edith Evans, dressed in the costume Oliver Messel had designed for her as Millamant in *The Way of the World*, stood ready to recite a poem written especially for the occasion. The audience, most of whom had no idea of what they were about to see, thought, since it was Christmas, it was a pantomime. They began to laugh. Dame Edith stood her ground until they fell silent then started to recite. As the words died away, the men exploded into applause, half in apology for their rudeness earlier, half because they realized they were in the presence of a great artist. The following acts went just as well and Gielgud, who was worried that Shakespeare might not be right, was given a rousing reception for his speech from *Henry V*, 'Once more unto the breach, dear friends.' A ship's captain told Gielgud that after the performance he had not had to deal with a serious crime for four days, the first time that had happened since the war began.

Once hostilities were over in North Africa, troops were accessible to stars flying in via Gibraltar or Morocco, and to companies sailing through the Straits. It was possible for an artist to fly in, play half-a-dozen major towns and return home within the space of a few weeks. This was a nice arrangement for those stationed in or near the towns and for the star who received the maximum publicity with the least inconvenience.

The first ENSA star company to reach North Africa was *Spring Party*, again organized by

Edith Evans above, in Gibraltar, costumed for her famous interpretation of the role of Milamant. Spring Party *was the first star company to visit North Africa and included Vivien Leigh, Beatrice Lillie, Richard Haydn, Leslie Henson, Dorothy Dickson, Kay Young and Nicholas Phipps.*

Vivien Leigh enchanted her audiences in wartime Tripoli with extracts from her most famous film role as Scarlet O'Hara in the legendary Gone with the Wind.

'Binkie' Beaumont, with Leslie Henson, Vivien Leigh, Beatrice Lillie and Dorothy Dickson.

'Perhaps my most vivid recollection of any show during the war,' says Roland Coombs, 'was sitting in an intolerably hot and overcrowded theatre in Tripoli watching Vivien Leigh on stage performing scenes from *Gone With The Wind*. As Scarlet O'Hara her cool, striking beauty was breathtaking. It aroused an aching nostalgia, a feeling of homesickness that almost shames me, even now, when I remember it.'

The *Fol-de-Rols*, revues, Geraldo and his Orchestra, George Formby, Noël Coward, Georgie Wood, Florence Desmond, Gracie Fields, *The Merry Widow* company with Cyril Ritchard, Madge Elliot and Diana Gould, Repertory companies, Emlyn Williams and his company, and many other individuals and parties followed *Spring Party*. A letter received by Emlyn Williams expresses how many felt on seeing such performers:

'I wonder, in spite of the rapturous reception you are receiving, if you really realize what it means to us to be able to see a company like yours? My own experience can, I know, speak for thousands of others. Since I left England I have seen nothing apart from a few concert parties . . . Time can dim the most vivid memories, however. It took a visit to *Blithe Spirit* to bring me to a full awareness of what I had been missing. The audience was different from any I have been in for a long time. It was more alive. I would like to convey to you and through you to the members of your company, my thanks for two of the best hours in three years.'

The big guns of USO were also beginning to fire. The Americans had entered the desert war in November, 1942 but the first entertainers had not arrived until February, 1943. That month, *The Sky Blazers*, the first US show to be formed from combat troops gave its initial performance in Cairo. Otherwise the US troops were like their British counterparts: they saw only the occasional ENSA show but mostly nothing. In May, Marlene Dietrich arrived to show her legs, sing and play a musical saw, closely followed by Bob Hope and Jack Benny. Benny was accompanied by Winni Shaw, Anna Lee and Larry Adler.

'We started in West Africa,' recalls Adler, 'and we were given our own plane which we christened 'Five Jerks to Cairo'. Our brief was to play only for Americans but I had been in England and knew the British well and I persuaded Jack to do shows for the Allies on Sundays, which were supposed to be our days off. Jack went down well everywhere. He was the most responsible entertainer I have ever known in my life. He insisted on doing a full two-hour show twice a day. Only twice do I remember a hostile audience. Once was when, through no fault of ours, we were held up and the audience had been kept waiting for several hours. While we were changing they started

Geraldo and his orchestra was the first top band to visit the Middle East. This concert on an airfield somewhere in the desert featured the singer Dorothy Carless. The Merry Widow toured North Africa and followed the invasion forces into Europe and featured Diana Gould (now Mrs. Yehudi Menuhin) in the cast.

singing filthy songs, the idea being to shock the girls in our troupe. When we came out they were very hostile. Jack always opened the show – there was no waiting for the star to appear – and he just walked out on stage and started his act. We finally won that audience over through his relaxed manner. The other occasion was also hostile and we couldn't understand why. It turned out that an entertainer who had been there the week before had kept telling them how lucky they were he'd given up his career in the States to play for them. It turned out he was being paid about 750 dollars a week! The troops hated to be patronized in any way. They referred to themselves as GIs and they didn't like the "Our brave boys" business one little bit. It didn't matter if we referred to the British troops as "boys" but we could never call the GIs that.'

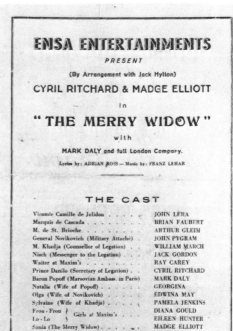

ENSA ENTERTAINMENTS

PRESENT

(By Arrangement with Jack Hylton)

CYRIL RITCHARD & MADGE ELLIOTT

In

"THE MERRY WIDOW"

with

MARK DALY and full London Company.

Lyrics by: ADRIAN ROSS — Music by: FRANZ LEHAR

THE CAST

Vicomte Camille de Jolidon	JOHN LFRA
Marquis de Cascada	BRIAN FAUBERT
M. de St. Brioche	ARTHUR GLEIM
General Novikovich (Military Attaché)	JOHN PYGRAM
M. Khadja (Counsellor of Legation)	WILLIAM MARCH
Nisch (Messenger to the Legation)	JACK GORDON
Waiter at Maxim's	RAY CAREY
Prince Danilo (Secretary of Legation)	CYRIL RITCHARD
Baron Popoff (Marsovian Ambass. in Paris)	MARK DALY
Natalie (Wife of Popoff)	GEORGINA
Olga (Wife of Novikovich)	EDWINA MAY
Sylvaine (Wife of Khadja)	PAMELA JENKINS
Frou-Frou } Girls at Maxim's	DIANA GOULD
Lo-Lo }	EILEEN HUNTER
Sonia (The Merry Widow)	MADGE ELLIOTT

Other stars followed: Humphrey Bogart, George Raft singing and dancing, Jascha Heifetz, Joe Louis and his boxing circus, Irving Berlin and *This Is The Army*.

The fighting may have been over in the desert and the Mediterranean may have been cleared of German ships and submarines but the war still raged in Europe and enemy planes flew in the skies. The first convoy to use the reopened Straits of Gibraltar after they were declared safe was attacked from the air. On board the last ship in the convoy were 122 ENSA artists.

'I was just going to have a bath before the second sitting for dinner,' remembers Chris Wortman, one of them. 'I'd taken off my jacket and just come out of my cabin in shirt and trousers, when – Zump! That's all I can say happened. It was just a zump. All the lights went out and there was horrible blue lighting around. The boat almost went on its side. I couldn't get back into my cabin since the door had jammed. Then it was action stations. After about twenty minutes, she more or

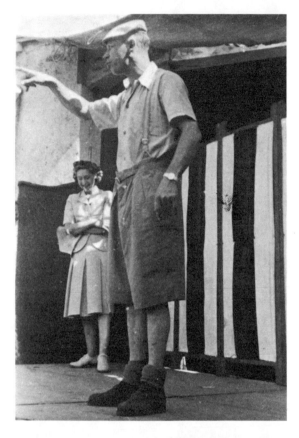

George Formby (and Beryl) in Cyrene was recalled by one soldier: 'I remember his long khaki shorts displaying the whitest knees ever seen in that part of the world'. Jack Benny (below, on the right) and Larry Adler, hand on hip, somewhere in North Africa.

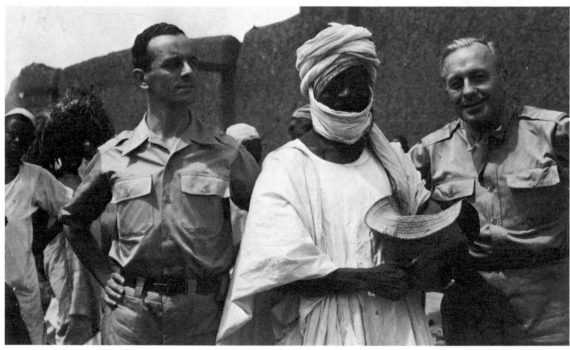

A REAL-LIFE DRAMA IN THE MEDITERRANEAN : The rescue by the Royal Navy of a large party of ENSA artists from an open boat after the ship in which they were travelling had been torpedoed by a German aircraft—*Drawing by Wm. McDowell*

less righted herself, enough for the lifeboats to be launched. We were told to go to lifeboat stations. There was no panic at all; we walked about like automatons doing what we were told. As I went up on deck there was an officer at all the hatchways where troops were saying, "I'll shoot the first man that moves!" That was a bit upsetting and I thought, It's them who are fighting the war, not us. But, I'm glad to say, we all got off safely.'

Ninety-seven people crowded into the same lifeboat as Chris Wortman and for half the night they floated around, drenched by rain, until their torches attracted a Royal Navy destroyer and they were landed at Phillipeville. At the bottom of the sea were their props, costumes and scenery. Other survivors were landed at different ports and it took some time before they could start work. Few companies managed to get together again and some girls suffered breakdowns and had to be returned to England.

Although everyone except those stationed in or near big cities like Cairo and Alexandria, com-

plained about the quantity and quality of entertainment, the one area of the Middle East that really was neglected was the Command known as Paiforce. Paiforce – Pai being typical Army abbreviation for Persia and Iraq – had been set up after the 1941 invasion of Syria, to safeguard our oil supplies. Centred on Baghdad, the Command stretched down to the islands of the Persian Gulf. It was a static force without a real war to fight. On some of the more remote stations the Artillery had not even been issued with live ammunition. Officers were forbidden to use a native tongue yet commanded troops that could not speak English. It was the only Command in which the unwritten rule of Army life, 'Never volunteer for anything', was consistently broken. Nothing the Army could find a man to do was worse than staying in Paiforce. A typical posting was Sharja, in the Gulf, several hundred miles from nowhere. During the summer, which lasted ten months, it was so hot that inhabitants used to joke there was only a thin piece of paper between them and Hell. One needed to be a masochist to take a shower; all the water was boiling, even if it came out of the cold tap. There was nowhere to go and nothing to do.

Upset by broadcasts from home that referred to them as the Parachute and Invasion Force, the Persia Aden and Iraq Force or, simply, Pay Force, the men of Paiforce felt abandoned. When shows eventually put in an appearance there were problems with the vast distances and poor communications.

'We were in Ahwaz,' says Reg Lever, 'when we heard that the Polish Legion was coming down from the Russian Front, passing through Persia and going on to the Western Desert. A signal had arrived to prepare for 30,000 Poles. This meant arranging bedding, tenting, food (cattle had to be rounded up ready to be killed because, of course, nothing kept in that heat.) They had only been given a period in which they would arrive, not a definite date. We went up to Andemiskt, which was only a posting station really with a few medicos, to do a show. They gave us a nice meal for which Rex Rashley, our conjuror, arrived all poshed up in his KD's, saying he'd had a wonderful bath. Everybody looked at him with astonishment and we found out he'd been in a bath of cold water which was their drinking water for the week. When we got back to Ahwaz the CO was in hysterics. I asked him what was wrong and he said it was the Poles. "Have they arrived?" I said, and he said, "Yes. They're over there." There on the ground were 30,000 telegraph poles!'

When the ENSA service to the Middle East started, it made little impression on the men in Paiforce. To visit troops there didn't have the same glamour as playing in the deserts of North Africa. Artists were reluctant to travel the huge distances involved, so far from the action they had told their friends and press agents they were going to see, and many fell mysteriously ill and had to return to England before they could complete the Paiforce leg of their tour. Bitterness against ENSA grew as week after week the local paper reported the cancellation of another star or company scheduled to tour the Command. Feelings ran as high as the standards of some companies that got through ran low.

Thoroughly alarmed, Basil Dean, who acknowledged the truth behind the criticisms, promised to take action. The news was greeted with the reply, 'You're three years late, Mr Dean!' Robert Harbin, who was in the Army as Major Edward Williams (his real name), was posted to Baghdad from Tobruk to salvage ENSA's tattered reputation and build up an entertainment service in Paiforce.

'Every couple of weeks I would meet the heads of Army, Navy and RAF Welfare,' he says. 'We would sit in my office, allocating shows and working out how to get them to places. The shows were all sent to Cairo and then routed up to me. I was told exactly what I could have – I could never just get shows I wanted – and what arrangements would be necessary; whether it was a big or small company, whether they carried scenery, whether they had to be billeted, whether there were more men than women, and so on. The biggest show we ever had was *No, No, Nanette* but most of them were small groups with a comedian, accompanied by his wife, probably, who was a soubrette, a juggler, a young conjuror and two little dancers. Very occasionally one had to bribe the RAF to transport people for you; bribe them by sending some girls for a dance or providing a band. If you did then you suddenly found three Dakotas at your disposal with Air Vice-Marshals to fly them!'

Even with Harbin in Baghdad pushing, chasing and cajoling, it was a struggle to persuade big stars to turn up. And, just as in the desert, men not stationed in the big towns received nothing. A handful of men guarding an oil well in Wafra or stationed several miles off a main route were inaccessible to a star or company that only had a week allocated for the entire Command.

'The greatest single artist I ever had was Joyce Grenfell,' says Harbin. 'Although I didn't meet them all, if I had to give a medal I'd give mine to her. We used to strap a small piano on the back of a lorry, put her and Viola Tunnard, her accompanist, in as well and off they went with just a sergeant. I never had any grumbling from them at all. Uncomplainingly they went round the whole circumference of Paiforce and entertained one man, two men, hundreds. She did an angel's job.'

Joyce Grenfell had been persuaded to join ENSA, the only means for a civilian entertainer to get overseas, by Noël Coward. Coward had visited Paiforce at the close of a Mediterranean hospital tour and what he had seen then had a profound effect as he recorded in his diary:

'Touring round these hospitals is certainly a salutary experience and I am profoundly grateful to have had the opportunity of doing it. No imagination, however vivid, could quite visualize the quality of these men. It isn't only their bravery in action, and, God knows, that's considerable

Noël Coward was one of the indefatigable and indestructable artistes who played to the services throughout the world. His concerts usually included his own mocking song 'Don't let's be Beastly to the Germans' which became a great favourite among the troops, despite the near condemnation of the number by the authorities.

enough; it's their magnificent capacity for overcoming, or at least appearing to overcome, the desolation, boredom, homesickness, pain and discomfort of lying day after day, week after week, and sometimes month after month, with nothing to do but swat flies, if they have an uninjured hand to do it with. Most of them have snap-shots of their mothers or wives or girl friends or children always close at hand so that they can look at them whenever they can bear to. Many of them haven't been home for two or three years. Some of them will never go home again. It is only after I have left the hospitals that any sadness comes into my mind. While I am there their own superb manners make any display of sympathy impossible. I can only hope that by just chatting with them for a few minutes I can at least temporarily mitigate their boredom and give them something to write home about; though why a man who has been through hell and carnage and been maimed for life should

derive any comfort from a few words with a healthy and successful playwright is beyond me.'

The troops he met were, he declared, men who 'deserved the best in the world.' On his return to Britain he did much to publicize their plight, especially in Paiforce. He suggested to Joyce Grenfell that a solo act was the best thing to take out and so she volunteered to work for ENSA's Hospital Section. Her first overseas trip took her and Viola Tunnard through North Africa, into Malta and Sicily, and finally to Paiforce. She was in the Command only two weeks on that tour but she covered two and a half thousand miles on the back of a lorry playing thirty nine shows (including nine in one day) one of which was to an audience of two. She appeared in hospitals, on gun-sites and in olive groves. She slept rough, at times on a deck-chair. It was under such conditions that she learned her art: when to be silent, when to make the audience laugh, when to be

137

Joyce Grenfell built up and established her repertoire of monologues and songs to the delight of the all but neglected Paiforce personnel. She and Viola Turnard toured tirelessly through dangerous terrain to the remote outposts of the war-weary men of Persia, Iraq and later India.

of talent and many careers first began to flower under the Mediterranean sun. One was that of Leslie Welch, a peacetime civil servant whose knowledge of accountancy had fitted him (the Army thought) to drive a tank. When his tank had been put out of action he had been sent back to Cairo.

'I was sitting in the Mess,' he recalls, 'feeling very cheesed off. I'd lost all my enthusiasm for the Army and was thinking about home. A sergeant major and another sergeant, both from Manchester, were having an argument about football. Neither knew what he was talking about and I couldn't stand it any more, so I said, "Excuse me, sir, but what actually happened in that match was that Mancester City beat Manchester United by three goals to two." And I went on to give them the scorers and the teams. There was a stunned silence while they tried to decide if I was taking the mickey. Then another sergeant, who'd got a little book of league tables, cup winners and so on, said, "Let's see if this cocky so-and-so knows what he's talking about." From that moment, Leslie

nostalgic. Her act comprised songs (anything sung by Vera Lynn or Rita Hayworth, standards, folksongs and her own compositions), monologues (about the society lady doing her bit by running a canteen, a piece she had to be careful not to do first, otherwise troops thought she was the society lady; and about ATS girls) and talking about any subject under the sun.

Individuals like Joyce Grenfell and Josephine Baker (who gave up her only chance to see the treasures of Tutankhamun to appear for men going on a special mission) did their best to make up for the stars who failed to make the trip, or only travelled with a first-class ticket. One entertainer refused all pleas to visit troops overseas; his reason, he couldn't find a dog-sitter for the time he'd be away.

As the fighting left the Middle East and moved back into Europe, the need to entertain those left behind increased rapidly. Official sources were unable to cope with demand; actors, musicians and entertainers of any description and experience were pulled out of their units to form new companies. It was a process that discovered a lot

Lines to a Remote Unit

When, at last, this desolate and bloody war is won
And the men who fought it, lived in it and died in it
Have done their job as best they could in rain and sand and sun
Without much time to take excessive pride in it;
When these heroic soldiers, sailors, airmen and marines
Are written of in poems, plays and stories.
The emphasis will be upon the more dramatic scenes
The sacrifices, tragedies and glories.
That this will be, that this should be is right and just and true
A very fitting Anglo-Saxon attitude;
But there are many fighting men stuck in one place like you
To whom we owe a lasting debt of gratitude.
It isn't only action, fire and flame that win a war
It isn't all invading and attacking.
It takes a lot of guts to keep your spirits up to par
When you know that the essential thing is lacking.
The battle area is wide, it stretches round the world—
There are islands, deserts, mountains, rocks and crannies;
There are many places where the flag of freedom's still unfurled
Where so many men are sitting on their fannies
And they, like you, just sit and wait, eternally prepared
Manoeuvering—parading.—doing courses;
They haven't even anything of which they need be scared
Except the nightly programme for the Forces!
They write long letters home and then re-write the things they
    wrote
Remembering the sharp eye of the censor,
And sometimes they are stationed in a place that's so remote
That they never even get a smell of E.N.S.A.
Try to remember now and then when browned off and depressed
And when you're feeling definitely out of it.
That everybody knows when it does come to the test
That you're ready and you're steady and you're primed to do
    your best
And that no one's ever had the slightest doubt of it.

Noël Coward

Noël Coward wrote this tribute to the men of Paiforce and it was published in Trunk Call.

Elizabeth Parry was voted sweetheart of Paiforce in appreciation of her work amongst them as the featured girl singer in the RAMC band. Dorothy Harbin (on the right), joined ENSA hoping to see her husband who was in charge of the entertainment forces in Baghdad.

Welch the Memory Man was born. I did my first show a few days later. A sergeant, who had been a dresser for Flanagan and Allen, had got together a concert party called *Out of the Blue*. The trumpet player, who didn't want to play in the band, was in the canteen knocking them back when his sergeant came in, livid, looking for him. He found me, surrounded by soldiers, answering questions. "I want you to come along to rehearsal," he said. "Not on your nelly," I replied. "I'm an established civil servant and I'm not allowed to speak in public. Me on stage? You must be joking!" "Please yourself," he said, "because if you don't come you're going to be on fatigues for the rest of your natural life." I said, "I'll come." '

Welch's encyclopedic knowledge of sports (he also answered questions on history and geography) appealed to the nostalgia the men felt for wet winter afternoons on the terraces. It was an easy act to stage, requiring no more than him and an audience. When a ballot was held to choose the favourite service and civilian acts to appear before Lord and Lady Tedder, he came third. The show was held at the Jeanette Watson Hut, Cairo, and the first time his name appeared on a poster, the printers got it wrong. He was billed as Trooper Tommy Welch, Memory Man.

Welch was seconded to ENSA and was then posted to Paiforce to do accounts by day and entertain at night, travelling there with Georgie Wood and Dolly Harmer who were nearing the end of their Middle East tour. His arrival in Baghdad coincided with that of Robert Harbin and while Harbin was getting to know his territory they teamed up in an unofficial two-man show, *Magic and Memory*. They worked together for nine months until Welch left for Italy. Also in Paiforce at the time was William Budd, mentor to *The Muddle Easters* and *Nomads of the Nile* in Egypt, with a brief to recruit uniformed talent for two Army shows to tour the Command. Among the men who answered his audition call was John Arnatt, suffering a posting on the mainland opposite the island of Abadan.

'I gave my lecture on The Rifle again,' he says, 'and was accepted at this vast public audition for which literally everyone in the Command had put in. I was immediately transferred to Baghdad which was marvellous, just what I wanted. We started to rehearse every day for the concert parties. We kept on rehearsing for about three months, getting nowhere, and then I left. While I was in Baghdad, King Faisal had a birthday party and wanted a conjuror; he was ten. Bob Harbin was, of course, the best, but he was ill and wasn't able to appear. Bill Budd was also a conjuror, of sorts, and Bob said to him, "You'll have to go on." Bill didn't know a good trick to finish so Bob told him to end with paper-tearing: making shapes from one piece of paper. "I don't know paper-tearing," said Bill. "Don't worry," Bod said. "I'll mark the paper and you just tear along the marks. It'll be all right." Bill did this, tore along the lines Bob had marked – and threw away the wrong bit! When he opened up the paper, instead of there being a little line of figures, all he had was a mass of torn holes.'

Similar attempts to produce local shows were being made in Egypt. Ralph Reader showed up to rehearse RAF units along Gang Show lines, while actor Torin Thatcher persuaded Army Welfare to let him set up Field Entertainment Units. Helping him were fellow actors John Woodnutt and Nicholas Selby, and a sergeant from the REME, Arthur Lowe.

Before the war Arthur Lowe had been working for Fairey Aviation. A keen rider, he signed on with a cavalry regiment in 1938. As soon as war was declared, the regiment was mechanized, lost its horses, and Arthur Lowe ended up in Egypt.

'My first contact with entertainment had been in Rafah on the Gaza Strip. There was a big Ordnance Depot there where the only form of entertainment was an open-air cinema. You couldn't go to that every night and you couldn't get pissed every night, so, since some of the chaps were sand-happy and there was nothing else to do, I hit on the idea of doing a play. I don't know why because I had had no experience apart from acting in plays at school. We got together a few keen people, stole or scrounged the wood to build a stage, and put on *The Monkey's Paw*, a one-acter. After that, wherever I was moved, I used to start a play group or play-reading group, and I also helped produce some revues. When Torin Thatcher asked if I would like to join his new units I said, yes, I would. What we did was to form a unit with an officer, a senior NCO, an NCO, a driver and a spare hand, and our job was to go out to lonely places in the desert and help them put on their own shows. We weren't allowed to play

ourselves, just help produce, stage manage or give them tips on how to build scenery. Since by this time there was a fair amount of stuff available in Cairo, if they wanted to start a small band, we could even provide them with instruments.'

The Field Entertainment Units were based in the major towns. Another Unit was taken over by John Arnatt. After his three months of rehearsing without performing in Baghdad, he had been hospitalized in Cairo. When he was discharged, Torin Thatcher invited him to become officer in charge of the Cairo Unit. In one of his shows was an unknown conjuror making a virtue of the fact that his tricks didn't always work.

'His name,' says Arnatt, 'was Tommy Cooper. He had not done anything before the FEU's, certainly not as a professional. It was in the desert that Tommy picked up the fez which has since become his trademark. His act then was exactly the same as today – conjuring that goes wrong with all the gags in between; same laugh, same everything. He was a bastard to be with as an officer because he delighted in getting you up on the stage to help him out and then he would take the mickey out of you something terrible. He had the entire audience on his side and if you weren't careful you came out of it looking none too dignified.'

Arnatt, like many servicemen who had been professionals before the war, was also loaned to ENSA to help with plays, revues and concert parties produced with local uniformed talent and visiting ENSA artists. Edward Stanley managed to put on a season of Shaw plays in Alexandria. Arthur Lowe, having got a taste for the stage, left the Field Entertainment Units to start a fort-nightly repertory theatre above the Pay Corps office, also in Alexandria, with Martin Benson, Neil Wilson and Henry Manning. For those lucky enough not to be sent into Europe or to the Far East to continue fighting, the lack of entertainment was a blessing. It gave the professional an opportunity to ease himself back into his profession, perhaps even try something new. It gave the amateur a chance to practise the craft he hoped to follow in a civilian life everyone knew could not be far away.

CHAPTER ELEVEN

BACK INTO EUROPE

THE ITALIAN CAMPAIGN

With the desert war over, the Allied leaders were faced with a problem: what to do with their battle-hardened, eager troops? General Marshall, the US Chief of Staff, favoured sending them to Britain in readiness for one massive strike against Western Europe even though there was unanimous, if reluctant, agreement that an invasion of France could not be mounted until 1944. Churchill, on the other hand, was keen to invade Europe through the Balkans. A compromise was reached. The Allied entry into Europe would be made through Sicily. If the campaign went well they would go on to invade mainland Italy. If not, they would be diverted to Sardinia and Corsica.

On 10 July, 1943, the 8th Army under Montgomery and the 7th Army under Patton landed in Sicily. By mid-August the island had been captured and the decision was made to strike on into Southern Italy. On 3 September Allied forces crossed the Straits of Messina and landed at Reggio di Calabria. Although the Italians surrendered the same day, hoping to save their country from total devastation, it was to take a further two years of hard, bitter warfare to dislodge the Germans.

During the invasions of Sicily and Italy and the months that followed there was little time for the unit performer to think about entertaining. Apart from an occasional impromptu concert (Harry Secombe's unit managed a few in Sicily while waiting to be sent to Italy) or a hastily thrown-on pantomime at Christmas, entertaining became the prerogative of the official organizations.

Among the first stars to reach Sicily were Jack Benny and Bob Hope, whose shows had been playing in Tunis. Hope arrived with his troupe three days after the fall of Messina and, on a football pitch at Palermo, immediately gave a show for 16,000 men. After it, Hope and his company were invited to dinner by General Patton. Patton deliberately hadn't attended the performance, thinking his presence might inhibit the men, so the troupe ran through their acts for him. As they were about to leave, Patton called Hope to one side. 'You know,' he said, 'you can do a lot for me when you get back home. I want you to tell the people that I love my men.' It was only when Hope got back to his hotel and discovered that Patton had struck a young soldier in hospital, accusing him of cowardice, that the general's words became clear.

The first British star into Sicily was George Formby. Formby wasn't much interested in playing for the battle-weary troops. His driving ambition, and that of his wife Beryl who went everywhere with him, was to be the first performer to reach Italy. He left behind a lot of disgruntled men when he cancelled the arrangements made for him to play to the 51st Highland Division and bribed his way across to the mainland. The Western Brothers were also criticized for trying the same trick and the sudden appearance of entertainers in the front lines in Italy, at a time when they were least welcome, did nothing to enhance ENSA's reputation with the top brass.

On 20 September Gracie Fields arrived in Sicily and made a surprise appearance at a hospital

Unquestionably George Formby and Gracie Fields were amongst the most popular artists to appear before the troops in the European and North African campaigns. They were swamped by appreciative audiences who could not have enough of them. Soon after the Italian invasion by the Eighth Army, George Formby sang his ribald songs before a huge gathering which included General Montgomery and Gracie Fields made an unexpected flying trip to a welcoming reception by the troops in Sicily.

show with Waldini's band. 800 people filled the hall. In the centre, with their nurses, were the seriously wounded and the stretcher cases. 'A breathless pause when Waldini announced Gracie,' wrote Virginia Vernon in her report to Drury Lane. 'They did not know if it was true or not. A continuation of this breathless pause when she walked on stage. They could not believe their own eyes. Then applause. She made them roar with laughter for half an hour, then sang 'Ave Maria' and had us all in tears. Then gave them a laugh to finish. Those wounded boys and everyone will always remember this Gracie Fields appearance.' In spite of playing to more than 60,000

men during her ten days on the island, Gracie's sudden departure for the States plunged her into the middle of an enormous row. In an interview with *Crusader*, the 8th Army newspaper, she had declared that the 8th Army had saved Britain and she wanted to stay with them for the remainder of the Italian campaign. The Army took her at her word and was bitterly disappointed when she cancelled her tour following pressure from her husband to return to the States to begin work on a new radio series. 'You and the rest of the top-liners have let the fighting soldier down,' complained a sergeant in a letter to *Crusader*. 'Blame it on ENSA if you like. Most of you do.' The letter was instantly condemned by the British press as being ill-advised, unfair and unchivalrous, but it did provoke a reaction. An MP raised the matter in the House of overseas entertainment and Tommy Trinder, one of the stars singled out for criticism, announced his intention of flying out in the New Year. Other stars who had been reluctant to become involved with ENSA also declared their availability for overseas tours.

The invasion itself did not go as smoothly as had been anticipated. Far from being the soft under-belly expected by Churchill, Italy was proving to be a very stubborn limb. The Adriatic coast as far north as Bari had been secured within two weeks, but at Salerno, on the west coast, where the Allies had landed on 9 September, it had taken seven days to secure the bridgehead. Kesselring, the German commander, pulled back to north of Naples and put up the first of his defensive lines along the River Volturno, determined to make the Allies pay dearly for every inch of Italian soil. The Allied advance reached Naples and ground to a halt. The entertainers moved in behind the front lines and began the task of amusing the troops.

As far as ENSA was concerned the invasion had gone well. With so many artists and administrators waiting in North Africa there had been little delay in getting entertainment to the front. Its forces had been divided into two columns and sent, one to Bari, the other to Salerno, and the slowness of the advance had made it easy to keep up. That's not to say that there weren't difficulties. The accusation of blue material raised its head again and there were constant crises of administration, but the major problem was the weather. It was winter by the time most performers reached Italy and ENSA hadn't realized that a winter there could be more severe than one in northern Britain. The countryside was blanketed by snow as

Diana Gould played Frou-frou as a soubrette and spoke most of her own outrageous lines in French which roused the Egyptian audiences to raucous laughter, to the bewilderment of those who could not understand.

companies arrived from North Africa equipped for the desert and artists arrived from London wearing khaki shorts and solar helmets. Lorries got stuck on impassable roads. Sandy Powell took eight hours to travel seventeen miles and the *Lucky Dip* company was marooned three days and three nights in fourteen foot drifts.

Diana Gould, who was playing Frou-Frou in Cyril Ritchard's production of *The Merry Widow*, recalls their arrival in Italy. 'We had been in Egypt for a month and we arrived at Taranto, at five in the morning, in an icy gale after a three day stormy crossing from Alexandria. Vesuvius had chosen that very moment to erupt and was showering us with pitch-black rain as we stood shivering on the quayside. We went to Bari to find that a recent raid on the harbour had shattered every window in the opera house, that no door would shut and the patched roof, mainly open to the sky, was letting in light squalls of snow. Madge Elliot, as the Widow, gave the entire show in her mink coat – looking ravishing with her osprey hat, I might add

– whereas I, as that inferior animal the dancer, could hardly expect the audience to accept a khaki duffel-coat over my tu-tu and was forced to fly around the stage flapping my arms like some elderly bird, a genuinely frozen smile on my face. It was torture, but with between three- and four-thousand soldiers packing the house, wrapped in their greatcoats, on a twenty-four-hour leave before returning to Campobasso to meet an almost certain death – that was why we were there. One exquisite moment I remember: we only took eight boys and girls with us and Cyril would borrow girls from the Naafi canteen to dress the stage for the final elegant scene in Maxim's. They were placed around the stage in beautiful off-the-shoulder dresses, with their hair up and lovely hats on. One night, in the quietest part of the duet between the Widow and Prince Danilo, one of these girls, shoulders sticking out of her tulle dress like a sentry, suddenly dived a large red paw into her bosom, drew out an immense and very dirty khaki handkerchief and proceeded to trumpet into it for the rest of the duet.'

It had been planned that *The Merry Widow*, and other similarly large touring productions, should go on to appear in Rome which the Allies confidently expected to take by Christmas. The Eternal City was not, in fact, in Allied hands until June, 1944 and Naples, which had been captured on 1 October, became the headquarters for all ENSA and USO operations. The US Special Services had immediately taken over theatres for live shows and started a programme of films. By the time ENSA arrived, in mid-November, there were only two theatres still vacant, the San Carlo Opera House and the Bellini. Much to the annoyed amazement of Drury Lane, local ENSA officials declined to use the San Carlo, which they thought would not be right for concert parties, and took over the Bellini, a much larger, less convenient theatre. The first show in, a concert party, was a disaster. After three days the cast took to its beds suffering from 'flu and depression and were replaced by an equally disastrous all-male band show. The Bellini was closed temporarily until it could be filled by a pantomime (the first ever seen in Naples) starring Victoria Hopper, Inga Anderson and Waldini and his band.

The San Carlo was reopened by the military authorities in November with an Italian revue complete with dancers wearing brassieres and G-strings, a band playing the latest swing numbers and a tenor singing 'Come Back To Sorrento'.

This was followed by *Flying High*, an RAF revue, *The Road To Rome*, an Allied show, and several other companies including Humphrey Bogart's USO troupe. The opera season belatedly began on 26 December with a performance of *La Bohème* and ran continuously until the end of the war with the exception of two weeks in 1944 when Irving Berlin's *This Is The Army* moved in.

North of Naples the fighting was at its fiercest. Stubborn German resistance, helped by the difficult mountainous terrain and fast-flowing rivers which were virtually impassable under heavy fire, made Allied progress painfully slow.

The grim realities of the life-or-death struggle demanded laughter. Two soldiers found themselves in hospital beds next to each other. 'Hello, Bill,' said one. 'Come in here to die?' 'No,' said the other, 'I came in yesterdie.'

But it wasn't just comedians troops wanted to see; it was any production of quality that would take their minds off the war and remind them of

The Canadian singer Inga Anderson decorated her sleeves with badges from most of the units she entertained.

Once Tommy Trinder went overseas to visit the troops he was energetic and appeared before the men wherever he could. He entertained them with gusto and visited emplacements to boost morale at the front lines.

home. Emlyn Williams's production of *Blithe Spirit* played to enthusiastic audiences wherever it went. 'The theatre in which I saw it,' recalled Victor Fawkes, a soldier, 'was very close to Cassino when the struggle for that unfortunate town was in full spate. I had just come down from the line, tired and dirty, and I entered the little theatre just as the performance was starting. It was traumatic because suddenly the actors were very real people, behaving in a manner that one had forgotten. I had been a private in North Africa and fought up Italy and to see people sitting in armchairs, to see them behaving as though in that other world we almost believed had ceased to exist, was a very emotional experience.'

To the south reinforcements arrived steadily, among them Joe E Brown, Hermione Baddeley,

Florence Desmond, Cicely Courtneidge and Tommy Trinder. Trinder, making up for not playing overseas earlier, threw himself into his work. 'An enormous success,' reported Virginia Vernon, 'the first star to play a really forward 5th Army location, British troops, and some of those who heard him are still talking about him. His material was often vulgar but his expert artistry in putting it across to the boys, and selling himself to them too, made it difficult for anyone to object or resist the fun.' Judy Shirley and Inga Anderson, a Canadian cabaret artist who, with just a pianist, was hitching her way round playing to troops wherever she found them, came in for similar praise. One person who did not was Leslie Henson. He and his star party had arrived in Italy before they were expected, owing to Henson

One of Stars in Battledress favourites was Tommy Godfrey (facing the microphone). Freddy Fowler and a bemused accompanist watch his hilarious French cook routine in Italy in 1943.

altering their routing himself. 'Because of bad weather,' commented Virginia Vernon, 'instead of flying across Italy from one Army to the other they had started across the mountains in an Italian civilian coach and had got stuck in the snow in a mountain village on one of the highest ridges. I went out to them next day taking all sorts of comforts. The only things they wanted were the whisky and gin that I had brought. They based their appreciation of all hospitality on the amount of alcohol provided. The troops did not like the show as much as an ordinary concert party. Henson was much criticized for having brought no new material at all.'

Italy gave many artists their first real taste of battle. Performers wandered across German lines while looking for audiences, came under fire, were shelled and bombed, and suffered all the hardships of living close to the front. Sandy Powell played a theatre on the Adriatic coast one night only to see it reduced to rubble the following day, while a

Stars In Battledress show was strafed by a German fighter. Kenny Morris was on stage as the bullets sliced it in half. He passed out. Such close proximity to the fighting proved too much for some stars whose main purpose in visiting Italy had been to attract personal publicity or avoid unfavourable comment at home. Leslie Welch, posted to ENSA in Naples from Paiforce, was detailed to accompany a "personality" to Anzio.

'Anzio was deadlocked at the time. We'd got the bridgehead but the Germans had surrounded us and we couldn't break out. We travelled up there in a tank landing craft and I was very sea-sick. When we landed, we had hardly walked fifty yards up the beach when the Germans started their first really intensive barrage for about two weeks. This star said to me, "I can't stand this. I'm going back to Naples right away." Which he did. But having gone through the tortures of that sea journey for five hours I wasn't going back for anyone. I spent the night under a gun-carrier.'

The next morning Welch met streams of troops heading for the front or returning for a rest. By the roadside he began to ask questions – 'Anybody from Manchester? Which team do you support?' – and was soon in the middle of his act, an impromptu performance which earned him a mention in despatches.

Tommy Godfrey, in Italy with a Stars in Battledress unit, was in the audience the night another top artist, later decorated for his work overseas, was due to give a concert north of Naples. 'We weren't working that night so we went along. We sat in the theatre waiting for him to arrive. When he finally got on stage a bomb fell about three miles away. "Come along, come along," he said, "we can't stay here. Back in the coach." And he and his company got in their coach and went back to Naples leaving a theatre full of soldiers waiting to be entertained. Of course we couldn't leave them sitting there so we went up and gave them our show.'

Fortunately such behaviour was rare. The majority of artists, famous and unknown, stuck to their job. When a bomb fell close to the building in which a Stars in Battledress Play Unit was performing *Someone at the Door*, Faith Brook, who was on stage, put out a hand to steady the rocking scenery and finished the scene to cries of 'Had your wheaties for breakfast?' The Play Unit had been sent to Italy with a repertoire of three plays.

'The idea was doomed from the beginning,' says Faith Brook, 'because we were playing to a moving population even in the towns. We could have stayed put in one place and done the same play week in, week out, and had a different audience every time. So, although we had taken three plays with us, we never did the others except when we got to Athens.'

The Athens visit came about because of Nigel Patrick, ENSA's man in Naples. When Greece was liberated his territory, which covered Italy, Sicily, Sardinia, Corsica and parts of North Africa, was extended to include it. He immediately went to Athens to find out what was wanted and was offered the use of the National Theatre, the hallowed shrine of Greek drama, provided he maintained the tradition of only the spoken word. 'I said, of course,' he recalls, 'and went back to Naples absolutely delighted, only to realize we didn't have enough big companies that didn't sing or dance. At that very moment, Stars in Battledress had sent out a very distinguished company with

John Longden, Geoffrey Keen, Faith Brook, Kenneth Connor and others. They were on their way to Bari on a bitterly cold day and we had them stopped at a road block and ordered to return to Naples. I've never seen a more livid, disgruntled lot of people in my life. Their faces changed completely when I told them they were going over to Athens.'

The Play Unit appeared in Athens for a month, then returned to continue its tour of Italy, playing in the out of the way towns most of which had a small theatre or opera house. Few had escaped the ravages of war. Roofs had been blown off, windows were smashed and facilities destroyed, but as long as the walls were intact the buildings were taken over. When lights failed, which was often, performances continued with the audience shining torches at the stage.

The design of most Italian opera houses follows the same pattern: tier upon tier of boxes. The best tiers were invariably reserved for officers and their ladies while other ranks filled the stalls and the levels above. During intervals the men indulged in their own form of entertainment. 'These were known as French Letter Ballets,' recalls David Benson, a marine who made occasional appearances on stage with a knife-throwing act. 'The OR's in the upper boxes would blow up their army-issue contraceptives like balloons, then drop them. Because of the heat rising these would float

Geoffrey Keen, who later gained fame in the TV series The Troubleshooters, *and Clive Brook's daughter, Faith, toured Italy and Greece with the Stars in Battledress play unit.*

down gently and by some quirk of the air currents always seemed to be drawn into the boxes where the officers sat, chatting up their ladies. It used to be very funny watching the officers try to beat them out before the girl he was trying to impress had seen them. Once, the CO was so annoyed he ordered the house lights to be put out. Everyone in the stalls then switched on his torch and these things were followed all the way down.'

The majority of performances took place far from theatres. 'Picture a long, raftered room,' a soldier wrote home, 'stone floor, light from two electric bulbs each end, long lines of beds, chaps in all sorts of positions, frames over legs, masks over faces, some very pale, some smoking; trestles with stretchers, on one a lad still under anaesthetic, another just arrived, asleep with morphia, a group standing together, able to walk. From the tents outside, nurses and orderlies. Two beds moved to one side, a piano inserted, and moving up and down among us all a sweet, most attractive girl, perfectly natural, charming voice, addressing herself to the chaps in turn, singing "Trees" and all the songs they like.'

The girl was Patricia Burke, the singer and actress who had just begun to make a name for herself with her first West End lead in the stage production of *The Lisbon Story*. Rather than tour with a company she had taken the advice of Joyce Grenfell and was playing in hospitals and to isolated units with just a pianist.

'The greatest problem I ever found abroad,' she recalls, 'was that men often forgot women need to go to the loo. They never made any provision for it. I was given a caravan to sleep in one night and, my plumbing requirements having been forgotten as usual, I was planning to creep off into the bushes after dark when no one was around. The only trouble was they were so concerned for my safety a Gurkha had been put on guard outside the caravan with orders not to allow anyone in. And he wouldn't let me out either! He didn't speak English, just kept smiling at me, refusing to let me pass. So I had to stay in and suffer. This story got round and the next unit I visited the officer who was looking after me kept saying, "Do you want to visit the, er er?" I kept saying no but eventually I had to, even though I didn't want to, so as not to hurt their feelings – they had built one for me!'

It was individual artists like Patricia Burke, and the small go-anywhere concert parties prepared to leave the towns and search out audiences, who earned the soldiers' gratitude most. 'It has not been the famous stars with everything laid on for them,' wrote *Crusader's* entertainments editor, 'who have given us the best entertainment. It has not been the big stars either who have stopped at all sorts of out-of-the-way places to give impromptu concerts to troops who have been cut off from civilization for months. The small concert parties have done that.'

The Allies finally entered Rome on 4 June, 1944 just two days before the invasion of Normandy. A campaign which had been expected to last three months had lasted almost a year. Although grim fighting lay ahead, the fall of Rome signalled, for the first time, that the end was in sight. There was a chance for the men to relax, to go sight-seeing, to watch a film or show in comparative comfort. Guide books on how to see Rome in three hours were issued by Army Education and lectures on Roman history and archaeology were arranged, and well attended. There were galleries to visit, bars, restaurants and night clubs. For men taken out of the line to rest, life in Italy had some compensations. For those still engaging the enemy there was a very real war on and it came as a shock to hear that Lady Astor had publicly described them as 'The D-Day dodgers, sunning themselves in Italy.' Lady Astor emphatically denied making the remark, which turned out to be part of a German propaganda campaign (the same campaign which had showered British troops with leaflets showing GIs in Britain getting up to all sorts of unmentionable things with wives and girlfriends). It backfired completely. The taunt was taken up and used as the basis of a lyric, sung to the tune of 'Lili Marlene', and became one of the most popular during the final year of the Italian campaign, sung at every concert and sing-song and by many men during the final offensive. Called 'The D-Day Dodgers', the last two verses ran:

Dear Lady Astor, listen hear to this,
Don't stand on a platform and talk a load of piss.
You're the nation's sweetheart and its pride,
We think your mouth is far too wide –
From the D-Day Dodgers, out in Italy.

Look around the mountains, in the mud and rain,
You'll find the scattered crosses, some which bear no name
Heartbreak and toil and suffering gone,
The lads beneath them slumber on.
They're the D-Day Dodgers who'll stay in Italy.

Christmas 1944 was celebrated by countless unit revues and pantomimes. Numerous Cinderellas, dressed by courtesy of the local opera house, appeared in theatres and Messes, and many uniformed artists made their first stage appearance since landing in Italy.

More companies and star names were brought out from Britain and the States. Irving Berlin arrived with *This Is The Army*; Katherine Cornell appeared in a Broadway production of *The Barrets of Wimpole Street* with Brian Aherne as Robert Browning; Jascha Heifetz, Barbirolli, Bebe Daniels, a big-game fisherman who lectured on the art of sea-angling, and Phil Silvers began to tour. Phil Silvers had with him in his company a young singer called Frank Sinatra. Sinatra was then very unpopular with the GIs who resented the adulation he was getting back home and the fact that he wasn't in uniform (he was medically unfit for service). Silvers hoped that his appearance overseas would help stem some of the criticism. It was only partially successful. Most GIs remained coolly indifferent and it was only after the war that they remembered they had been entertained by one of the greatest of popular singers. The Italians, too, found Sinatra a puzzle. At one impromptu concert, the cooks and servants lined up to hear this great Italian singer from America. As Sinatra ran through his repertoire, Silvers noticed frowns of incredulity, then disgust, creep over their faces; they expected a great baritone to be singing opera.

Leslie Welch appeared on the bill with Sinatra at a special concert in Rome. It was the first time Welch was asked a question which stumped him.

'I hadn't been doing the act very long when I was put into this show, sandwiched between Phil Silvers and Frank Sinatra. The theatre was packed and there was bags of brass in the front rows. This cocky little Irish sergeant, half way back, got up and asked me to tell him the last man to box Gentleman Jim Corbett. Well, I had no idea so I talked round it, padding it out. "He won the world championship in 1892," I said, "held it for five years and lost it to Bob Fitsimmons." I went on like that naming all the people I knew he'd fought, until in the end I had to say, "I'm sorry, I don't know the last person to box him. Can you tell me?" "Yes," said this smart bloke. "The undertaker."'

From October, 1943 after the Italians had declared war on Germany, a gesture that made them allies, it was permissible to utilize the talents of Italian artists entertaining troops. Singers, dancers, musicians, jugglers, even a hypnotist who couldn't speak English but still managed a successful act, appeared in front of the Allies. An RAF audience entertained in a cowshed by a local variety company was amused to see that the soprano's dress had been made from Allied parachute material. They were not so amused when the fire-eater began his act, breathed flames into the rafters and they were deluged by singed spiders.

Italian artists meant, mostly, musicians and, in particular, opera singers. 'It was incredible to watch,' says Nigel Patrick, 'in that lovely phrase, "the brutal and licentious" queuing outside the San Carlo in Naples to pay their thirty bob to go in, which was a lot of money to a soldier. They became absolute addicts. They were the sort of people who would never, in a million years, have gone to opera in Civvy Street. They went first out of a feeling of "What shall we do? What's this Ayeeda? Who's Ayeeda? Singing? Well, might as well go anyway?" They went and loved it and became mad about it because, of course, one heard the best. It was not unusual to hear two squaddies discussing the merits of various sopranos in the most strong barrack-room language.'

Marlene Dietrich began her now world famous career as a solo entertainer when she toured the US, Europe and North Africa for USO.

Opera and ballet (the Anglo-Polish Ballet filled the 4,000 seat theatre in Bari every day), enjoyed surprising popularity. In the first year after the Allies captured Naples nearly half a million Allied troops went to the San Carlo and the house was full for seventy-five per cent of performances. In Rome, the Compagnia dell' Opera gave troops a free performance of *La Bohème* in appreciation for support during the season. Men may have gone in the first place because they were bored and there was nothing else to do, but having been once, they went again and again. And, as was pointed out in a local Army paper, the military population was changing constantly so it was not the same people who packed out the San Carlo month after month. And, of course, they did see the best with artists of the calibre of Tito Gobbi and Mario del Monaco. If the chorus in *Aïda* was wearing wristwatches because it wasn't safe to leave them in the dressing-room, or the hero was a foot shorter than the heroine, it only added to the enjoyment.

One star who did not appear for the Allies for some time was Beniamino Gigli. Soon after the Allies entered Rome Gigli had been invited to sing at a special concert but the US authorities objected. He was accused of being a Nazi collaborator, of hoarding food, of making derogatory remarks about the States. The Italian stage hands refused to work with him and he was banned from taking part. 'What the Italians do about paying to hear Gigli is their business. But if I were back in the States I would fight to keep him out of our theatres. In Italy I will go to see a class C movie instead,' an irate corporal wrote to *Stars and Stripes*. Other correspondents echoed his sentiments. Gigli prepared and published a booklet outlining his defence: he had never said America was finished; with a family of twenty to support it was quite natural he should have 600 kilos of flour at his house; he had not collaborated with the Germans – his art was international and he performed for anybody; he was the victim of attacks by a jealous baritone. 'The charge that Gigli was a collaborator always puzzled me,' says Nigel Patrick. 'Since he was a member of a nation that was an ally of Germany, I don't know how he could be accused of collaboration.' Patrick fought for Gigli to be allowed to sing to Allied troops and eventually he made his first appearance, lasting seven minutes, at a show Patrick organized for ex-POW's. But it was a long time before Gigli could appear on an Italian stage without being hissed and booed.

THE MASKED BALL

Wednesday, April 11th 1945 - At 19,00hrs

CAST

Richard	Gustavo Gallo
Renato	Tito Gobbi
Amelia	Maria Pedrini
Ulrica	Pina Ulisse
Oscar	Amalia Remi
Samuel	Iginio Riccò
Tom	Antonio Picillo
Silvano	Raffaele Aulicino
A Judge	Carlo Giorgianni
A Servant	Pasquale De Rosa

Orchestra Conducted by

FRANCO CAPUANA

The 1945 production of The Masked Ball *was performed in Naples in the San Carlo, the house for which it was written in 1859.*

Symphony concerts also attracted new audiences. Five hours after it was announced that a concert would be held in the San Carlo every Sunday, all seats were sold and the performance had to be given on three nights. 'In my thirty-five years,' wrote a Sapper, 'I thought I had my likes and dislikes pretty well sorted out but I must confess that recently I discovered one glaring exception. Blame it on a day's leave which I have just had in Rome. I somehow bought a seat for a symphony concert. I went into the theatre. I sat down and tongue in cheek, I listened. They started with Mozart's *Marriage of Figaro*. In spite of myself, I was impressed. Then came *Fountains of Rome*, what they call a tone poem. I began to feel the depth of the music. I closed my eyes, relaxed, and then during the next quarter-of-an-hour I discovered a beauty of sound and harmony I never believed existed. Technically I know nothing of the make-up of music. And I say, leave that to the experts. But let us through our schools and in our homes make the thrill of beautiful music more widely known.'

The Italian campaign did much to change the attitudes of many men. Entertainment which was considered highbrow and not for them was discovered to be very much for them. They acquired a love of music and, in particular, opera which they would take back home with them, into civilian life, once the war was over.

150

CHAPTER TWELVE

THE SECOND FRONT

In January, 1944 Montgomery left the 8th Army in Italy and returned to England to help plan the Allied invasion of Normandy. Operation Overlord, as the D-Day landings were code-named, was the greatest amphibious operation of all time. Preparations were meticulous and elaborate but, as the build up of troops in southern England grew, impossible to keep secret. Everyone knew why the forces were gathering, including the Germans. The invasion was talked about in pubs and discussed in the press. What was not general knowledge was the place and time it would happen.

Early on, almost before the idea became public property, Basil Dean, thinking well ahead as always, had started to plan ENSA's contribution to the Second Front. He knew from his experience of the first foray into France in 1939, from criticism of ENSA's Middle East and North African campaigns and the rumblings of discontent that were beginning to emerge from Italy, that one of his main problems would again be transport. This time he was convinced he had the problem solved. Instead of being abandoned, leaving artists to make their own way as best they could, ENSA vehicles which broke down (as they did frequently) would be repaired by the REME. The system, which seemed such a good idea when Dean set it up, didn't work in practice. As camp followers, ENSA came low on the list of priorities and transport was to remain a headache until the advancing troops were on the threshold of Germany. By then ENSA was threatened with a total breakdown of its service and finally decided to set up its own transport section.

At the beginning of 1944, however, Dean was satisfied with the arrangements he had made with the REME and turned his attention to the more important task of finding artists. There was no lack of stars volunteering to make the crossing. People he had spent years unsuccessfully badgering to give a few weeks to ENSA were suddenly available to lead ENSA's troupes to France. Dean loyally stuck by those who had helped him in the past and in the spring of 1944 was able to announce ENSA's plans. 144 artists, including stars, had been booked. Not one of the dancers – the 'lovelies' as the press called them – was over twenty-three. All acts had been vetted by a quality committee and were waiting at ENSA's country HQ, bags packed, ready to leave at twenty-four hours' notice. The various companies, including stars, had been divided into twelve columns, each column consisting of two parties; all that was needed was the signal to move.

The US Special Services were also preparing for D-Day, organizing its forces into columns. Each column contained a variety show, a dance band, boxes of baseball bats, yo-yo's and other sports equipment, films and books. The shows would be provided by USO or specially selected GI companies such as *Broadway in Khaki*.

Meanwhile southern England was swarming with Allied troops. Strict security had been imposed to prevent leaks and men were lodged in secret tented camps, behind barbed wire, not allowed out for any reason. Elated by the thought of so many captive audiences, ENSA Area Organizers applied for permission to take shows into the camps only to be met by blank stares. If the camps did not exist, how could shows be put on in them?

The situation changed dramatically in May when the invasion was postponed for a month. The men resented being caged up, with nothing to do. Discipline deteriorated and there were break-outs. ENSA and USO parties were begged to enter the camps which they did under armed guard, forbidden to talk to anyone. Special Entertainments Officers were drafted in to organize anything that would keep the men amused. At one camp a Brains Trust was set up at which the question was asked, 'Who first invented the phrase, "Don't shoot until you can see the white of their eyes?" ' Before any of the panel could reply the answer rang out from the back of the hall: Dr Marie Stopes.'

The month's delay gave shows waiting to go to France an opportunity to try out their acts on the Servicemen and the rumour spread that they were being used as a threat: face the Germans or attend another performance. 'In the face of such a challenge,' recalls a soldier, 'the lads fought like heroes.'

In spite of the precautions, security at the special camps was never total. After playing for troops billeted at the West Ham Football ground,

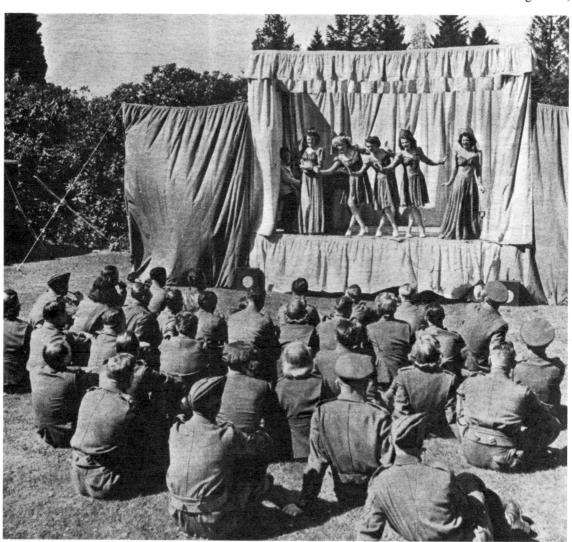

The ENSA concert parties rehearsed in their country headquarters in Hindhead to be prepared to follow the troops into Europe. Once the second front was established, the entertainers were to be there to keep up morale.

Fred Astaire and his sister, and one-time partner Adèle, were among the many stars who dropped in to celebrate the opening of the London branch of the USO Stage Door Canteen in 1944.

Geraldo and his musicians were asked to sign autographs on the only pieces of paper the men possessed – French francs issued that morning. And Brian Oulton was told by a Naafi manager that something must be happening because the boys had all been paid in francs. Tommy Trinder went to give a show at Canning Town with 'Monsewer' Eddie Gray.

'When we arrived a sergeant came up to us and said, "Who's doing the announcing?" I thought he meant who was compering the show so I said that I was. He gave me a list of troop movements and I knew the invasion was going to start that night. I looked at this list and thought, I'm not supposed to have this! I went to the CO and asked if he really wanted me to announce it. He was horrified and made me promise not to divulge what I had read to a soul, otherwise he was going to keep me there until the operation was over.'

Operation Overlord began on 6 June. For the first time since Pearl Harbour the Statue of Liberty's torch was switched on as a signal that US Forces had at last reached the land from which the statue came. Despite Basil Dean's vociferous clamourings, ENSA was left firmly on the English side of the Channel. None of the military men masterminding the landings wanted to be bothered with civilian entertainers at such an early stage and Dean's frequent requests to be allowed to send in his forces were refused. The first official entertainers to reach Normandy were members of Stars in Battledress. Five parties, under Sergeants Rudy Jess, Bif Byfield, Sid Millward, Arthur Haynes and Harold Childs, made the crossing on 14 June. Two days later Edward G Robinson, who was in Britain making a propaganda film for the RAF, became the first American to play for US troops in France. Eddie le Roy was a member of Jess's Stars in Battledress party.

'Before the invasion all our gear had been packed and garaged at the Duke of York's Barracks in Chelsea. All we had to do was report every day. We would turn up each day and be told to come back tomorrow. This went on for weeks. I was living in Pimlico at the time and I used to be home by nine o'clock every morning. So, I reported as usual one lovely, sunny Saturday morning. I remember it particularly because my wife had managed to get hold of an egg and I was looking forward to having it for my breakfast after I'd reported. When I got to the barracks, Stanley Hall, the QM, said to us all, "Get your kit bags and rifles." We looked at one another and said, it's only a rehearsal, nothing to worry about. We were there for about an hour and three big troop carriers drove through the gates. That was it. We piled in and were taken to Charing Cross station. We then went to Lewes by train, where we were shunted backwards and forwards until we eventually arrived at a station just outside Southampton. They marched us to a camp site called Folkswood, where we were billeted under canvas with the Guards. We were there some days, then one morning they put us on a train and took us to Southsea where we got on these little barges. We sat and waited for hours and when we eventually left I was so sea-sick I just laid down. All you could hear was the noise of the barges and the sound of the shells – Gerry was shelling us like anything. The barge behind ours was sunk. Somehow we managed to get to the other side.'

On the beaches of Arromanches, waiting under an umbrella of fire, was Captain Richard Stone, newly appointed Entertainments Officer of the 2nd Army.

'I think, quite honestly, that we were a couple of

Eddie Le Roy (brother of Monsewer Eddie Grey) a member of the first Stars in Battledress shows into Normandy, leading men of the Sixth Airborne Division in community singing in June 1944.

days too early. We were in the way and were a bit of a nuisance. I remember standing on the bridgehead, shells still falling, with this curious selection of chaps who, by Army rules, ought not to have been there because they all had flat feet or were C3 when you had to be A1 to go in with the Second Front. These fellows stood there with their instruments and goodness knows what and Cyril Lagey, the coloured dancer from Sid Millward's band, said to me, "I's got flat feet, Cap'n, and I's not moving." And he wasn't going to.'

In the confusion that followed the parties split up. Some people wandered off on their own, others jumped on trucks. Eddie le Roy and Louis Almaer went into a field and fell asleep. When they awoke, the place was deserted. Stone had rounded up as many as he could and, promising them a truck would be along soon, set them off to march the ten miles to Bayeux, the town which was to be

their headquarters. When a truck did catch them up it didn't have room for everyone and most had to continue on foot, the longest march any of them had ever done. One artist tried to hitch his own ride on the back of a slow-moving lorry, swung himself over the tail-gate and disappeared head-first into a bin full of swill.

Their billet was a former nunnery and Gestapo headquarters in the village of Sommervieu, just outside Bayeux. Improvising beds as best they could, they flopped down on the flag-stones to enjoy as comfortable a night's sleep as the German barrage would allow. In the morning the door was kicked open by a British soldier. Covering them with his bren gun he demanded to know who they were. 'Ve are zee Stars in Battledress,' replied Rudolf Jess, nearest the door, in his thick German accent. Jess, a naturalized Briton, had been a star of the Berlin State Opera. A variety of regional

154

accents hastened to assure the suspicious soldier that Jess was telling the truth. The man summoned his sergeant. 'Had a good night?' the sergeant asked from the doorway. 'I'm pleased to hear it,' he said when the artists, relieved the soldier hadn't opened fire, chorused that they had, 'because, for your information, you're all sitting on a load of bloody mines.' The retreating Germans frequently booby-trapped buildings as they vacated them and the nunnery hadn't been checked. A search revealed two such devices.

Although the actual landings had gone according to plan, it did not prove as easy as the Allied commanders had expected to reach the first objectives. The fierce German resistance took them by surprise and it was several days before anybody was ready or able to enjoy a show. By the time the first parties had recovered their props and equipment, most of which had travelled separately, a second wave had arrived, including Charlie Chester's unit and the music unit compered by Terry-Thomas.

It had always been Ralph Reader's ambition that his RAF Gang Shows should be the first official entertainers to play in Normandy and as soon as the first airstrip had been laid, he took out the first show himself. They flew from Northolt not knowing the Army had beaten them to it.

'We were very excited,' recall the Cox Twins, Fred and Frank. 'It was a gorgeous day when we arrived over France and as we circled the strip to make our landing, we looked out and there was Charlie Chester with his unit, laughing and giving us rude signs. We were terribly disappointed. When we got down and met them, they were in a really bad condition and were having a very tough time. Kenny Morris, with whom we'd worked in a kids group before the war, hadn't eaten for a couple of days. What food there was was very bad. The first thing we did was to give them a decent meal.'

The original plan of attaching Stars in Battledress parties to fighting units had not been working. Units didn't want them permanently and had no rations for them. If the parties moved around looking for audiences instead, everything had to be scrounged with the result that they were missing out all the way round. The problem was only eased when Basil Dean, anxious to obtain permission for ENSA to proceed to France, arrived and set up a system of routing and rationing, in conjunction with Entertainments Officers, which could be utilized by all entertainers in or out of uniform.

Montgomery's original plans had included the capture of Caen, a town less than a dozen miles from the sea, on the first day. The British 3rd Division found itself unexpectedly opposed by the crack 21st Panzer Division which was garrisoned in the town itself. 'Nothing seemed to move the Germans,' remember the Cox Twins. 'They were like a solid granite wall and we had no air support. We thought they were invincible supermen. It was beautiful weather and we were living in an orchard. In the field next to us were hundreds of bodies of the boys who'd been killed, lying in khaki lines. It was so silent. There were apples on the trees and we stripped off and sunbathed, until we were told our white bodies made good targets for the German fighters. When we arrived we were told that if we wanted to live we had to dig a hole, a deep one, so we dug this hole which had corrugated tin to cover us. About eight o'clock every evening everything happened: snipers, machine guns, bombs, mortars, the lot. The noise was terrifying and although most of the stuff was passing overhead there were bits of shrapnel flying around. One evening Ralph Reader came in our hole with us. Suddenly there was a knock on the tin and we froze with terror. We heard the voice of a flight sergeant: "Is Squadron Leader Reader in there?" Ralph said he was. "Would you like to see a film, sir?" "Who's in it?" "Errol Flynn." "Sure, we'd like to." We climbed out of this hole and crawled behind the flight sergeant, across the orchard and into a tent where they were showing *The Sea Hawk*. We forgot about the barrage completely and sat watching this film.'

Charlie Chester also remembers Caen vividly for the heavy summer storms which turned the fields into quagmires. 'The mud was unbelievable. I was standing waiting to get my boys together talking to Arthur Haynes who had a great big moustache. We were by a slit trench which was more like a little grave topped up with oozing mud, and millions of little frogs. Arthur looked at me and said, "That's a slit trench." I said, "I know it's a bloody slit trench." "Well," he said, "you wouldn't get me in there for all the tea in China." Just then two Focke-Wulfs came out of the sky and he was in there so fast! I threw myself on the ground and when I looked up there was Arthur with frogs coming out of his ears and out of his moustache!'

Caen was captured on 9 July and the Allies began the long march towards the Falaise Gap

In July 1944 George Formby (and the ubiquitous Beryl)
entertained a group of sappers in Caen. Three weeks later
ENSA sent the play Love From a Stranger *to France.*
Ivor Novello and Diana Wynyard were among the stars in
a cast that also included Margaret Rutherford, Joanna
Benham, Daphne Page and Robert Andrews.

and the roads that led to Paris and the Low
Countries. Janet Brown and Frances Tanner had
been allowed to rejoin their Stars in Battledress
units and, much to the relief of an exasperated and
impatient Basil Dean, ENSA was given permission to make the Channel crossing. On 24 July, six
parties, led, inevitably, by George Formby and
Beryl, landed in France. Four days later eight
USO Camp Shows arrived on the Utah beaches
and within two hours gave a combined performance from the back of a thirty ton ammunition
carrier before setting out on their own.

A few days after the first ENSA contingent,
further stars arrived. Forsythe, Seamon and
Farrell led the second wave, with Richard Hearne
in charge of the first star party. On 19 August,
Alice Delysia, Gertrude Lawrence and Ivor
Novello landed. Novello brought with him a
production of *Love From A Stranger* in which his

co-stars were Diana Wynyard and Margaret Rutherford. Their first performance was given in a Normandy orchard to the accompaniment of German gunfire. The build-up of entertainment continued with the arrival of Sandy Powell, Kay Cavendish, Flanagan and Allen, Emlyn Williams and his *Blithe Spirit* company, Jessie Matthews and Billy Scott-Coomber.

Dean was in France himself, supervising operations. He was not surprised to be told one day that Alice Delysia, who was annoyed at not being included in the first party, had gone missing. Paris was on the point of being liberated and Dean knew at once where she had gone. Anxious to be there himself for that historic occasion he set out in pursuit. 'I joined the endless crocodile of vehicles, nose to tail, kilometre after kilometre, pouring through the Falaise Gap, still heavy with the scent of the dead,' he recalled in *The Theatre At War*. 'As we drew near the capital we were borne forward upon a relentless flood of vehicles of every sort and description: giant American trucks, tank transporters, mobile guns and staff cars ... Crowds of enthusiastic bicyclists with British and American flags tied to the handle-bars or worn as scarves, surrounded the Etoile and Avenue des Champs-Elysees ... At Fouquets the crowd and the noise seemed greatest. An impulse of curiosity drove me inside the place. There, standing on a marble-topped table surrounded by a wildly excited mob of cheering and singing Parisians, was Alice Delysia ... She flung her arms round my neck and promised to return to her troupe in due course. She did for a short while, but really her gallant pilgrimage was over: France was free.'

Dean had another reason for wanting to visit Paris, apart from finding his missing star and seeing the city liberated. He had set his heart on turning the famous theatres of Europe into ENSA Garrison Theatres and planned to start in Paris. In most cases his plans were premature. By the time he could bring over prestige companies such as the Old Vic, the men who should have formed the audiences had drawn breath and rushed on across Europe. Not until the invasion force became an army of occupation, able to get to the theatre, did his idea really work. The first major show he organized was a concert for Allied troops at the Marigny Theatre in Paris on 15 November. On the bill were Noël Coward, Frances Day (who created a sensation by throwing her underclothes into the audience), Will Hay, Bobby Howes, Nervo and Knox, and Geraldo.

Not long after the Liberation of Paris the USO Stage Door Canteen was inaugurated in imitation of the successful New York, Hollywood and London predecessors. A splendid cabaret performance by Noël Coward and others, backed by an American Service band, became legendary in the annals of theatrical history.

Paris had become the temporary headquarters of USO and the city proved a big lure to touring artists, so much so that troops at the front began to complain they were being ignored. Towards the end of October the US Military Authorities banned all performances in the city by American entertainers and ordered those who were there out. First to go was Marlene Dietrich who had been in Paris for two weeks with her company and not given a single show. She was packed in a jeep and sent off towards the front.

The front, by this time, was moving rapidly through Belgium, into Holland and towards the German border, and entertainers were doing their

The beloved Frances Day, who began her wartime career as a member of the very first ENSA show, continued to appear to the forces throughout the war. She followed the Liberation forces from France to Belgium and into Germany.

best to keep up. 'It was cock-eyed,' recalls Charlie Chester. 'You never knew where the front was. We never knew if we were going in the right direction or if we might finish up behind German lines.' Several artists did just that. Bing Crosby, touring foxholes with just a guitarist, had been told to follow the telephone cables until he reached the lines. 'The advance was so rapid at this time that the troops would frequently get ahead of their lines of communication. The advice was that if we didn't see our telephone lines, turn round and come back. Suddenly I noticed we were out of lines but we pushed on to a little town and took a look ahead. We saw some strange-looking equipment.' The town was still in German hands.

Even while giving a show, performers were never allowed to forget that there was a war on. Three members of a Stars in Battledress party were singing 'Nobody Loves a Fairy When She's Forty', dressed in ballet costumes, when the stage was strafed by a German fighter. The sight of the 'ladies' diving for cover a split second before the backcloth was peppered with bullets produced the biggest laugh of the day. An ENSA unit was in mid-performance when bombs fell outside the theatre. The artists on stage were hit by flying shrapnel and the dresses hanging outside were cut to ribbons, but the show went on. Dinah Shore was asked to open a temporary bridge, named after her, over the Seine. After cutting the tape she sang for forty minutes. Only when she had finished did a German sniper climb out of a tree and surrender. He had been watching the entire performance through his telescopic sights.

All units playing near the front had experiences similar to Charlie Chester. 'We played to a commando unit. The men sat there, faces blacked, clutching rifles, with all their equipment. Suddenly a man crept in and said "First four rows." The first four rows got up and went out. Later on they would come creeping back in and you'd see the boys counting to check how many had been killed.'

Even behind the lines life could be dangerous. There were booby-traps and snipers everywhere. Richard Hearne's driver was killed going to get petrol and when Hearne drove into s'Hertogenbosch to look for a hall in which to perform, his jeep was pinned down by sniper fire. He eventually got through and found a suitable building. When he returned later, with his company, the hall had vanished, blown to pieces.

Although the end of the war seemed in sight it was still too early for the really large companies to move up. Entertainments close to the front line needed to be small and mobile. Winifred Doran was a member of a six-handed ENSA party.

'The biggest part of our job at that time was really off the stage. We played to small units wherever we found them and the reaction was always tremendous but being sociable after the show was always more important. They were desperate to talk to someone who wasn't in the Army and who could remind them of home. We had two dancers with us who were an indifferent act but were very, very pretty and, quite frankly, we couldn't have done without them.'

Dinah Shore, like Bing Crosby, was another of those artists who refused to stay well behind the lines and insisted on going as near the front as she could. On one occasion she and Crosby joined forces to give a concert to men of the 3rd Army. During his six weeks in Europe, most of them with

*Bing Crosby followed the US army into Normandy and, accompanied by his guitarist, frequently showed up without any
ceremony in the front lines and on one occasion ahead of them . . . in Eindhoven.*

just his guitarist, Crosby covered 1,500 miles. He
always closed his programme by singing 'White
Christmas', the Irving Berlin hit from his film
Holiday Inn, and hoping that his audience would
be back home for Christmas 1944. 'They'd holler
for it, they'd demand it and I'd sing it and they'd
all cry,' he remembered later. 'It was really sad.'

His wish was never fulfilled. That winter Hitler
launched his Ardennes counter-offensive and the
war, which everyone confidently predicted would
be over by Christmas, spilled over into 1945.
During the autumn of 1944 all had seemed to be
going well. Montgomery had pushed on towards
Germany leaving the small pockets of resistance to
be dealt with by his subordinates. City after city
had fallen to the Allies. Brussels was liberated on 3
September. 'There was tremendous excitement on
the streets,' recalls Richard Stone, who arrived the
same day, 'people singing, cheering, waving flags,
crying even. The ABC Theatre there still had up

the bills for the German opera. Outside it said,
'*Monday, Tuesday, Wednesday: Der Rosenka-
valier.*' I posted up, '*Thursday, Friday, Saturday:
Flanagan and Allen.*',

Brussels became ENSA's European headquarters soon after the first columns arrived and
remained so until the end of the war. The
administration moved in in force. All shows, from
the smallest concert party to the Old Vic Company
and the Sadler's Wells Ballet, were routed through
Brussels and many played there before heading on
towards Holland and Germany. It probably goes
without saying that the muddle and inefficiency
that marred so much of ENSA's previous work
also arrived. Star parties were put into small,
sordid hotels and converted brothels while lowly
ENSA officials moved into large, comfortable
houses; Gertrude Lawrence had to catch a bus to
the theatre while the same officials drove past her
at the bus stop in their cars.

Gertrude Lawrence, who worked for both ENSA and USO, was one of the most popular of all entertainers with Allied troops. She had landed in Normandy and stayed with the Forces until they reached Germany. Felix Barker wrote an account of a performance she gave to men of the 51st Highland Division in his diary:

'September 8th. Etretat, Normandy.

Gertrude Lawrence and her company are going to play in the Casino again, as in this weather it is hardly feasible to perform in a field. We've put in all our own lighting and curtaining to cover the bizarre interior set for our show and theirs, and the ENSA company, which played here yesterday, in the dimmest gloom, were very pleased ... G Lawrence, back from America after her tour, was in tremendous form. What can one say of her show and performance? That it was great and she tremendous? Well, the supporting company was average and she won a triumph out of what looked like defeat. Either from experience of troop shows, or from an idea of her own, she made the initial mistake of playing down tò her audience. Almost, one could see her saying to herself, "I have to deal with a bunch of unsophisticated, braw Highlanders. I must fire every gun I've got." And so, during her first number, we were treated to a full salvo of every trick she knew. But the braw Highlanders, who'd been under fire before, were not impressed. In fact, they thought it rather grotesque. For a ghastly five minutes one of the greatest artists of our stage looked like getting a grouse straight from the moors. But she was too clever for that. A Cockney number, a couple of wise-cracks at the expense of officers and padres, a lovely number from *Lady In The Dark*, and she was back. By the time she was smashing over "All's Well, M'moiselle", the whole audience was with her and the show ended in one of those red-white-and-blue, First World War, Tipperary-type finales.'

She stayed on after her performance to watch the Division's own concert party, *The Balmorals*, give their show. She wanted to see, in particular, a sketch Barker had written about a star refusing to tour France for ENSA because she was not allowed to take her complete entourage, including two dogs, with her. 'We were worried about her reaction,' says Barker, 'Because we thought she might feel we were getting at her type of ENSA star, but she was delighted. She paid us the compliment of missing her dinner and staying for the whole show.'

Sylvia Handel and Dorothy Carless, together with Cyril Ornadel, toured Belgium and Germany as a three-handed ENSA unit. They performed at the Victory celebrations on Lüneburg Heath the night the European war ended.

In early spring 1945 the Allies crossed the Rhine and were poised to strike at Berlin. Dispirited German troops surrendered in droves and on 30 April Hitler committed suicide. Among the parties that had kept up with the victorious Allies was a three-handed ENSA company. 'There were just the three of us, Dorothy Carless, Sylvia Handel and myself,' recalls composer Cyril Ornadel, whose first job after music school was to join the show as pianist. 'We were a unit on our own, playing anywhere. We followed the Army into Eindhoven, then to Kiel and eventually landed up at Lüneburg, waiting to go and do a show in Berlin which was the prime prize at that time. While we were at Lüneburg we were told Peace was going to be signed and there would be official celebrations that evening at which we would appear. The performance took place in a whacking great field, in front of all the top brass, on a small rostrum with a piano and chair, and no microphone. About six jeeps were placed at strategic positions with their headlights on, and that was it. During the performance the wind started to blow and my music went flying; all the things you see in comedy films happened that night. Afterwards there was a party in a huge marquee and everybody got absolutely plastered.' It was 8 May, 1945. The war in Europe was over.

CHAPTER THIRTEEN

FAR EAST

The war in Europe may have ended but in the Far East in May, 1945 the Allies were still locked in a desperate struggle against the forces of Imperial Japan. To the British Forces fighting in Burma and South East Asia the events in Europe were a world away. The public at home took little notice of their war and not for nothing did the 14th Army call itself the Forgotten Army.

The prelude to the long hard campaign to retake Burma had been played out over Christmas 1941 when the Japanese had driven the meagre British forces from Singapore and chased them through Burma into India – the longest retreat in the history of the British Army. Fortunately, the Japanese territorial teeth ceased champing on the borders of Assam, giving the British time to regroup, await reinforcements and prepare a counter offensive. Out of the dark days following that retreat grew the first official entertainment in India, BESA – the Bengal Entertainment Services Association. Under the patronage of Lady Mary Herbert, in June, 1942, BESA was formed to provide entertainment for British, Indian and US troops throughout Eastern Command and 14th Army areas. It was based in Calcutta, where it was run voluntarily by civilians, and employed services' talent. Laurence Neal, serving with the RAF, was a founder member:

'BESA sprang out of a concert we organized in a Forces' canteen in Calcutta, which we persuaded Lady Mary Herbert to attend. We then talked her into having a general and an air vice-marshal to tea and she persuaded them to release some of us, gave us some money and helped find us a theatre and some equipment. The first real difficulty for most of us came in getting seconded from our units, even with pressure from above. At that time, for instance, I was one of only a few experienced fighter controllers in India so it was understandable that my CO wanted to retain me.'

Neal and several other airmen and soldiers stationed in and around Calcutta obtained their release from regular duties and six weeks after Lady Mary Herbert's tea party the first BESA company opened in *Besabuzzin*, a variety show with a cast of twenty, including the band and eight girls from the Calcutta Amateur Theatrical Society. Some of the cast had to return to their units when the curtain came down on the production but the remainder and the band set off on a month's tour of Chittagong. The reports that reached Calcutta of the show's success, coupled with the enthusiasm of Lady Mary Herbert and her civilian helpers, convinced the most sceptical of officers that BESA meant business. Support for the project was found everywhere. There was no other entertainment for troops in India and everyone was desperate for it to succeed. A school hall was taken over as the BESA Garrison Theatre and headquarters; auditions were held and new performers recruited, some just for a show, others permanently; a dramatic society was formed; boxing tournaments were arranged; Indian entertainers were engaged to take shows to the Indian troops. By the middle of 1943, nearly one hundred Servicemen were appearing in twelve full-scale productions, two Miniatures and touring throughout Bengal, Bihar, Orissa and Assam.

(Above) The BESA Miniature party 'The Greenflies' performed in Tinsukia in 1943. This was the first BESA Miniature to go on tour and play to audiences in various conditions to British, American and Indian troops throughout Bengal, Oressa, Bihar and Assam.

The Miniatures were six-handed parties designed to be sent to the forward areas of Assam. They travelled light, carrying just costumes, bedrolls and a mini-organ – there were few props and no scenery – and were all-male. Women were not allowed into the front lines though one or two of the girls (who were nearly all civilians and took part in BESA productions in their spare time) did play within twenty miles of the Japanese. The names of female impersonators Yvette (Alex Purdie) and Patricia (Vic Paternoster) became as well-known in that part of India as those of Betty Grable and Ginger Rogers.

Welsh comedian Ivor Owen was in *The Grasshoppers*, the first BESA Miniature. 'The boys loved us. They had nothing else, except their food, and that wasn't very good. The basic diet was

dehydrated spuds, dehydrated onions, soya link sausages – there was no fresh meat – a vitamin C tablet every day and a Nepracin tablet. The only treat they got was when one of our little travelling shows, with no star names, appeared. They knew we'd travelled sometimes 200 miles where there were no roads, only a dust track and sometimes not even that, just to be with them; that we'd walked behind mules; that we were sleeping rough where they did, in a slit trench or a foxhole, or under a mosquito net tied to a bush. On any unit we played we were treated, at all times, like royalty.'

BESA's area covered over a quarter of a million square miles and presented the part-time administration in Calcutta with an enormous headache. It took a year of one-night stands for one party to get round all units. Communications were poor, which meant parties arrived unannounced or unexpected. There were problems with transport and in a country without roads, companies were frequently lost. They had to cope with intense heat and the prevalence of strange illnesses. Sir William Slim, Commander of the 14th Army, was later to pay tribute to BESA for 'the grand work they have done during the past two-and-a-half years in providing such a high standard of entertainment with a minimum of properties and under difficult conditions. The BESA parties, through the warm welcome given them by the troops themselves, know how much they are appreciated by all ranks of the 14th Army . . . In particular I would like to thank the Miniature parties which have toured so regularly among Divisions and forward troops, under jungle conditions, during the difficult monsoon months. Many units have depended upon BESA Miniatures for their sole entertainment, and the success with which they have toured is a very great credit to them.'

'We used to do two or three shows a day, starting in the morning,' recalls Ivor Owen. 'After the first one we'd go thirty miles down the road, over rough country, to do the next. Then on to the next unit and a final show about six o'clock. After the show and a bite to eat, we'd sit around until the sun went down, singing and chatting. This was the lovely part of evening and the best thing the boys liked outside the shows themselves were the sing-songs. We had a little accordion and they would request songs from all over the place. As soon as the sun went down, it was silence. The law of the jungle was very strict in those days: when the sun went down nobody moved. A lot of boys were

'Yvette' (Alex Purdie) star of BESA and later ENSA shows in the Arakan, performed for the men of the 36 Division at the bottom of the Nyakdauk Pass in 1944. During the war, without question, Purdie was one of the most popular of the female impersonators in India.

killed because they moved after dark. Those on guard used to have hessian tied to their wrists and if anything happened they used to pull it so that the other man knew something was up. The Japs never used a gun. You never heard a shot; it was always the knife. People suffering from dysentery would get up in the night and in the morning, we'd find them dead, knifed.'

Large though BESA's area was – almost three times the size of the British Isles – it was no more than a small hand on the body of India. Anyone based elsewhere on the sub-continent had to be content with whatever entertainment could be devised and produced locally. The RAF station at Drigh Road, Karachi, had its own show which played the camp and neighbouring bases, and also managed a production of *The Mikado*, with full

Jack Hawkins reformed the First World War Cross Keys divisional concert party in Poona. In 1944 he maintained traditions in mounting a Christmas pantomime production of Cinderella *near Ondaw. In spite of the appalling heat nothing was skimped in the costumes.*

chorus and orchestra drawn from RAF and local amateur musicians. Singing with the station band was crooner Jimmy Young. In Poona, Jack Hawkins reformed and ran the Cross Keys Divisional concert party for the 2nd Division, on the order of General Grover. 'He gave me authority to scour the Division for talent, and what was virtually an open cheque on Divisional funds,' Hawkins wrote in his autobiography. 'It was astounding just how much talent was available in the Division. Within six weeks I had assembled a cast, and a large dance band, as well as all the scenery and costumes I needed ... We had no band parts, but they played by ear, and someone scored the various parts. New tunes we picked up from records and broadcasts. My own great starring role was a female impersonation of Carmen Miranda ... I wrote the sketches and gags, although I must admit that I shamelessly robbed material from every revue I could remember seeing. The reception to our opening

performance was overwhelming; so much so that the army engineers built an astonishing folding stage which we hauled out to camps throughout India, and indeed followed the 14th Army into Burma.'

One artist who started his career in India was Norman Wisdom. He had joined the Army as a bandboy at fourteen to learn the clarinet and was posted to India with the band of the 10th Hussars.

'The band used to play and sing sea shanties at concert parties,' he recalls. 'I knew there should be some sort of solo in them and said to the Bandmaster one day, standing very smartly to attention, "Excuse me, sir. Why doesn't anybody sing the solos?" "For the simple reason, Wisdom," he replied, "that we don't have anybody who can." I said I could. I couldn't, in fact, but I just chanced it. "Sing me something," he said, so I sang a very old Jack Buchanan number, 'You Must Say Yes To Mrs Brown'. He was satisfied and from then on I was singing the solo parts in the sea shanties in front of the band. I was very, very nervous but I began to get a feel of what it was like to appear on stage. Then I went into the wash-house and gradually taught myself to tap-dance, with Army boots on, of course, because I had no tap shoes. I went to the Bandmaster and said, "Excuse me, sir. How do you think a tap dance, in front of the band, would go down?" "Don't tell me, Wisdom," he said. I said, "Yes, sir." '

'Now at that time I wasn't very proficient on the clarinet, I was still learning. The band used to go away on three month engagements up in the hills and I was one of three blokes lumbered to stay on the plains, in the hot weather, to blow bugle calls – Lights Out, Reveille and Cook House. In the store-room I found a xylophone which I got out and taught myself, parrot fashion. After re-hearsals the Bandmaster would usually ask if anybody wanted to try something new or special. When they came back from the hills I said, "Yes, sir. 'Snow Flakes'." "But that's a xylophone solo," he said and everybody laughed. I told him I'd taught myself to play the xylophone, I got it out, played it and he was very pleased. That meant I was in front of the band playing the xylophone, singing and doing a tap dance. I was getting applause and I thought, This is it. We then went to the Officers' Mess to do a concert and there was me, tap dancing and everything. As I started to

dance the officers began laughing. I'd never had that before and for a moment I was peeved and worried. Then I suddenly realized that dancing in Army boots and uniform, doing a Fred Astaire-type number, was, to a more sophisticated audience, let's face it, very funny. I was a member of the boxing team at the time and used to train by shadow boxing; to amuse the fellows I used to let my imaginary opponent hit me back. So, when I came out and started to dance in my Army boots and they began to laugh, I changed to eccentric dancing and fell over. They shrieked with laughter and the laughs were so good that, there and then, I decided what I would do – comedy.'

When he returned to England, Wisdom was transferred to the Signals, joined the concert party and began to perfect the comedy routine that was to make him one of Britain's biggest box-office successes. He was one of the very few, certainly the most talented, artists to be refused a transfer to Stars in Battledress. He was star of the concert party, in the boxing team, the cricket team, the football team and the cross-country team. His CO was adamant: he stayed put.

Another Divisional concert party to become a full-time entertainment unit was the Chindit Road Show. In 1943 General Orde Wingate had taken his first Chindit expedition (named after the Chinthe, a mythical Burmese beast) deep behind

Having started his stage career in front of a band in India Norman Wisdom (saxophone) was returned to England to join the Royal Signals Corps and played in their dance band.

enemy lines beyond the Chindwin river to strike at Japanese outposts and lines of communication. The toll was heavy – a third of the men and all the equipment were lost – but Wingate had proved his theory that the way to fight the Japanese was to take them on at their own game, living rough and avoiding roads, with food and supplies being dropped by parachute. A second expedition was planned for 1944 and in late 1943 jungle training started for the new Chindits in Ceylon and Southern India. Their strength was equivalent to two divisions, including one whole division stationed at Bangalore. This division had its own concert party built round a band, under John Lancaster, playing Glenn Miller-style music. Wingate saw the show and decided on the spot that the Chindits must have its own entertainment unit. The concert party was taken over and renamed the Chindit Road Show. While training continued, the Road Show entertained and made brief forays into the cities of India to raise money for instruments and pay for the productions.

In March, 1944 the second Chindit expedition

started. The columns into which the Chindits were divided didn't all go behind Japanese lines at once and the Road Show stayed in the forward areas of Assam playing to those waiting to leave or men returning from the jungle. Peter Watts was a member of the company.

'The Road Show was armed and organized as an infantry platoon and at the seige of Imphal, when the cooks, the bottlewashers and everybody were called in to help, we were called upon to be just that. The show was basically the sixteen-piece band with acts in between. They played popular music by Ellington, Bob Crosby, Glenn Miller and so on but they also had Kenneth Moore, a violinist who had been with the BBC, and he played the classics. We had a tenor, Stanley White, who sang opera and the band also used to play the Warsaw Concerto and Ravel's Bolero. The acts in between were current general humour, with army stuff spliced in – cracks about the local colonel or sergeant major – but what went down really well were the sentimental pieces. Bill Slater used to do a monologue about London and his home being

The third Chindit Road Show was called You Shall Have Music *and played, in among other places, Bangalore to raise funds for their unit. John Lancaster, in white dress clothes, produced the show and conducted the band.*

bombed. It was real cod but I've seen them sitting in rows with their handkerchiefs. Bill would know he'd hurt them and they were unhappy, thinking about the folks at home who might have been smashed up, and at the end he had to say. "Of course, I'm only joking." We also had female impersonators: Arthur Smith, who was very good, and Harry Brydges. Harry also did an act as the Chinese magician Foo Wong as well as a ghastly female impersonation in a comedy sketch. I remember a drunken major taking a fancy to him and Harry, who was as normal as anything, lifting up his skirts and fleeing into the jungle, hotly pursued by the the major.'

The second Chindit expedition ended badly. Sixty-two of the gliders used in the launch from the south hit the trees, resulting in wholesale slaughter, and Wingate himself was killed when his plane crashed into the jungle. The other columns failed to reach their objectives and were sent north to help General Stilwell. Four members of the Road Show, who had been due to be dropped to the Forward columns by parachute (it was said Wingate wanted to be the first man to take entertainers behind enemy lines) never made it. Ten minutes before their scheduled take-off, news reached them that the Japanese were mortaring the landing zone. They rejoined the Road Show in the Forward areas, playing to any troops they could find. As soon as they heard of any Chindits returning from operations they would rush, sometimes hundreds of miles, to give them a show.

'It was really tough with not enough sleep and not enough food,' remembers Peter Watts. 'Sometimes I used to wish to God I was a field medic again it was so physically exhausting. We drove around in a truck, nicknamed "Maisie Lou", and if we found anybody who wanted a show we gave them one. The saddest part of all was at the end when the Chindits returned out of the jungle. We rushed to meet them in the camps they went to, to try and make them laugh. They came out looking like men who had been in Belsen. One camp they were put in, in the north, was bloody awful. The sanitation was appalling and everywhere was swarming with flies. We could feel their disappointment: they had expected so much when they got back and it was so bad. Having gone through all they had in the jungle, to come out alive and find such awful conditions was too much for one man – he committed suicide.'

The winter of 1943-1944 heralded the beginning of the offensive to drive the Japanese from Burma.

Noël Coward who seemed to be everywhere at once was the first star to appear in India. He did this at the personal request of Lord Louis Mountbatten. He was invariably accompanied by his pianist Norman Hackforth.

It coincided, too, with the arrival of the first outside artists to reach the 14th Army since the war had started. First to make it was Noël Coward, answering a desperate personal plea from Lord Louis Mountbatten, newly appointed Supreme Commander of South East Asia. Concerned by the lack of entertainment he found when taking up his post, Mountbatten cabled Coward, who was in South Africa on a fund-raising tour, to break his journey home. Coward agreed immediately and arrived with Norman Hackforth, his accompanist.

'You might have thought Noël would be far above the dear boys heads but don't you believe it,' says Hackforth. 'He was tremendously popular and they adored him – except for one memorable flop on the Ledo Road, the main route on the borders of Assam. The audience was mainly coloured and had never heard of him and didn't know anything about him. He went out with all this tremendous chi-chi and they didn't want to know. To make matters worse, we were on a stage with a tin roof and the audience was out in the open. It was pouring with rain and the noise of the rain on the roof and the lorries coming past all the time meant he couldn't be heard. Everything conspired against him and the audience, out in the rain, got a little bit restive. The whole thing was not a great success. Apart from that occasion we played in the most unlikely places, off the backs of lorries and so on, and they simply loved it which, on the face of it, was quite extraordinary because, starting from the premise that entertainment for troops had to be broad, practically "Who was that lady I saw you with last night?" kind of gag, Coward was doing anything but that. He sang all his own songs and the parodies of "Let's Do It". Half way through the act I did a piano medley of all his tunes while he went off to, as he said, shoot himself. Then he came back and did recitations, of Clemence Dane – a poem called "Plymouth Hoe" and another called "They've dropped a bomb on St Paul's" – a Shakespeare sonnet and a poem of his own called "Lie in the dark and listen". Then we went on with songs like "Don't Let's Be Beastly To The Germans", which the troops loved, and "That Is The End Of The News".'

Even though Noël Coward was given star treatment he arrived to perform for one small detachment to find no piano available. He pressed on with his act, telling stories and singing unaccompanied, while the redundant Norman Hackforth sat on an ammunition box at his side, applauding politely at the right moments. His tour was also in the middle of the monsoon season as Ivor Owen tells:

'They had put up a beautiful marquee for him at one unit and all he had to do was come out and walk on to the stage, a platform made out of bamboo. It even had a canopy over it because of the monsoon. Some water must have got on to the bamboo because as he ran out of the tent he slipped on his backside and went into the mud. His language! You've never heard anything like it! He was wearing the most beautiful, immaculate, white sharkskin suit and he had to have a complete change, only he didn't have a change with him. He couldn't go on as he was so there was a twenty minute delay while he cleaned up, during which American actor Melvyn Douglas, who was a major in the US Army, went on. Eventually Noël got on stage. There were about 2,000 troops massed there, officers, their wives, ladies, everybody you could think of. The first thing he said was, "I'm most frightfully sorry, but fucking awful weather!" He then went straight into his act.'

At the same time as Coward was in India, ENSA started an Indian service. For the first three years of the war, India had been totally ignored as a destination for troop shows because of a squabble over who would pay for them. The Indian Army had its own canteen service which did not want the Naafi setting up shop and without the Naafi, ENSA could not afford to provide entertainment. Basil Dean was unable to find anyone else prepared to underwrite the operation. Until the conclusion of the Desert War, which opened up a quicker route to India, ENSA had deliberately closed its eyes to the plight of the 14th Army. Mounting criticism from India and in the press at home had its effect. Although the financial problems had not been resolved, a decision was taken in London to send out a small number of parties to see how they fared. 'We had not been neglectful of India and Burma,' explained Virginia Vernon, ENSA's Chief Welfare Officer. 'We hadn't been able to put it over in a big way until then. We could not be everywhere at once.'

Anxious to eradicate any impression the troops in India may have gained that they had been neglected, ENSA staff arrived at the end of 1943 with flags waving. At last the men of the 14th Army were to be saved from those dreadful amateur entertainers in uniform.

'They didn't pull any punches,' says Ivor Owen of BESA. 'They let us know right away that they were the professionals and they treated us like dirt, although their shows were inferior. I say this because we had had three years experience of entertaining in India. They came out from Blighty expecting to walk into a country they didn't know and do the same things they'd been doing in England. It didn't work. Shows were folding up, left, right and centre, because the troops just didn't know what they were talking about. They didn't know what was happening back in England. You couldn't sing "We'll Gather Lilacs in the Spring Again", at 108 in the shade, unless you wanted to be sent up.'

The first ENSA show to reach India was the *You're Welcome* concert party with Scots comedian Alec Halls. Halls had been a one-man band for ENSA since it started, touring the British Isles extensively before heading to the Western Desert and on to India. When he spent a spell in hospital he left his bed to entertain in the other wards. Later decorated for his work he set a high standard others found hard to follow.

Within a year of its arrival, ENSA had taken over BESA and all BESA's shows with the exception of the Indian companies. But for the contempt with which some ENSA staff treated any artist not wearing its uniform, the take-over could

An Indian artist giving a demonstration of classical Manipuri dancing for the Indian troops which were about to return to Burma in 1943 to cut a new road through the jungle. This type of entertainment was provided by the Indian Service of BESA, which was the only department not taken over by ENSA.

have been amicable. It was certainly sensible. With the push into Burma under way, BESA, run by Calcutta-based civilians and relying upon donations for finance, had neither the administration nor the resources to follow the road to Mandalay. But, as usual, ENSA in London underrated the job. Unaware just how large India was, ENSA was sending companies from the Middle East to complete the last few weeks of their tours. It would have been better for most of them if they hadn't bothered. There was time only to give a handful of shows before embarking on the voyage home, and the standard of much of their entertainment was not high. Typical of the many cables that flew between ENSA officials in the field and Drury Lane is this one: 'In my opinion this show is not up to standard. Of the seven artists four should not have been sent to India at all and should be returned to the UK. The comedian is vulgar and not funny. The singer has no voice. The two dancers cannot dance.' It was not a masterpiece of

tact to send a West Indian band, billed as a 'Coon' band, to play to Indian troops.

'We called ourselves the arse-end charlies,' wrote Jack Hawkins who was seconded to ENSA, 'for we were at the end of a very long line. So far as ENSA headquarters in Drury Lane were concerned, we were not only at the bottom of their catalogue of priorities, we *were* the bottom. All their talents went into finding entertainers for the European theatre of war, starting with the Italian front, and eventually spreading to France and Belgium. After that came the Middle East and various parts of Africa, and finally the flotsam and jetsam no one else wanted would be forwarded to us. We would receive telegrams from ENSA in London telling us of the imminent arrival of an exciting musical act, but all we would receive would be a lonely pianist who had been deprived of his violinist, or a distraught dancer without her partner . . . The result, from our point of view in India, was a complete shambles.' Hawkins's move fully turned out; and, of course, they weren't young but they went everywhere. They were super, absolutely charming.'

With them had arrived Stainless Stephen only to disappear almost immediately. He was later discovered in Imphal, entertaining in the foxholes. Throughout his stay in India, Stainless Stephen travelled from unit to unit by jeep, on his own, performing for anybody who wanted to see him whether the audience was two or 200, entertaining thousands of men. Shortly afterwards, Vera Lynn arrived, her evening dress crumpled into a ball in her holdall, all the luggage she possessed.

All artists wanted to play the Forward areas, forgetting that men stationed thousands of miles behind the front lines were also suffering the heat and were in desperate need of entertainment.

The incredibly popular Doris and Elsie Waters were the first ENSA stars to reach India. They made a farewell broadcast from Delhi at the end of a tour that took them into the heart of the Arakan.

to ENSA was a fortunate one. His tireless enthusiasm and ability won the respect of all who came into contact with him. His reward came when he met Doreen Lawrence, an actress who had toured West Africa and Egypt for ENSA and was sent to India with a production of *Private Lives*, and later became his wife.

The first ENSA stars to reach India, following closely in the wake of Noël Coward, were Elsie and Doris Waters.

'One or two stars came up to visit us in forward areas and joined in our shows,' remembers Peter Watts of the Chindit Road Show. 'The ones the Chindits really fell for were Doris and Elsie Waters. The chaps described them as real ladies and they really were. They had style and they came over marvellously. There they were, in paddy fields and in the jungle, immaculately dressed, beauti-

The indestructible 'Sweetheart of the Forces', Vera Lynn, did her first tour for ENSA by going to the Near East. She went to India and Burma with a minimum of luggage and a maximum of cheerfulness.

'Some stars,' wrote an exasperated Basil Dean, 'expected the order of the battle to be changed to suit their convenience.' But it wasn't only stars who proved difficult. Some performers arrived in pleasant towns in the hills and stayed, doing no work. An accompanist who failed to appear at a concert gave as his reason the fact that the unit was too far away. Others gauged their appreciation of hospitality by the amount of alcohol provided, a yardstick that did nothing to improve their performance on stage. Complaint after complaint about the quality of artists and the material they were using poured into ENSA.

'A stream of entertainers began to arrive,' Jack Hawkins remembered, 'a deluge of fragmented acts; bottom-of-the-bill comedians, contortionists, conjurors, the remains of dancing troupes, strident lady vocalists and booming baritones. To a man (and woman) they would bounce into my office demanding to be sent to the front line to "entertain our boys", and invariably they would add that they did not have much time because they had promised to appear at the Palladium. One had to admire their spirit, but the fact was that the nearest they were ever likely to get to the Palladium was a show at the end of Skegness Pier.' In some outlying districts it was only the tireless work of individual artists like Douglas Byng and Joyce Grenfell, who were prepared to get on with the job they had been sent to do, that saved ENSA's reputation at all. Joyce Grenfell, continuing the work she had started in the Middle East with ENSA's Hospital Section and still with Viola Tunnard, was astonished to be welcomed by a chaplain in Poona who thanked them 'for coming all this way to entertain the men in bed.' Another artist who caused a stir on her hospital rounds was Doris Ingham who sang 'Bless This House'. She couldn't understand why the lines 'Bless the people here within, Keep them pure and free from sin' should get such a big laugh – until she found out she was in the VD ward.

Although ENSA had taken over responsibility for official entertainment, local concert parties continued to flourish. Army Welfare tried to promote concerts through the Army Central Entertainment Services and RAF Welfare sent Bill Sutton and Norrie Paramor, from the RAF Gang Shows, to tour RAF stations and organize six new Gangs. Most of the men they found, like drummer Eric Delaney, were professionals and welcomed the chance to perform again even though it meant a cut in pay.

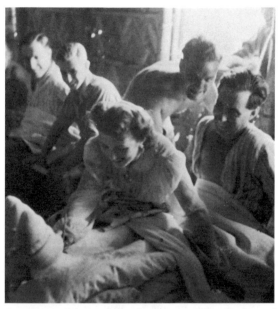

Patricia Burke, daughter of singing star Tom Burke and actress Marie, arrived in Burma from a five month tour in Italy. She visited hospitals as well as camps accompanied only by Jimmy Bailey, her pianist.

The highlight of many a small concert party's existence was the visit of a star who would top their bill. Patricia Burke had flown to Burma from Italy.

'We went down the Arakan to Akyab, Ramree, Cox's Bazaar and all those little places. In one of them I was supposed to do a show for some commandos. Their CO came to me and said they had their own concert party and since his men had been fighting for such a long time he wanted to make it a really big concert; would I mind if his boys did their bit first. I said of course not. They did their concert and there were some quite good things in it: a Welsh boy with a very good voice and a Cockney bloke who told the Tale of the Three Bears in a terrible mixture of Cockney and Urdhu. I was supposed to do three concerts there and at the end of the first one, one of them came up to me and asked if they could do the next one with me. I said, "Well, I don't know. Wouldn't we have to ask the brigadier or something?" "Don't worry," he said. "We'll fix him." So they did the next concert, and the next, and the next which was at Headquarters. The following day I was going across to Ramree and they said could they come with me. "But I'm going for about ten days," I said, "What will your brig . . ." "Don't worry. We'll fix him." And they did. When we got to

Ramree I told them that if they were going to be with me for ten days they would have to rehearse, cut their acts and become professional. At nine o'clock the next day I got them on the beach for a rehearsal and I made them work. I cut their stuff, tightened it all up and divided my own act into two so that they started the show, I followed, they did some more and then I finished. It made a good evening's entertainment.'

A soldier who saw Patricia Burke in Burma wrote to his mother: 'I saw a young lady who did just that one thing, gave the boys a real show off her own bat, except of course for the help she received from her pianist. She's that very talented and exceedingly attractive Patricia Burke, and believe me, she was the berries! I believe panto's been her speciality back home but however good she was in that role, at entertaining a service audience miles from home, she'll take a lot of beating. Perhaps it's because I haven't seen any star female entertainment – only one poorish one – that I enjoyed her show so much – but she certainly went down well here. She's had plenty of experience at this game and she's come direct from a five month's tour of Italy. She's very versatile, sings all manner of songs and even cracks a few jokes. Her best kind of number is "Honeysuckle Rose" or "Good Morning". She jumps, skips and shakes her hips in grand style and her voice is really grand. I was charmed, as you may have guessed! . . . If ever she comes to the Empire after the war, I'll spend my last bob (if times are bad) to see her.'

While playing on Ramree island, Patricia Burke's show was strafed by a Japanese fighter and she ended up under a table with an air vice marshal. When she got back to the mainland a letter was awaiting her from Lord Mountbatten. He thanked her for visiting Burma and South East Asia. 'I hope,' he wrote, 'that you will come out this way again before the war ends and tour the forward areas.'

The US Forces in South East Asia and the Pacific had been suffering from neglect just as much as the British. The American front against the Japanese extended from the Aleutian Islands off Alaska in the north to the Coral Sea off Australia in the south, a front several thousand miles long. Entertainers had been flying to the Aleutians since Jolson, Joe E Brown and Bob Hope had pioneered the way in 1942. Being so close to the mainland, the posts there never seemed so far away and it was good publicity without too much trouble to play there. The Southern Pacific was different. GIs were spread out across hundreds of islands, miles apart. The main staging post for the area was Hawaii, just over two thousand miles from San Francisco. On 22 December, 1942 fifteen artists, the first USO entertainers to reach the South Pacific, had flown there and a month later, at the beginning of 1943, Joe E Brown, with guitarist Johnny Marvin, was the first star to arrive. Brown gave twenty shows on Hawaii and then struck out for the islands. 'We covered the whole Pacific front, clear up to where the bullets were flying,' he wrote in his autobiography. 'Show time was any time at the front. Often we would begin our first show early in the morning. Once when I was taking a 9 am plane in the New Hebrides Islands I jeeped sixteen miles out into the jungle and did a show for Carlsen's Raiders and still got back before the plane left. The smallest audience I had . . . was one youngster on lookout duty who had to miss all the shows. I shinnied up the tree to a platform where he was sitting. He was from Houston, Texas, and I asked him "How come you got this assignment in a tree?" "Well, I'll tell you," he said with a grin and a nice soft drawl. "Fact is, I didn't have me no shoes. So I couldn't work any other way." That was on the island of Canton which was pretty short of supplies just then: no bread or butter, and not even an extra pair of shoes to be had.'

'One of the difficulties,' Brown recalled of working in the Pacific, 'was rain. It was hard to do anything in the kind of rain they had on those tropical islands. It was almost impossible to do a show. But the boys didn't see any reason why sheets of rain couldn't be used as a backdrop for our act, and I got so I could accept it myself. It just meant screaming a little louder to get above the roar of the rain. Once in New Guinea, when I got to a certain place where we had scheduled a show, I found it had been raining for hours. The mud was almost knee deep, and I couldn't imagine how I could stand on some rickety, wobbly platform, much less try to do my act. I asked the Special Services officer to announce that the show would be postponed until the next day. Then I heard a terrible outcry. "What's that?" I asked the colonel who was putting me up in his tent. "That's your audience," he said. "Listen!" I listened. "We want him now. We want Joe E, we want Joe E," they were chanting. "They're waiting in the rain," the colonel said. "They've been there for two hours – twenty-five hundred of them, Mr Brown." I don't

Joe E Brown was probably the most widely travelled American star in the years 1942–1944 and his popularity was matched only by that of Bob Hope. Of all the men who toured the USO circuits in 1944, he alone received an award that acclaimed him as 'Father to All Men Overseas'.

need to add any "PS They got their show." And not one kid left throughout the whole hour that I sloshed about on that stage trying to keep on my feet and deliver the goods they had ordered. Many times in the Pacific I stumbled along in utter darkness to reach a makeshift platform of boxes where my guide would say, "This is the stage, sir." I'd look round and say, "But where is the audience?" "They're all around you, sir." And sure enough they were, crouching there in the darkness waiting for the show.'

Small wonder few Hollywood stars were prepared to risk their reputations or health in such conditions if they could possibly avoid it. The official answer to complaints about lack of star visits and USO shows in Europe and North Africa was always that the major concentraion of effort was in the Pacific, but that didn't mean the Pacific islands were overrun with film stars. It proved as difficult for USO to get stars to tour as it was for ENSA. There were notable exceptions. Jack Benny, Larry Adler, Carole Landis, Paulette Goddard, Gary Cooper and Bob Hope were among those who joined the innumerable small-time USO troupes. There were also some limited local attempts to form GI concert parties. Maurice Evans, the noted stage actor, formed *The Hourglass Players*, a variety company, from members of the 7th Division in Hawaii and also produced *Hamlet* with himself in the lead. But the majority of men never saw a show with or without stars and the complaints increased. In October, 1944, the

Singer Frances Langford and moustached comic Jerry Colonna with Bob Hope in the South Pacific. Frances Langford, who frequently toured with Hope, was voted the most popular female entertainer by US Servicemen.

CBI *Roundup*, the US Army's weekly paper in the Pacific, lambasted Hollywood stars for not visiting them or for cutting short their trips because 'the going was too tough'. Paulette Goddard, Ann Sheridan, Joe E Brown, Al Jolson and Joel McCrea were all singled out for criticism. The marines leapt to the defence of Brown, who had collapsed with exhaustion, saying he was the best entertainer ever to visit the Pacific. Ann Sheridan was furious; if she had wanted publicity, she said, she would have stayed at home. She had been kept waiting in New York for a month before leaving on her tour and had to return to fulfill a contract. Joel McCrea had also spent a month in New York and was eventually told to go home. Al Jolson had never been asked to go. There were faults on both sides. USO, who specified where an entertainer was to go, was disorganized. Equally, many Hollywood stars who had volunteered their services earlier had kept very quiet when the time came to fulfill their promise. Alarmed by the bad publicity, the Victory Committee held a big rally at which Victor Mature, Clark Gable and Robert Montgomery spoke for the men in uniform and Jack Benny, Gracie Fields, Kay Francis and Bob Hope told what it was like to entertain overseas. As a result, more stars did express willingness to visit troops overseas and USO did its best to slot them in. After VJ Day the War Department requested the number of shows to be stepped up and by November, 1945 there were 1,205 USO artists playing to men in the Pacific and South East Asia.

On 6th August, 1945 the first atomic bomb was

dropped on Hiroshima. Three days later a second bomb was dropped on Nagasaki and the war in the Pacific came to an abrupt end. Singapore, scene of that humiliating defeat for the British three years earlier, surrendered without a shot being fired and four days later ENSA party *Keep Moving* was performing on the dockside to five hundred ex-POW's awaiting embarkation. The first star to reach Singapore was Gracie Fields, touring for USO. No theatre could be found large enough to hold all the people who wanted to see her so she appeared in the football stadium. It was filled to capacity with servicemen, the wounded and ex-POW's and Gracie Fields gave one of the best performances in her life. It was seen by Donald Sinden who was in SEAC with an ENSA Play company.

'I had to fight to get in and I was sitting high up in one of the stands. All the stands were packed and the pitch was covered with the wounded and POW's. Down in the middle of the pitch, on a tiny stage like a boxing ring, was Gracie, singing her

Jack Benny also toured the Pacific Islands. In Hawaii the 299th Army Ground Forces band, the Jungleers, presented him with one of their uniforms.

heart out. She gave us everything and when she started the first few notes of "Sally" I looked at all the faces around me. Tough men, who had seen a lot of the war and all the horror, were crying; uncontrollable tears rolled down their cheeks. It was a memorable occasion.'

Douglas Byng reopened the Victoria Theatre in Singapore and was followed in by John Gielgud and his company playing *Blithe Spirit* and *Hamlet*. The theatre was in a poor state. The wall behind the stage had been demolished and the stage was separated from the outside by a curtain; the doors had been blown off and there was no glass in the windows. Swifts flew in and out during the performance and the actors couldn't be heard when the audience in the concert hall next door applauded Solomon who was giving a recital. In spite of the conditions, the audience loved *Hamlet* because, says Gielgud, 'Of the colour, the lights and the costumes. We had taken the full stage costumes from London rather than doing it in modern dress, which would have been much easier and much more comfortable in the heat. The troops responded to the care and trouble we had taken.'

Gielgud had been worried about taking *Hamlet* on his ENSA tour of India and South East Asia; it was not a play he felt was suited to troop audiences and, on a purely personal level, he was concerned that audiences would find his performance as Hamlet, arch and mannered. He need not have worried. He found it exhilarating to play in front of English audiences, many of whom didn't even know the story. Forced to rethink his approach to the part and shorn of West End mannerisms, he found a new intimacy with the audience through playing in the round (in Rangoon), and gave, so he felt, some of his finest interpretations. Acknowledged as the finest Hamlet of his generation, he felt that he never wanted to essay the part again and gave his last performance to troops in Basil Dean's Cairo Drama Festival on his way home.

Without the excuse of the war being on, ENSA's shortcomings were again exposed. Although plays, ballets, variety and all types of entertainment were sent out, an increasing conflict with the commercial theatres was developing. Artists, who had been reluctant to visit India in the first place, no longer felt it was their duty to entertain troops and were far more concerned with carving out careers in the West End or on radio. To make matters worse, the 14th Army's demob was deferred. Once more they were in danger of becoming the Forgotten Army. Army and RAF Welfare encouraged the formation of any units that could entertain and anybody with experience was asked to audition. There were some surprising rejections. Michael Langdon, the internationally-known operatic bass, auditioned for a major and sang 'The Floral Dance'. He was told he was all right to take part in a barrack-room sing-song but not good enough to go on the stage. Kenneth Williams, who had joined the Royal Artillery for the last year of the war and been posted to Ceylon, was constantly told to forget any ambition he might have to be an entertainer. Only perseverance got him into his unit concert party which included Stanley Baxter (another earlier reject), John Schlesinger and playwright Peter Nichols. A singer who met with better success was tenor Charles Craig. He was requested for an ACES unit after he had been heard at a divisional concert by Slim himself, and in spite of being posted deep into the jungle by his CO, who didn't want him to leave, joined the unit and began a career that has taken him to La Scala, Milan.

RAF Welfare, taking over responsibility for the six RAF Gang Shows produced by Bill Sutton and Norrie Paramor, decided to produce Welfare Road Shows along similar lines. All airmen were eligible to audition and among the successful ones was Harry Illingsworth, a fitter, who had always harboured a dream to go on the stage. To get his name on the bills he later shortened it to Harry Worth.

'I don't think I was a very good fitter,' he says, 'I just passed my test, that's all. I don't want to do injustice to a lot of reputable people but after the war there used to be advertisements in the papers: Fitters required – RAF need not apply. We were taught, in effect, to take one component off and replace it with another. The actual repairing went to somebody higher. I was posted to Burma with 62 Squadron and we came back to India to refit. While we were there the bomb went off and all the people who had been considered too important before because of their jobs – fitters, mechanics and so on – were asked to audition for these Welfare units. Before the war I had been a miner, in the local dramatic society and appearing occasionally in the Working Men's Clubs. I

auditioned in Delhi and within a week I was in. I took part in everything but my main act was as a ventriloquist.'

Conjuror Stanley Watson also auditioned successfully for the Road Shows.

'To keep my hand in while stationed in the jungles of Assam I used to amuse the chaps in their billets with card tricks galore and as the Mosquito aircraft we had were all equipped with Merlin engines, my unofficial name became "Merlin". At the auditions the most frightening thing for most blokes, and me in particular being a conjuror, was that we had to sing. Anyway, I got through! At most camps the show was well received but occasionally we came up against people who thought we were a load of poofs, particularly as most of us had to don drag whether we wished to or not. At one camp they very pointedly put a "Gents Only" sign over the door of the Sergeants' Mess.'

'It's marvellous how the shows utilized the talent of people,' says Harry Worth. 'The show, with eight or ten of us, lasted two hours. Each contributed his own bit but in the midst of this were the sketches, the songs and the music. No person's talent was stretched too far. I don't know why we weren't sent up. It's rather amazing but we got great receptions everywhere. They were in the most awful places and to see anybody dressed up on stage, with a few lights on them and with the minimum of talent (though some had a great deal more than that) was a change. It wasn't a Hollywood production, or anything like that, but it did take them out of the hum-drum existence they were leading.'

The war being over audiences and shows began to dwindle as men received their signals to pack up and return home for demob. The Road Shows and other concert parties struggled on with decreasing numbers; what had once been ten-handed shows were reduced to five performers, until they, too, set sail for England and Civvy Street.

'From my point of view,' says Harry Worth, 'those last few months in uniform were marvellous. I had six months in which to appear at least once, mostly twice a day in front of an audience, to get used to the idea of doing the job professionally. It was invaluable experience.'

KEEPING
OCCUPIED

By the close of 1945, thousands of troops who had answered their country's call to arms were kicking their heels around the world, waiting to return home and get on with the business of living. Demobilization didn't happen the moment Peace was signed, and the laborious process of recalling overseas forces, sorting everyone out, issuing demob suits and signing everyone off lasted well into 1946, and 1947 for the really unlucky ones. The war was over but the need for entertainment was greater than ever.

Since there weren't enough camps in Britain to

Jay Morris's company Let's Pretend, *accompanied by an American band, was the first ENSA show to be given in Germany. The company celebrated the event by dancing on the lawn at Regendal.*

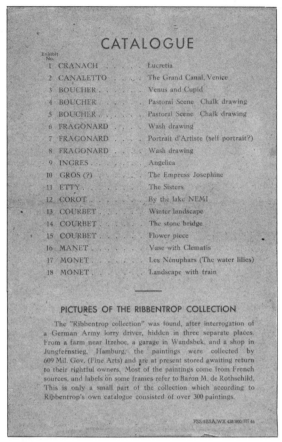

CATALOGUE

Exhibit No.		
1	CRANACH	Lucretia
2	CANALETTO	The Grand Canal, Venice
3	BOUCHER	Venus and Cupid
4	BOUCHER	Pastoral Scene Chalk drawing
5	BOUCHER	Pastoral Scene Chalk drawing
6	FRAGONARD	Wash drawing
7	FRAGONARD	Portrait d'Artiste (self portrait?)
8	FRAGONARD	Wash drawing
9	INGRES	Angelica
10	GROS (?)	The Empress Josephine
11	ETTY	The Sisters
12	COROT	By the lake NEMI
13	COURBET	Winter landscape
14	COURBET	The stone bridge
15	COURBET	Flower piece
16	MANET	Vase with Clematis
17	MONET	Les Nénuphars (The water lilies)
18	MONET	Landscape with train

PICTURES OF THE RIBBENTROP COLLECTION

The "Ribbentrop collection" was found, after interrogation of a German Army lorry driver, hidden in three separate places. From a farm near Itzehoe, a garage in Wandsbek, and a shop in Jungfernstieg, Hamburg, the paintings were collected by 609 Mil. Gov. (Fine Arts) and are at present stored awaiting return to their rightful owners. Most of the paintings come from French sources, and labels on some frames refer to Baron M. de Rothschild. This is only a small part of the collection which according to Ribbentrop's own catalogue consisted of over 300 paintings.

PSS/BSSA/WX 438-900/III 46

The war was well over when the von Ribbentrop collection of looted European art went on an eleven day exhibition in Hamburg from 12 to 23 March in 1946.

accommodate all the troops many men, who had been in North Africa or the Mediterranean, found themselves posted to Germany, to await demob, where they became part of the Army of occupation. The service Welfare and Education branches went to town organizing lectures on current affairs, how life had changed back home and what to expect, adult education courses, painting classes and career guidance. In Hamburg an exhibition of the Impressionist paintings found in von Ribbentrop's collection went on display and recitals by classical musicians, plays, revues and concerts were organized to supplement the work of the official service entertainment units, ENSA and USO.

At the request of the War Department, USO sent a further sixty units to Europe, including fifteen play companies and eight large scale musicals, with casts of up to fifty. Jack Benny and Larry Adler arrived with Ingrid Bergman and on 4 July gave a show to 40,000 GIs in the Nuremberg stadium where Leni Riefenstahl had shot *Triumph of the Will*. Marlene Dietrich, at the end of a year's tour of Europe, caught pneumonia and had to return to the States for an operation, but not before she had seen her sister Elizabeth released from Belsen. As soon as she had recovered she returned for her third overseas tour, lecturing, visiting hospitals and still singing.

The many ENSA companies in Europe at the close of war continued to tour, and for the first time the presence of prestige West End productions was really appreciated. Companies could take over a theatre for a week at a time and troops could get to see them without suddenly being ordered on. Anna Neagle, Rex Harrison and Roland Culver starred in *French Without Tears*. After one performance, Anna Neagle, who was known mostly from her films, especially her role as Queen Victoria, received a letter. 'I think you'll be amused,' the soldier wrote, 'by a remark I heard when I came out of the theatre after the performance. Two young soldiers were talking and one said to the other, "Do you know, I've only ever seen her as Queen Victoria before? I never knew she had legs like that!"'

Emlyn Williams starred in *Blithe Spirit* and his own play *Night Must Fall*, productions he had already taken to North Africa and Italy; the Old Vic Company, with Sybil Thorndike, Laurence Olivier and Ralph Richardson, played through France, Belgium, Holland and into Germany. Many people, to whom the idea of Shakespeare was taboo, had a free chance to see some of the finest artists of the century. They went in the first place because there was little else to do; they stayed to cheer.

'I remember one night,' says Jeffrey Segal, 'a sergeant who had seen the Old Vic's *Peer Gynt*, with Richardson playing Gynt magnificently, saying, "You know, I've never been to the theatre before but I'll tell you what my favourite play is, it's *Peer Gynt*. It's smashing. After that comes *Richard III*. It was great." This sort of thing happened with people from all ranks. The Old Vic productions were elaborate and the German theatres had every facility, of which they made full use. When they went to the Atlantic Theatre in Hamburg, with far more facilities than the New in London, it really was a magnificent, exciting theatrical experience. It was magic for the boys –

(Above) The cast of French without Tears *met the staff of 55th Military Hospital at Sterkerl in June 1945. Sitting on the lawn, looking very English, are the nurses and the members of the company including Anna Neagle, Roland Culver and Rex Harrison. (Right) Dame Sybil Thorndike toured France and Germany with fellow members of the Old Vic company.*

like a kid going to his first pantomime at Drury Lane. And the sheer difference of what they were seeing. They were used to concert parties, having somebody with various degrees of sequined dress on come out and sing, 'We'll Meet Again', watching the odd, not very sophisticated sketch with jokes about officers. Here was something so outside that, it had a tremendous impact.'

Another company sent out from Britain was the ABCA Play Unit with its repertoire of current affairs plays, which were seen as a valuable adjunct to the programme of informing troops of what was going on around them.

Ralph Richardson and Laurence Olivier, seen here sightseeing in Hamburg, were other members of the lengthy 1944–45 Old Vic tour which brought several productions of the classical stage, including Richard III *and* Arms and the Man *to the occupying armies.*

'We were called the Army Topical Theatre for our German tour,' recalls Stephen Murray, 'but such is the way of Army Welfare that we found ourselves being routed as the Army Tropical Cabaret and the men came in expecting to see hula-hula girls. When they found it was us, they still raised the roof, I'm glad to say! The first show we gave was in an RAF Mobile theatre, a quite big canvas theatre, which for some extraordinary reason had been pitched in a swamp. They had dug trenches all around and they had pumps working, trying to keep the water down. We had three tons of equipment and were due to give two shows. Half way through our first performance the water started to rise and they just managed to get in another pump to keep it down. Half-an-hour before our second performance the water rose

dramatically and we decided we had to get out. Within thirty minutes we were up to our waists in it and we carted our three tons of equipment the three hundred yards to a lorry, waist deep in water. The audience was marched rapidly away!'

The period between the end of the war and demob gave many uniformed artists their first chance to entertain. Germany was divided into Commands and what happened in the area around Hanover, occupied by 30 Corps, was typical in most of them.

'I was a staff officer at Brigade headquarters,' recalls Ian Carmichael, 'when a decree came from General Sir Brian Horrocks, the Corps commander, after VE Day, that now we had settled down to occupy Germany it was essential we provide enough entertainment for the troops. Since ENSA was not supplying enough, we therefore had to make our own and he decreed that anyone, regardless of rank or experience, who had talent or who wished to entertain, should go to Nienburg to attend auditions.'

Like many professionals anxious to get back to work and utilize the remainder of their time in uniform, Carmichael jumped at the opportunity. He went to Nienburg and found himself being auditioned by Richard Stone, the newly appointed Corps Entertainments Officer. Although in different years, he and Stone had been at RADA together. Stone recognized him and invited him to join his staff.

Another audition hopeful was Jeffrey Segal, who had just started his career as an actor touring plays for troops in Britain, when he was called up and sent to North Africa. After fighting in Italy, he was posted to Germany a week before the end of the war. His REME unit was reshuffled and he became surplus. At the unit's farewell party, the adjutant (who had been in Segal's concert party only on the strength of his rank) told him about the new 30 Corps Pool of Entertainers.

'My new CO, who really had no idea what to do with me, was so delighted when I told him about the auditions,' remembers Segal, 'that he gave me his car and driver to get there. I arrived and it was a highly-civilizing experience because one had rushed from the hurly-burly of hairy-bottomed soldiery to the garden of a manor house at Nienburg which Richard Stone had managed to obtain as his headquarters. I was greeted by a man who said, "Have you had tea? This is the piece we would like you to do but go and have some tea first. I think there are some strawberries and

In 1945 Ian Carmichael was stationed at Nienburg in Germany. One of his tasks was to supervise rehearsals of a production for 30th Corps. He began as assistant to the Corps Entertainment Officer and subsequently took over the position himself.

cream, if you'd like to ask one of the serving wenches. Anyhow, get your breath back, settle down, then come and do this for us, if you would be so kind." There was an added piquancy because I was a sergeant and I did my audition for a private. At the end he said, "Right, I'll let you know." I went back to my unit in the CO's car and as I walked in his face fell. He thought he'd seen the last of me.'

A few days later Segal heard that he had been accepted and was sent to join the cast of *Men In Shadow*, a regimental production which had been taken over by Army Welfare. Entertainers of every description and talent, not just actors, made their way to Nienburg and, following Horrocks's decree, acceptance had nothing to do with talent. One of the first shows Richard Stone managed to get on the road, a dance band, had a colonel playing trumpet and was conducted by a private. Joining the queue of hopeful singers, jugglers, reciters and comics was Bombardier Francis Howerd. Before the war Howerd had been running an amateur concert party in Eltham, London, while working as an insurance clerk. He tried unsuccessfully to join ENSA, was called up into the Royal Artillery and applied three times for a transfer to Stars in Battledress. Three times he was rejected. 'Of course I was very sad and upset I couldn't get into Stars in Battledress,' he says,

Private Gordon Brown directed a highly professional regimental production of Men in Shadow *in 1944 which was taken over at the end of the war by Army Welfare. It was this production Jeffrey Segal was sent to join after V.E. day.*

'because I considered I would have been much more useful doing that than what I was doing, which was to impede the progress of the war. My sergeant major used to refer to me as the "Unknown Quantity"! But, thinking back, I'm not surprised they turned me down – I think I would have turned me down as well. It was very difficult trying to be a comedy smash hit on a grey winter's day, in a cookhouse, to an audience of only one grim-looking officer. I remember one of my auditions in South Wales: it was a very cold, wet day and this little major sat at the back of the cookhouse, on his own, where it was so dark I could hardly see him, and said, "Make me laugh." I was so cold and nervous standing among the pots and pans at my end, and it is extremely difficult to make an empty cookhouse laugh. He didn't think much of me.'

Posted to Germany, all his chances of entertaining stopped until the war was over and he was working in the Military Government office. His CO saw a show he put on and sent him to Nienburg to audition for Richard Stone and Ian Carmichael.

'I remember him at that audition,' says Car-michael, 'as being almost exactly the same as the Frankie Howerd we know today. He did a bit of patter and sang a song. I don't think one can say it's a lack of discipline in so great a comedian but, in some ways, you feel he cocks up as many jokes as he makes good ones. He has this tremendous flare for capitalizing on apparent mistakes and making something funny out of what seems to be total disaster – which it would be for anyone else – that gives him the style that is Frankie Howerd. He had this sort of lack-of-control then and I remember, after he had left the stage, Richard Stone said, "Fine, we'll book him. He was good. We can build a show around him." I said, "But he's terrible!", and went on to say everything I've just explained. If it had been left to me I would not have booked him; and I now think he is a very great comedian!'

The show built around Frankie Howerd was *The Waggoners*. It toured for six months and folded only because Howerd's demob came up and he left Germany and the Army.

Although Richard Stone was not officially permitted to use Germans to entertain Allied troops, it was not long before he was calling on the talents of local performers, all of whom were anxious to get back to work. Horrocks, eager to give entertainment its head, was happy to turn a blind eye to the breaking of the No Fraternization rule. Some German performers were recruited in a most unexpected manner. One night just before hostilities ended, a Rifle Brigade unit was waiting to cross the river Elbe. In front of them they could make out what were obviously camouflaged German vehicles on the edge of a wood. They commenced rapid firing and when it wasn't returned, advanced cautiously. The 'vehicles' were two elephants and cowering beside them were the frightened performers of the Circus Belli. A signal was sent back to HQ: 'Two lions brewed up, two bears escaping, two elephants and circus staff captured.'

'My colonel saw this signal,' recalls Stone, 'and said to me, "Marvellous. We'll have a circus." I dashed off to find these two beasts and from them I worked back to various other circus acts that were knocking around. Since we weren't allowed to use

Germans at that time we had to prove that all these people were Displaced Persons; Russians, Latvians or anybody so long as they weren't Germans. Gradually we collected together a circus and re-established the Circus Belli. Belli hadn't got a big top; his had been burnt down. In my innocence I went and requisitioned the big top of Hagenbeck, who was undoubtedly German, and gave it to Belli, his big rival. I'm told that years later Hagenbeck is still looking for the Major Stone who requisitioned his big top on an army form! We put the tent up in the middle of Hamburg and played three times a day to capacity houses. I remember the dress rehearsal because Olivier, Richardson and Sybil Thorndike, and that very famous Old Vic Company which was playing at the Opera House, came to it. Herbert Menges, the Old Vic's musical director, didn't like the noises the band was making so he dashed up to the platform above the animals' entrance, where the band sits in a German circus, and took over the baton.'

When Richard Stone left 30 Corps his job was

The two elepants captured by the Rifle Brigade passing through Hamburg to join the Belli Circus company.

Under the auspices of the Army Welfare, members of various companies were organized to join the Circus Belli which proved to be an enormously popular show with both the occupying forces and the citizens of Hamburg.

taken over by Ian Carmichael who discovered for himself the German fascination with circuses.

'There were dozens of them of various shapes and sizes,' he remembers 'After Richard had gone a man came to me from the Circus Ahltoff and said would I like to route him to the troops. I went to see him, thought it was a good circus and gave him two dates, a week in one town, a week in another. At the end of the second week he came back to me. "The first week I do good business," he said. "The second week no business at all because Circus Belli came to town. This musn't happen again." I went to see Circus Belli and said we didn't want this clash again as neither of them were doing good business. Belli agreed I should route him as well, to keep them separate. At the end of the week they both came back to me and said it was all very well but in each town I'd sent them to, another circus had appeared. This snowballed and although I didn't want the bloody things, I ended up with six or seven circuses. Not only did I route them all, they used to come to me with their problems like where to get fodder for the elephants.'

Outside 30 Corps the search for people with talent to amuse also continued. Anyone who had ever had a hankering to appear in the spotlights was encouraged to come forward, among them Eric Sykes. Sykes's war in the RAF had been far removed from entertainment. A wireless operator with a mobile signals unit, he had been posted to Normandy shortly after D-Day and achieved the distinction of spearheading the Allied advance for two days, although he didn't know it at the time. His unit had set up camp in a French village two days before the advance guard arrived to liberate it. Ending up in Germany, he answered the call for entertainers, although he had had little experience, and was put into a revue run by Flight Lieutenant Bill Fraser.

In Italy, where after the long struggle morale was low and desertions were high, the Central Pool of Artists set up an Italian section, which attracted two men from the Royal Artillery, Harry Secombe and Spike Milligan. Their paths had first crossed in North Africa when Harry Secombe, asleep under a hill guarded by a large gun, was awakened by the sound of the gun rolling towards him. The man who came to ask for it back was Milligan.

In England, the Central Pool redoubled its efforts to find artists. In its early days, the Pool had been able to recruit established performers from the ranks. Now, it had to use young, untried talent. Actor Jack Carlton, the Pool's new CO, who had taken over from Basil Brown, outlined his new policy in a newsletter: 'It takes years to make stars, so we can't expect to find many new stars. The concert party, as such, has served its purpose in this war, and served it well. To produce a concert party one needs stars or a star on whom to build the show. In the place of concert parties we will produce revues which will depend for their success on team work.'

A scriptwriting unit, to which Sidney Vauncez, the show business journalist, and Charlie Chester were attached, was set up to prepare material for the new revues.

'There was a room full of artists downstairs,' recalls Chester, 'waiting for some young officer to say, "I'm the producer and I want seven people." He'd then pick out the ones he wanted and sent them up to us for material. They sent one boy up to me who said he sang comical songs with a ukelele. I asked him what kind of songs he sang. "The officer downstairs said you would write one for me," he said. "I will," I said, "but what type of songs have you been singing?" "The officer said you would write all my material." I said I would and asked him to play the ukelele for me. "The officer said you would teach me how to play," he said. The poor kid had never done anything.'

Some of the new talent taken into Stars in Battledress may have been young and untried but

Bob Hope continued to combine his professional career with tours of personal appearances for US forces long after this event in the Royal Albert Hall in 1945. His wartime exploits won him a place in the American Hall of Fame.

they were, like Secombe and Milligan in Italy, to become the stars of the future. Reg Varney, who had tried to join the Pool before and had been stopped at the beginning of his audition with a curt 'Thank you very much', was accepted and put in charge of a party that included actress-singer Stella Moray. Another unknown, who got his first chance with the Pool, was Benny Hill. Having applied to join them and hearing nothing, he took leave from his unit and went to the Pool's headquarters. His previous experience had been playing small parts, before the war, while working as an assistant stage manager. The Pool had enough stage managers and scriptwriters (which Hill wanted to be) but were short of comics. Hill was told to come back for an audition the following day. He had no act and no ideas but that night he went to the Windmill and saw Peter Waring at work. He wrote a shaggy dog story and gave it the next day in the style of Waring. He passed and was cast as the comedy lead in the musical *Happy Weekend*, a production he stayed with until Stars in Battledress disbanded.

While realizing that Stars in Battledress would soon be finishing, Carlton was determined that the high standards of the previous years should not slip during the last few months and he started a drama school, a sort of khaki RADA, under Michael Denison, to teach newcomers to the Pool their trade. Denison's assistant was James Donald, a method actor, who disagreed violently with everything Denison tried to teach. He would stand at the back of Denison's lectures expressing his disapproval of every point made until he could take no more and burst in with his own theories on the art of acting. Denison won all the arguments simply by pulling rank.

The war may have been finished but there was still one more casualty to come – ENSA itself. It was inevitable that the various organizations providing entertainment should be gathered under one umbrella. A central body, which knew where troops were and where the artists were, was essential if the wartime mistakes, that some areas received all the shows while others received none, were not to be repeated. ENSA would have been the logical body on which to base this organization but for the fact that ENSA's own body was dying, riddled with stab wounds. As the war came to a close, animosity towards Dean grew. He had never been popular. His brusque, dictatorial manner aroused antagonism but he had achieved results of which any man could be proud. Things had not

always run smoothly for ENSA and it had suffered from its share (perhaps more than fair share) of incompetent artists and administrators. But, whatever the difficulties, ENSA had provided an entertainment service that reached around the world.

With no war to unite them in a common purpose, the generals and artists, on whose toes Dean had frequently stepped, turned on him. He became the victim of a bitter and vindictive witchhunt that found its way into Parliament and ended with the disbanding of ENSA. The attacks on Dean were felt by the thousands of men and women who had loyally worked for him, and through him for the fighting men, for the previous six years. Although every conceivable form of war service was recognized in the Victory Parade in London, not a single ENSA artist took part.

ENSA's work finished on 31 August, 1946. The new organization that took its place, formed by the Welfare Departments at the War Office, was Combined Services Entertainment, or, as Tommy Trinder, who took the last ENSA show to Burma, explained the initials, Chaos Supersedes ENSA.

Back in London for his demob, Richard Stone was asked to become colonel in charge of CSE and under his command came all the ENSA shows still on the road and all service entertainments, including Stars in Battledress, the RAF Gang Shows and Army Welfare productions. Reg Varney was flying from Cairo to Singapore with his Stars in Battledress company when the take-over occurred, and had never heard of CSE. Their papers had been inadvertently sent to Italy and when they reached Singapore no one knew who they were or what Stars in Battledress, the organization to which they claimed to belong, meant.

The work of CSE, taking entertainment to British troops anywhere in the world, continues today, but by the end of 1946, its wartime job was over as the last of the conscripted Servicemen changed their uniforms for mufti.

In the United States, USO continued a little longer. USO clubs were gradually handed over to local communities and USO Camp Shows entered its final phase entertaining the wounded in hospitals. By 31 December, 1947 both USO and USO Camp Shows were out of business. Their operations started again in 1951 for GIs fighting in Korea, continued throughout the Vietnam war and are still going today.

In their various ways, all the men and women who set out to entertain during the Second World

In September 1945 Puccini's Madama Butterfly *was taken by the Sadlers Wells Opera Company to Hamburg. The Hamburg Philharmonic Orchestra was conducted by Sir John Barbirolli. Parry Jones sang Pinkerton and the title role was played by Sybil Lloyd.*

War succeeded. For perhaps only a half-an-hour they managed to distract men's thoughts from the realities of why they were in the jungle, desert, Arctic or sitting by a lonely gun overlooking the North Sea. They took with them a reminder of the world left behind, the world the troops were fighting for.

Audiences saw a lot of rubbish, only one remove from barrack-room horseplay, but they also watched people who were destined to become stars and performances by some of the greatest artists of the century. Cultural barriers came tumbling down as opera, ballet, classical music and drama were discovered to be as enjoyable as variety or a band show. The one thing troops would not stand for was a performance that was shoddily presented or underrated their intelligence. Quality, whether in a juggling act, Gielgud playing Hamlet or a fine needlewoman demonstrating her art, was readily appreciated and accepted.

The saddest of all the war casualties was, perhaps, ENSA, which stood in the middle of the battle between quality and quantity. People complained if they didn't see ENSA shows, they complained when they did. The basic fault with ENSA was, not in what it did or did not do, but that it was not run by Servicemen. It was a civilian organization living in a military world and the men in uniform resented its presence. If a show was good, Army Welfare took the credit. If it was poor, it was dismissed as another ENSA show. Richard Llewellyn, author of *How Green Was My Valley*, was Basil Dean's right-hand man during the formative days of ENSA. He is in no doubt that had Dean been a general he would have been properly acknowledged for his work with ENSA.

'Without Basil Dean it would never have been. He was a martinet, a son-of-a-bitch bastard, a monolith, a kindly – sometimes – tyrant, a bully, but he knew what he wanted and others didn't, and he got it and the rest were in the ruck. His was the influence, the hand on the wheel that never faltered. He made enemies. The enemies were never of the slightest use until it was all over, then they slipped in the poison.'

Nigel Patrick agrees. 'ENSA was a very easy target. It was terribly easy to say that the shows stank and were no good. There was perhaps one sixth of truth in that. Some of the shows were appalling but the vast majority were in the "all right, not bad at all" bracket. The remainder were absolutely first class whether they had stars or not. And they did a lot, all people who entertained during the war, did an enormous amount of good in maintaining morale and taking the minds of the serving man and civilians working in factories off the terrible humdrum routine of their ordinary lives.'

The men and women at war needed to be taken out of themselves, desperately wanted to be able to forget the horror, the sweat and the blood that surrounded them. ENSA, USO, Stars in Battle-dress, the RAF Gang Shows, GI shows, Unit and Divisional Concert Parties, the amateur companies – every single person who ever stepped out in front of a troop audience no matter how large or small nor how safe or remote – helped them do just that.

INDEX